Be Ready When the Luck Happens

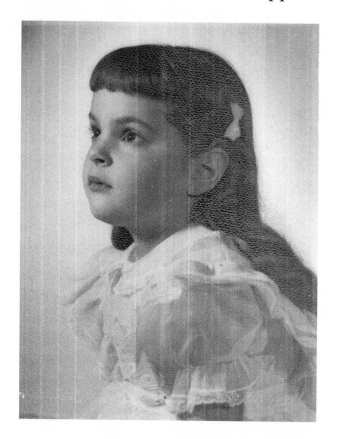

ALSO BY Ina Garten

Be Ready When the Luck Happens

A Memoir

Ina Garten

CROWN
NEW YORK

Published in the United States by Crown, an imprint of the
Crown Publishing Group, a division of Penguin Random
House LLC, New York.

All photographs courtesy of the author unless otherwise
noted.

Library of Congress Cataloging-in-Publication Data
Names: Garten, Ina, author.
Title: Be ready when the luck happens : a memoir /
    Ina Garten.
Description: First edition.
LC record available at https://lccn.loc.gov/2024007070
LC ebook record available at https://lccn.loc.gov/2024007071

ISBN 978-0-593-79989-5
Ebook ISBN 978-0-593-79980-2
Premium edition ISBN 978-0-593-80022-5
Signed edition ISBN 978-0-593-80021-8
Williams Sonoma box set ISBN 979-8-217-03377-5

Printed in the United States of America on acid-free paper

crownpublishing.com

Editor: Gillian Blake
Editorial assistant: Amy Li
Production editor: Terry Deal
Production editorial assistant: Taylor Teague
Design manager: Andrea Lau
Book designer: Marysarah Quinn
Production managers: Heather Williamson and Philip Leung
Copy editor: Aja Pollock
Proofreaders: JoAnna Kremer, Tracy R. Lynch, and Eldes Tran
Publicist: Kate Tyler
Marketer: Allison Renzulli

Printed at LSC Crawfordsville

1st Printing

FIRST EDITION

Do what you love. If you love it, you'll be really good at it.

—*Jeffrey Garten*

Contents

Prologue

"No, I'm not doing it, I'm not climbing that hill."

My words, on a chilly fall day in 1965: a memory that's so vivid to me even today. There's no recipe for writing a memoir, but the best part of being the author of your own story is that you can look back on your life and find the moments that really made a difference. One of my big moments happened at Balch Hill, in Hanover, New Hampshire, of all places.

I was visiting my boyfriend, Jeffrey Garten, a brilliant and *very* cute sophomore at Dartmouth. I was a high school senior, and while we had been dating for several months, we were still figuring out our relationship. Something was a little off that day, because I'd arrived on campus dressed in party clothes, ready for a social weekend, but he was in the mood for an outdoor trek at a nature preserve.

He gave me a pair of his blue jeans to wear (which seemed way too intimate to my seventeen-year-old self), and we drove to what seemed like the steepest hill I'd ever seen. Hill, ha! It looked more like a mountain to me! After we'd been hiking for a while, I realized that I'd had enough, and I said so. Something you need to know about me: there wasn't much room for disagreement in my

1965, Jeffrey at Balch Hill

childhood. My parents had more of a "my way or the highway" approach to child-rearing, and any attempts at noncompliance were met with pretty serious anger. Even questioning what they expected me to wear, or when to do my homework, was totally unacceptable.

Yet here I was, saying no to Jeffrey when I *really* wanted him to like me. While I stood there stubbornly, he said, "Just keep moving!" He even tried to get behind me and push me up the hill, which made me laugh, but I didn't move one inch.

Then it occurred to me that there was something in between doing it and not doing it. What if I kept moving, but I did it my way? Instead of huffing and puffing straight up the trail, I walked back and forth, back and forth, across the path, barely making it any higher up the hill.

I was afraid to look at him. *He's going to be really mad,* I thought. *It's over.* That's what I expected, given my experiences at home. But when I finally got up the nerve to look back, I saw that Jeffrey was doubled over . . . *laughing*! He thought it was the funniest thing he'd ever seen. In fact, he thought I was really clever!

In that moment I learned two things. Lesson one: There would be many Balch Hills in my future; there always are. Challenges, disappointments, heartbreaks, problems that hit like a ton of bricks, days when I didn't want to get out of bed. The solution is rarely obvious, and it's never a straight line up and over the hill.

Lesson two: For all those Balch Hill moments, I wanted Jeffrey by my side, laughing, understanding, and encouraging me to find my own way. I felt safe, accepted, and appreciated. Better still, he had a great sense of humor. And he just was so adorable.

Three years later, I married him.

I can't wait to tell you my story.

xxx /nu

1967, Jeffrey's fraternity house

1978, The original Barefoot Contessa

Over the Wall

"There has to be something more fun than this," I said to myself, probably for the millionth time, as I sat at my desk drafting nuclear energy policy at the White House. I should have been thinking about enriched uranium, but more often than not, I was looking for distractions. I was most likely planning a weekend dinner party and wondering which ingredient would make the flavor of my chocolate cake POP (it's coffee, by the way).

My ongoing frustration was that nothing ever happened in government, and even if it did, it took a really long time. Working in the Office of Management and Budget was exciting in the beginning because the issue papers I worked on went directly to the president—first Ford, then Carter. But after four years of shuffling what seemed like very important papers and pulling numerous all-nighters, I realized that despite my working on multibillion-dollar federal budgets, nothing ever seemed to get done. And when it did get done, somehow the next year, it got undone.

The only good thing about having a low threshold for boredom is that I've always been willing to take crazy risks just to get out of that miserable state. In my bureaucratic job, I was just part of a larger process, but I wanted to *be* the process—to do my own thing, either in real estate or in the food business, and, for better or for worse, to make my own decisions and mistakes, risking my own money. I also need immediate feedback, and there was nothing immediate about government work. The issues I was working on involved $50 billion budgets and $25 billion construction projects; I knew I'd be so much happier if they involved only $25, but *my* $25. I distinctly remember thinking, *If I were asked to be the head of OMB, would I want it? And if not, what was I even working toward?* I also knew that my success there would depend on a man *choosing* me to be the head of the organization, and in 1978, that would *never* happen. I needed to find an alternate track where my success would be measured by my own business skill and nobody could stand in my way.

I didn't whine—no one wants to hear someone complain about working in the White House!—but I was withering a little more each day. Jeffrey, who knew all too well how unhappy I was, encouraged me to find a passion and follow it. "Pick something you love to do," he urged. "If you love it, you'll be really good at it. And don't worry about whether you make money. Just do it!"

I was sitting in my office, exhausted, and it was only ten a.m. I had the whole day in front of me, so I decided to catch up on *The New York Times* instead of working. There it was—in the Sunday, April 2, 1978, Business Opportunities section, where they advertised everything from dry cleaners in the Bronx to a coffee shop with an apartment upstairs, or the hottest new food fad in the seventies: a frozen yogurt store (though it was hard to predict if frozen yogurt had a future).

I had never even *seen* that section of the paper before. As I studied the tiny print, I spotted an ad for a specialty food store called Barefoot Contessa, for sale in a place I'd never been: Westhampton Beach, New York—all the way at the end of Long Island. The ads were written in a shorthand that was difficult to decipher, and the word *opportunity* seemed like quite an overstatement. To this day, it's hard for me to imagine why this ad spoke to me, but I'm so glad it did, because it changed the entire trajectory of my life. This was the ad:

> **CATERING, GOURMET**
> **FOODS & CHEESE SHOPPE**
> Shoppe. Top #1 loc w/unlimited poten-
> tial. . All new equip & decor. In the
> Hamptons. Gross over six figures in
> summer alone. (914)591-7263

Honestly, it sounded like a prediction you might find in a fortune cookie, especially the "gross over six figures" part. And cheese *shoppe*? Who would answer that ad?

That night, I went home and told Jeffrey that I really needed a new profession, and that's when he reminded me that I should think about doing what I love. "Funny you should mention it! I just saw an ad for a specialty food store for sale in *The New York Times*."

"Let's go see it!" Jeffrey said cheerfully. Looking back, I imagine that he was probably just humoring me. We lived in Washington, DC, and Jeffrey had an important job writing issue papers and speeches for the secretary of state. How in the world could I work in Westhampton Beach? But Jeffrey always had the most positive attitude—*If this is what you want to do, we'll work it out.* We got in the car the very next weekend and drove to Westhampton to see the store and meet the owner, Diana Stratta.

On the way, I reminded myself that there was no reason on earth why this was a good idea. Yes, I had taught myself how to cook and I loved being in the kitchen, but I'd never worked a day in the food business. In fact, I'd never hired an employee, I'd never even set foot in the Hamptons, and this certainly wasn't its most welcoming time of year. Signs of spring were everywhere in Washington, where the air was warm and the cherry blossoms were a week away from their stunning peak moment. But Westhampton in early April was cold and cloudy, a sleepy summer resort town reluctantly waking up from its long winter nap. By the time we parked in front of Barefoot Contessa, the place we'd traveled more than five hours to see, I'd decided that it was a crazy impulse and predicted we'd take a fast look, then turn around and drive home.

The shop, a white clapboard building on a corner in the center of the village's Main Street, was small—only four hundred square feet. It was so small that the stove didn't fit in the tiny kitchen in the back and was instead right there in the store. There was one employee who was taking care of absolutely no customers (in fact, there seemed to be no one in the whole village), but she was baking big chocolate chip cookies. Instantly, the scent triggered a rush of good feelings, like endorphins on steroids, and my first thought was, *I need to be here!* I didn't want to write papers about enriched uranium; I wanted to bake cookies, not just because I liked them (and I do!), but because I saw a completely different life from the one I was living. The food business, *this* food business, would give me the freedom and creative outlet I craved. You bake cookies, you sell cookies, and if the cookie doesn't sell, you make something else that customers will love and that WILL sell. It's a business problem to solve, and it involved chocolate chip cookies! *How great is that?*

Standing in this adorable little place named after an Ava Gardner movie (it's about being elegant and earthy), surrounded by beautiful baked goods, gorgeous prepared salads, and ripe exotic cheeses, I experienced a true "ruby slippers" moment. I felt as if I had clicked my heels and finally come home. I enjoyed everything about cooking, from planning menus to shopping for ingredients, from following a recipe in the most scientific way to making something up just for fun. Most of all, I loved serving the delicious results to Jeffrey and my appreciative friends. It was my favorite escape from my intellectual but totally uncreative job. *What if the thing I love to do for fun could actually be my work?* I thought. I kept hearing Jeffrey say, "If you love it, you'll be really good at it."

We spent the night at a local hotel that had the ambience of an insane asylum. The room was white, the bed was white, there was not a single glint of metal or sharp object in sight—the perfect setting for two lunatics who were discussing a move that was certifiably crazy.

I'd like to say that I bought Barefoot Contessa on the spot and boldly stepped into a brand-new life, but it didn't happen quite that way. Remember, I was only thirty and still a little nervous about committing to a life-changing decision as important as this one. Diana was asking $25,000 for the business, and Jeffrey and I discussed offering her $20,000, figuring it would give me time to think about it while we negotiated the price.

But the universe had other plans for me, and they were big. On Monday morning, back from Westhampton Beach, I was sitting at my desk, working on some nuclear energy budget and sinking into my daily stupor, when the phone rang. It was Diana, who said simply, "Thank you very much. I accept your offer."

I remember sitting there stunned, thinking, *Oh shit! I just bought a specialty food store!*

What Goes in Early
Goes in Deep

Thirty years old, not one minute of experience in the food business, walking—no, *running*—away from a really good job in Washington, and leaving my beautiful home and all my friends behind, and my husband (who would have to commute back and forth on weekends) on his own. It sounded a little crazy, but I was out of my mind with excitement. I didn't know if it would be the best decision or the worst mistake I ever made.

My parents were horrified when I told them what I'd done. "You bought a food store?!" I thought I was being entrepreneurial, but in their minds, I was moving down in life, going from being a professional with a promising career in government to a shopkeeper, like my grandfather who had opened a candy store when he arrived in this country from Russia.

Their reaction wasn't surprising. We never saw eye to eye on anything I did. In fact, they expected very little from me and generally registered strong disapproval of any decision I made that was different from theirs. They were all about checking boxes and keeping up appearances, while I always ran as far from the "box" as possible in order to make my own way.

Our disagreements began early.

For the first five years of my life, our family, including my older brother, Ken, lived in Brooklyn, initially with my father's parents in their two-story attached house on Avenue A. It was remarkable that Morris and Bessie Rosenberg even *had* a house, because they were immigrants who moved to America from Eastern Europe—Russia and Poland, respectively. Despite the fact that they spoke only Yiddish when they arrived, they found jobs (Morris was a dance instructor and Bessie worked in a clothing factory on the Lower East Side), saved their money, and started their own businesses, including the candy store and a scrap metal company, *scrap metal* being a euphemism for *junkyard*. Morris bought large metal objects like cars, separated the parts, and sold the scrap metal by the pound.

The junkyard was located right next to the house, which was a huge bonus for everyone who worked there because Bessie welcomed their employees into her kitchen. She was always cooking, and like all good cooks, she was happiest when she was feeding people. Her steaming pots were filled with traditional Jewish dishes that were probably overcooked and underseasoned, but simple and delicious. Grandma Bessie, generous and good-humored, and Grandpa Morris, perpetually reading his Yiddish newspaper, created a warm home filled with relatives, friends, food, and love.

My mother's side of the family . . . not so much. I suspect I would have loved my grandfather. Irving Rich was a respected doctor, a champion bridge player, and a painter. He had a studio behind his office, so if he didn't have a patient, he could go back there and paint a still life. My grandmother, to put it politely, was challenging. She was referred to as "Diamond Lil," even though her name was Annette—a reference to the Mae West character who dripped diamonds and attitude. Chilly and demanding, she was the polar opposite of Bessie, whose arms and heart were always open to me, her granddaughter who looked just like her. There was no generosity or warmth, let alone gifts, coming from Annette—only harsh criticism.

Bessie and Morris had enough money to take a trip to Europe and came back with my favorite present: my Paris dress. I loved it—a flouncy little off-the-shoulder number, not the usual practical, inexpensive clothing my mother picked out for me. I loved the way it made me look and feel—pretty and ready for a party. I didn't know where Paris was, but I was sure it was a special place and I wanted to go there someday. Realistically, however, the only destination in my immediate future was a suburb in Connecticut.

When I was five, my parents moved to Stamford, where my father, a surgeon, was setting up his medical practice. Our house on Vineyard Lane was a "ranchburger," like several of the houses on the street, brand-new with a two-car garage, a wide front lawn, and all the modern (for the 1950s) conveniences. The neighborhood was actually very pretty in that Connecticut way, with long winding roads, mature trees, old stone walls, and the classic babbling brook in a nearby ravine. And here we were, the all-American family: Dad, Mom, brother Ken, me. It certainly looked good from the outside, but it was all about appearances.

My parents were definitely products of their very different families. My father was classically tall, dark, and handsome, a Clark Gable type with a giant personality and a wonderful sense of humor. He loved his friends, and he was happiest when he could pull up a chair at the center of a group and tell stories to entertain them. When my mother looked anxious, which was often, he'd say, "There's a black cloud over your head. Let's just wave it away," moving his hands back and forth to dispel the cloud.

My dad had a tremendous sense of style, wearing cashmere sports coats to the office long before everything was cashmere.

When most doctors had their offices painted in antiseptic hospital green, my father hired a decorator to design his in bright colors. Shouldn't patients feel good waiting for the doctor? His waiting room was always full, partly because he was a very good doctor and partly because he loved chatting with his patients and gave them far more attention than their appointments allowed.

My mother was a pretty woman, brunette, slim, neat, always composed. Weirdly, given how gregarious my father was, my mother was not social. There was something missing that prevented her from really connecting with people. When we were older, my brother, a physician, and I speculated about the reason for her emotional detachment. He thought she might have been an anxious depressive with a spectrum disorder. Whatever her condition, my mother liked to be in control of her image, her thoughts, her feelings, and her children. But children can't always be controlled, which she found very frustrating.

Her approach to child-rearing was basically making sure that we did what she thought we were supposed to do. I dutifully went to ballet school for years, although there was nothing about me that screamed ballerina. Even when we went to concerts or museums in New York, which we did frequently because art was one of my mother's interests, there was never any discussion of how music or a painting made us *feel*—it was all about checking that box. And there was certainly no lunch at Rumpelmayer's, or even an ice cream cone as a treat afterward.

Occasionally I showed signs of the rebellious streak that would help chart my path later in life. I was a Girl Scout for about ten minutes during a time when there were only four varieties of Girl Scout cookies. I tried to organize some of the other girls to do something that probably wasn't in the handbook, and when the scout leader pulled me aside and snapped, "Shape up or ship out," I smiled and said, "I think I'll ship out!"

We had all the accoutrements of a comfortable life, but for me, it was a dour existence. Every activity had to have a purpose: it couldn't be just for fun. My mother enrolled Ken in two different Book of the Month clubs—history and biography—when he was in third grade. Toys had to be educational or they weren't worth having, so there were no dolls, stuffed animals, or fun games in our house. There was no sitting around after dinner and playing Monopoly as a family. But my mother was so wrong about that. When kids play, they develop their brains, and it doesn't matter if it's chess or Mr. Potato Head. The only frivolous toy I do remember was a gift not from my parents but from my favorite great-uncle—the biggest pink tea set with little cups and plates. I just adored it. I played with it constantly, setting and resetting the table, serving treats to my imaginary guests at pretend parties. Funny. Now that I'm thinking about it, that tea set was *really* educational, considering what I do today.

In our house, my brother and I had one job—to excel academically, which meant that we spent most of our time alone, in our rooms, doing homework. We were raised as if we were only children, with little interaction between us. Neither of us remembers ever setting foot in the other's bedroom. We played chess (considered educational) at breakfast—Ken always won. And when we sat around the dinner table, we didn't have a conversation; we were quizzed on multiplication tables or state capitals. And, inevitably, the daily question I dreaded the most from my father: "What did you accomplish today?" If I proudly said that I'd won a tennis tournament or made a fisherman knit sweater, as I liked to do, he'd say, "Those are things you *wanted* to do, but did you accomplish anything?" I was confused. Why couldn't succeeding involve something you enjoyed doing?

If we disappointed my father in some way, we saw the dark side of his personality when he had temper tantrums and administered harsh punishment. I was only three when I begged our babysitter not to tell my father I had done something he would disapprove of because I was terrified of the consequences. When he got angry, which was often, anything could happen. He'd hit me or pull me around by my hair. Then, as if shocked by his own behavior, he'd leave the house, or go down to the basement until he could control himself. I spent hours in my room, crying, wondering what I had done to provoke him, too young to understand that I wasn't the problem. I kept my door closed, hoping he wouldn't come in and scream at me. I was lonely in there, but at least I felt safe.

I remember thinking that Ken had it worse because he was the firstborn—and the only son—and more was expected of him. But he recalls that *I* had it worse because I was trapped in a cycle of neglect and abuse. My parents didn't believe in me or my potential, but they held me to impossibly high (and arbitrary) standards, nonetheless. If my father told me to do six things, and I accomplished only five, there was hell to pay.

We all lived in the shadow of his anger. My mother was terrified of his outbursts, which is probably one of the reasons she set so many rules. It was her way of maintaining order and control, and she was rigid about our roles. I wanted to cook but my mother always refused, saying, "It's my job to cook. It's your job to study," so the kitchen remained off-limits. Dinners were more nutritious than delicious, and no one ever asked what we wanted to eat except maybe on a birthday. Plain broiled chicken or fish, steamed broccoli, canned (not even frozen!) peas and carrots. Always margarine, no butter allowed in the house. No carbohydrates *ever*. Spaghetti and meatballs? Never. I spent my early life searching—no, *begging*—for flavor. My father figured out that if he went to the local diner for breakfast and lunch during the workweek, he could secretly indulge in all the delicious food that was forbidden at home—corn muffins dripping with butter and jam; warm, spicy pastrami sandwiches; anything with carbs, cholesterol, fat, or *flavor*.

I wasn't so lucky. My mother sent me to school with lunches no sane child would consider a good trade. Sardine sandwiches, tuna without the mayonnaise, a handful of raw carrots. I was dying for a gooey peanut butter and jelly sandwich on fluffy white bread, comfort food, but it was never an option. If I asked for a snack, she would snap back at me: "Oh, just eat an apple!" Whatever happened to warm homemade cookies and milk after a long day at school? Not in my house! Not ever.

If it sounds like a cold and lonely life, it was. Parenting was different in the 1950s. I wasn't aware of any helicopter parents, today's moms and dads who hover over every activity and want to be their child's best friend. But even at a time when parents were supposed to be authority figures, my mother and father surpassed the stereotype. They made the rules, set the goals, and expected us to comply. Period. Not open for discussion. Their motto was, frighteningly, "Being a parent isn't a popularity contest," which translated to, "I really couldn't care less what you think."

When we look back on our childhood, Ken and I agree that our parents were not people who should have had children. My father actually told Ken, his own son, that he hadn't wanted children because he was afraid they would interfere with his career. They did so because of social pressure: young couples were expected to have children in the 1940s. But parenthood did not come naturally to them. Child-rearing was an unwanted responsibility, and children were messy, spontaneous, and an endless imposition. My mother had no maternal instincts. If I got sick and had to stay in bed, she gave me a bell to ring. When I needed something, she'd deliver it and leave, never lingering to offer any comfort. To the outside world, we looked like the family who had everything—everything material, that is—but what we missed emotionally is what counts the most.

I was fortunate to have an alternate universe at school, where I had wonderful friends and did perfectly well in my classes without working all that hard. I lived for having fun and spending time with my friends, who made me feel accepted and *connected*, unlike at home, where everyone was so distant and cold. We collided in our day-to-day lives, but we didn't actually *connect* at all. I was hungry for authentic relationships, and I found them with my friends: Buzzy, Janet, Liz, Wendy, Sybil, Barbara, Sue, and "Jimmy," who is still my dear friend and who grew up to be the Pulitzer Prize– and Tony Award–winning writer and director James Lapine. They were all smart and fun and I felt alive when we were together.

We skied in the winter, played tennis and swam at the club in the summer, went to the library, the Buttery, and the DQ, and had occasional (though very tame) coed parties in basement rec rooms, with more than a few clandestine rounds of spin the bottle. Those parties were never at my house. Everyone knew about my parents and their strict rules, and no one would ever think of coming to visit me.

At school, science was my thing; I loved the process of coming up with an idea for an experiment and testing my hypothesis for the annual science fair. The boys—the science nerds—spent months planning and researching their projects, but my ideas came to me in lightbulb moments, usually at the last minute, when I'd pull together an experiment and see where it would take me. I liked it when anything could happen—when I didn't know the results before I started. Surprises were what made science fun.

One year, I got it into my head that I wanted to use mice for my science experiment, the cute white laboratory ones that look like Disney characters. I wanted to test how they learn and remember by putting them through a maze at different time intervals, which meant I had to dye half of them purple so they could be on separate teams.

I can't believe my mother allowed me to keep them in cages in the basement while I tested their memory skills—I called the project A-Maze-Ing Mice. The most "a-maze-ing" thing about the mice was that they staged a jailbreak and scattered throughout the basement. My parents were furious. I had to find them one by one and put them back in their little cages.

The ending of the story was typical of my family; I won first prize in the citywide science fair two years in a row, and since my parents were sure I was a loser, they didn't even bother coming to the ceremony or, after I won, say that they were proud of me. But I didn't care. I loved winning those science fairs. So many years later, I think of writing recipes as little science projects, and I still feel good about each success. I have a hypothesis, I test it, and I find out whether it was a good idea—or not—and then test it again. But instead of ending up with smarter mice, I end up with the best mashed potatoes, which is so much more satisfying.

It was a transitional time for young women, marked by a crazy confusion of ideas and expectations. We were supposed to do well in school and get into college. My friends were smart. We were in advanced classes and excelled in different ways, but the ultimate goal seemed to always be to get married. Even high school sports had an ulterior purpose. The reason to learn how to play golf was so we could play with our future husbands. I took one golf lesson, hated it, and—rebellious streak surfacing again!—simply refused to play. My father's overreaction was that with my attitude, no one would ever love me, and he was sure no one would want to marry me. *Really?* I was only fifteen, but he had already decided I had no future.

Teenagers are trying to figure things out, and the process is usually one of trial and error, mostly error. But my brother and I weren't given the freedom to make our own choices—or mistakes. Everything from what friends we saw to what shoes we wore was decided by my mother. If I had an idea of my own, my mother's response was, "You think it's a good idea, but it'll turn out badly." How did that make me feel? Discouraged. Unmotivated. I believed my ideas weren't good. Worse still, anything I tried to do would have negative consequences. This was the endless loop in my head: *You'll never amount to anything.*

Feb 2, 1965

Dear Sara,

First, let me say that Roy has
nothing to do with this little note.
Matter of fact he wouldn't give me your
address for about a week.

Anyway, I have the impression that
Roy's attempt to get me a date with
you affected you the wrong way. If
you felt that he was trying to
"pass you off" you could not be more
mistaken. Truth is ... I saw you
(but we were never introduced, unfortunately)
when you were up here this Fall.

"Don't Even Waste the Stationery"

In the autumn of my junior year of high school, my parents decided to visit my brother, Ken, who was a sophomore at Dartmouth College in New Hampshire. We hadn't done this before, so I thought it might be fun to spend a weekend at an all-male Ivy League school. Although my high school boyfriend was a terrific guy, my mother didn't particularly like him, so she asked Ken to fix me up with a classmate. She was probably hoping to derail our relationship, which, honestly, had started to wane as soon as my boyfriend had left for college.

We arrived on a beautiful fall day. Hanover is so scenic at this time of year—the picture-book image of an Ivy League school— and there were boys everywhere. I'd dressed in my best blue skirt, my favorite blue-and-white wool and angora sweater, the new blue Pappagallos that I'd bought with my own money so my mother couldn't refuse to buy them for me, and a blue grosgrain ribbon in my hair. Maybe a little heavy on the blue, but I felt very pulled together.

As we toured the Dartmouth Green, the heart of the campus, I was surprised to run into my high school boyfriend, who'd heard about my trip to New Hampshire and raced to Dartmouth from his college in Boston to remind me that we were still a couple. I guess he was afraid that an all-male school was a dangerous place for his girlfriend? I was a little annoyed that my soon-to-be ex was trying to control me. I had enough of that at home! I convinced him to go back to Boston and felt incredibly free. I remember thinking this was all very risqué, with one boy coming to see me from Boston during the day and another boy, a Dartmouth freshman (a friend from our tennis club at home), taking me to the movies that night.

At some point, I passed the library, a building right off the beautiful Dartmouth Green with huge windows and an elegant New England steeple. And here's what happened next.

The story, which I've told countless times, usually begins with "I was fifteen," until I learned another interesting thing about writing a memoir: Your own life can be full of surprises. The stories we tell repeatedly don't always hold up to fact-checking. When I did the math for the first time in decades, I was stunned to realize that I was *sixteen,* not fifteen, on that fateful day.

Nonetheless, while I was standing outside the library, admiring the architecture, I later found out that a Dartmouth freshman was inside, admiring *me.* As he tells the story, Jeffrey Garten looked up from his book and glanced out the window. He saw me on the Green and, in an instant, was *smitten*! He liked the way I stood, the tilt of my head, my clothes, and especially the blue ribbon in my dark hair. "Look at that beautiful girl," he said to his roommate, who followed his gaze, then recognized me.

"I know her. That's Ina Rosenberg and we're going to the movies tonight."

Jeffrey's roommate was Roger, my date for the evening, and they had been studying together in the library. The last thing Jeffrey expected to hear, the last thing he *wanted* to hear, was that Roger had a date with the mysterious girl who'd caught his eye.

The next day, Jeffrey asked Roger about the date (we went to see *A Shot in the Dark*) and was relieved to hear that Roger considered us "just friends." Jeffrey asked if it would be okay for him to write to me. Apparently, Roger teasingly held out for about a week, then gave him my address and agreed to make the introduction, which he didn't get around to doing until January. Eventually, Roger wrote, thanking me for "making a dull Saturday night not so dull," and went on to tell me about his roommate. "A friend of mine, Jeff Garten," he wrote, "was very impressed when he saw you and would like you to come up. He's from Tampa, Florida, and a true southern gentleman all the way. I think you'll have a great time with him, because he's one of the nicest guys you'd ever want to meet."

Okay, I admit I was annoyed. There was something about the idea of these two college boys discussing me—one handing me over to the other—that rubbed me the wrong way. Poor Jeffrey, thinking romantically about the girl with the ribbon in her hair and wanting to meet me, while I was feeling insulted.

Letters flew back and forth—Roger to me, me to Roger, then Jeffrey, defending himself and Roger.

I saved Jeffrey's letters, every single one, so I know exactly what he wrote, and it still amuses (and thrills) me to read his words. Handwritten (remember those days?) in the most beautiful script.

First, his explanation:

> Dear Ina,
>
> . . . I have the impression that Roger's attempt to get me a date with you affected you the wrong way. If you felt that he was trying to "pass you off," you could not be more mistaken. Truth is . . . I saw you (but we were never introduced, unfortunately, when you were up here this Fall) . . .

Then, his challenge.

> If the idea of dating a Jewish freshman from Flor-
> ida whom you have never seen doesn't repel you,
> how about dropping me a note and we could work
> something out. If you are not at all interested, don't
> even waste the stationery.

Don't even waste the stationery?! It was our version of meeting "cute," with sparks flying. Such confidence. So charming. Who
wouldn't respond to that? It helped that he'd enclosed a photograph of himself. Curly hair, a wide smile, and bright, engaging
eyes that pulled me in—the handsomest boy I'd ever seen. And he
was smart, too! Game on!

I want to pause for some terrifying what-ifs. What if I hadn't
walked past the library at that moment? What if Jeffrey had
picked a different seat, not by a window? What if he had never
looked outside? What if Roger hadn't been there to tell him my
name? What if he'd seen me and hadn't said anything to Roger?
How many times have we done that? Fate had a pretty fragile grip
on this precarious chain of events, like many events in my life, but
somehow it all fell into place, and we started sending letters back
and forth.

Jeffrey took letter writing very seriously. Years of being away
from home at boarding school, then at Dartmouth, taught him to
be a great storyteller. He wrote about his classes, his friends, how
he spent his day, and what was on his mind.

To be honest, I wasn't the best correspondent. I'd much rather
have a conversation than write a letter. First, I obsessed about
what to write, and then I had to endlessly edit it until all the spontaneity was gone. I hated writing letters!

But Jeffrey was the best. His immediate focus in those early
days was setting up our first meeting, which he finally pulled off

in March. He planned a trip to New York to interview for a summer job and wondered if he could come to Connecticut to take me out. I remember peeking out the window when he arrived and thinking he was even better in person than in the photograph he'd sent. And, just as Roger described, he was a "true southern gentleman," who politely came in to meet my parents. They were impressed and maybe even a little shocked that this exceptional guy would even be interested in me.

When we were alone, Jeffrey asked me what I'd like to do—he'd never been to Stamford, so I was in charge. Thinking quickly, I answered, in my most mature voice, "Would you like to go for a drink?" Pretty nervy of me, considering I was underage, I'd never even been to a bar, and I had no idea where to find one. In Connecticut, the drinking age was twenty-one, so that wasn't an option. But across the state line in New York, it was eighteen, so I knew Jeffrey could legally get into a bar. How I thought I could get in is one of life's mysteries, but there I was, suggesting we go to Port Chester, New York, to a bar I'd heard people talk about called Hilltop. The only thing I knew was where the exit to Port Chester was on the New York State Thruway, but as I was telling Jeffrey where to get off, I realized I had no idea how big Port Chester was, nor any idea whatsoever where to find this particular bar. Remember, we're not talking about GPS to get you somewhere. You needed a map! You needed directions! How did I think this was going to work out? And then, totally my luck, there it was! Right in front of us was a sign that said HILLTOP. I was saved!

But was I? We parked the car and headed for the door, where a large man, the bouncer, stopped us and demanded IDs. No problem for Jeffrey, who pulled out his license. I just stood there—silent—and finally admitted that I didn't even know what he was asking for. ID? What's that? Jeffrey looked at me quizzically.

"What do you mean you don't have one?" he asked. He'd assumed I had a fake ID, like every underage teenager in America who wanted to go to a bar. But I didn't even *know* I needed one, which made it so much more embarrassing.

Jeffrey came to my rescue by suggesting we drive back to Connecticut and do something else. I remembered there was a coffeehouse in Westport—college students in the sixties liked coffeehouses and Peter, Paul and Mary music, right?—and we headed there. No alcohol, but plenty of caffeine and conversation, a little guitar music, and a chance to get to know each other.

Our families were so different. Jeffrey looked at my life and saw stability and sophistication: our house in an affluent part of Connecticut; my parents, a successful doctor and his attractive wife—it all looked perfectly lovely. I, in turn, was intrigued by the Gartens and their adventurous life, who were not like any families I knew. His father, Colonel Melvin Garten, a much-decorated veteran of World War II and the Korean conflict, was in the army paratroopers, a "cloak-and-dagger type" (according to Jeffrey) who jumped out of planes and performed secret missions for the State Department. So secret that "no one in the world knows where he is until he comes back to tell them where he *was*"—it could be Africa, it could be Vietnam, Jeffrey said, making the Colonel sound more like a character in a Bond movie or *The Man from U.N.C.L.E.* than someone's dad.

The vagaries of military life had made Jeffrey independent, even for a college student. He figured things out because he had to, hustling for summer jobs, driving himself to and from Florida when he wanted to go home, thinking about how his choices today would affect his future tomorrow. He was an old soul in a young man's body. From my point of view, the combination was irresistible.

Many years later, I asked Jeffrey what he could possibly have seen in that clueless girl who didn't even know how to get into a bar with a fake ID. Apparently, our date, disastrous as it was, awakened a feeling. He saw that I plowed full speed ahead and didn't recognize a big problem—say, the bouncer?—until it was right in front of me. "I thought you needed someone to take care of you," he told me. And happily, he wanted to be that someone.

Meet the Parents

When Jeffrey dropped me off at my house after our first date, he invited me to come to Dartmouth for its famous spring Green Key weekend. *You really don't know my parents,* I thought, *because hell will freeze over before that happens.* What I said more politely was that there was no possibility my parents would say yes. Always looking ahead, Jeffrey continued, "What about when you're a senior?" It didn't seem too outrageous to imagine a visit in the future; I'd ask when the time was right. I couldn't believe he thought he wanted to see me again, let alone the following year!

I was in the process of applying to colleges, so freedom was in sight. Everybody thought I should go to a small women's school, maybe Skidmore or Smith, but I didn't listen. I was always being told what to do. College was the very first decision I was allowed to make completely on my own (which was a little crazy). I wanted to have fun at a party school where I wouldn't have to study hard to get good grades. And, after a childhood filled with anxiety, I was terrified of rejection. Looking back, I now realize that I was looking for a school that would never turn me down.

It didn't occur to me to see college as part of a long-term plan—that I should go to a certain school to study a specific subject so that I could get a particular job. I was living in the moment. I wanted the freedom to figure out who I was, then I'd take it from there. I rushed through the admissions process as quickly as possible, applying "early decision" to Syracuse University so I would never have to think about it again. If I got in, by September of my senior year in high school I'd be done with the college decision.

Meanwhile, I'd lined up a summer job with a local architect. At the time, my dream was to be an architect, and Jeffrey was amazed by that. He said that he never knew a girl who wanted to be an architect and predicted I would be written about in *Esquire* or *Time* for my bold choice. The reality was that I spent my time filing and doing chores at the office, but it was a golden summer because I enjoyed that bit of daily independence, and thinking about Jeffrey made me so happy.

He worked at the Concord Hotel in the Catskills for the first part of the summer, until business at the resort slowed down and he was laid off. He rebounded quickly—he always did—and knocked on doors at the New York World's Fair until he found a job at the Oregon pavilion, where, in the shadow of a giant statue of Paul Bunyan, he spent the rest of the summer preparing barbecue sandwiches. I can safely say it was Jeffrey's first, and *only,* job cooking. The job was a great development for us because he stayed with relatives in Long Island and we could see each other on his day off.

Whenever Jeffrey came to take me out, the whole house lit up. He had an idealized image of my family—he saw two very traditional parents, who, unlike his dad, were home all the time, focusing on their children—and when he was there, that's who they were. He brought out the best in my parents. Jeffrey didn't see the darker side, my mother's iciness and my father's rage, and I wasn't ready to reveal all that. My father loved talking to him, and my mother cooked meals she would never make for us. I think there was actually fried chicken and cake in his honor! Jeffrey's charm was so irresistible that he somehow inspired my mother to embrace carbohydrates! No wonder my father liked him.

We played tennis and took long walks, using our time alone to find out a little more about each other. I remember the two of us standing on a highway overpass at dawn, watching the cars go by on the Merritt Parkway, and thinking that Jeffrey could make anything fun.

The good news was that in early September I was accepted to Syracuse, so *that* was done. I was almost a college student, so I casually mentioned to my father that Jeffrey had invited me to homecoming weekend at Dartmouth. Did I say casually? His reaction was anything but casual.

He went berserk. *His* daughter spending a weekend at Dartmouth? Over his dead body. My father had once berated me for wearing lipstick, calling me a "slut." If wearing lipstick made me a slut, well, *this* . . .

On the other hand, he really liked Jeffrey, who in addition to being polite, personable, and handsome was attending an Ivy League college and thinking about becoming a doctor—every Jewish father's dream! While my father was extremely skeptical that I could hold on to him, he didn't want to do anything to discourage the relationship. He looked for advice, consulting first his therapist and then his rabbi, but he just couldn't decide what to do.

He kept me in suspense for a month. When I couldn't take it anymore, I broke down and said, "Just tell me! I can't stand not knowing!"

My father had come up with a plan that left him feeling in control. He said I could go to Dartmouth exactly three times during my senior year, warning I would have to plan my trips carefully.

Okay, I thought, *I can work with this,* and in my true "jump first and worry about tomorrow when it comes" approach to life, I flew up to Hanover to see Jeffrey three times before the end of October. Oops! What do we do now?

The first trip was for Dartmouth homecoming, the weekend of October 9. The flight cost all of twelve dollars, but I felt like a jet-setter going off to New Hampshire all by myself. I was so excited to see Jeffrey but equally excited to be on my own, at last. Behind me were two people for whom I could do nothing right and in front of me was a smart, funny guy who thought everything I did was a total revelation, and frankly, to this day, whenever I see him, I feel the same way.

Autumn in Hanover, again—nearly a year after my first visit to see my brother. But this time, I was with my *boyfriend.* I stayed at an inn near campus that had converted its attic into a dorm for girls who were visiting Dartmouth students. Not that I spent much time in the room. The weekend was packed with events. We went to parties, the big football game, a Peter, Paul and Mary concert. I could feel myself coming alive. I really didn't want to go home.

Jeffrey wrote to me while my flight was still in the air, claiming it was the best weekend he'd ever had. That's why we quickly burned through our three allotted weekends. Now we needed to figure out how to outsmart my father and his rabbi.

Jeffrey realized that if he visited me in Stamford the weekend before he wanted me to come to Dartmouth, and asked nicely, my father invariably agreed to "just one more weekend." Manipulative? Absolutely! But happily, we got through the whole year that way.

When we were apart, we found other ways to be close: phone calls and letters—long letters that deepened our relationship. Jeffrey said it best: "I would like for you to be around so I could think with you," he wrote. Sometimes we were playful, competing to see who could be more sarcastic. Other times we were soul-searching, earnestly discussing the meaning of the universe (*so* "college"—we decided we didn't know).

It was the late 1960s. The war in Vietnam was bitterly dividing the country, and women were joining "consciousness-raising" groups to liberate themselves from the constraints of the traditional expectations that had held them back. College girls were burning their bras and women were trying to get *out* of the kitchen. And what was I doing? I was demanding that my mother let me *into* the kitchen to bake brownies to send to my boyfriend! I'm astonished now by how out of touch I was. But was I? Why couldn't I be an architect or an entrepreneur, as I told Jeffrey's friends (where did I get that idea?), and enjoy cooking at the same time? I wanted to be independent and self-determining after an overly regimented childhood, and I suppose you could say I'm still that person. I love traditional pursuits; I just want to do them my way and make my own decisions.

It was at this time that I found out how much I loved cooking. I adored the process of baking something (well, truthfully, it was probably a Duncan Hines mix!), I loved the smell in the house, but most of all, I loved taking care of Jeffrey and making him happy.

This was the very first time I thought of food as an expression of love. Before I started cooking for Jeffrey, food could be good, bad, or mediocre like the food at home, but it didn't matter because it was just sustenance, not pleasure. Now baking something delicious was a way to express my feelings and to connect with Jeffrey—I'd think of him while I cooked, and when he reached for one of my cookies or brownies, I knew he'd think of me. It was a sensory win-win. I think those homemade brownies were for Jeffrey the culinary equivalent of a low-cut dress: irresistible and guaranteed to make an impression!

The year was all fun and games—we carefully negotiated more weekends for me to visit Dartmouth, we spent that memorable day hiking at Balch Hill, and we celebrated the end of my senior year, with Jeffrey escorting me to my prom in his red Chevy convertible. We fantasized about how nice it would be in September, when I started at Syracuse, far away from my parents and their rules. Happy times, all the time.

Until reality intruded with the worst possible news. Jeffrey's father was seriously injured in Vietnam. He had been riding in a jeep in the middle of a convoy. The first half of the convoy had safely rounded a turn on a dirt road, but when Colonel Garten's jeep followed, a mine exploded. Apparently, his vehicle had been targeted by the enemy. He was always concerned about that, so he never allowed any young soldiers to ride in his jeep. Jeffrey's mom received the dreaded telegram and raced to Walter Reed hospital in Maryland, near Washington, DC, to be with her husband during his one-year recovery. Jeffrey was so concerned about his father that he accepted a summer job at a telephone company in Washington.

In June, Jeffrey decided it was time for me to meet his family. He knew a visit from the two of us would be a happy distraction for his convalescing father, and he needed me in the family circle during this difficult time. I wanted to be there for him, but my mother had a different perspective. No, she didn't want me going to Washington with Jeffrey. I think she saw the visit as an indication that we were way too serious about each other.

And I'm sure she was not happy about Jeffrey's new ROTC scholarship. With his father's injury, he wasn't certain his parents would be able to afford his tuition at Dartmouth, so he applied for, and won, an ROTC scholarship. It was a great deal for him, covering most of his expenses at school for the next two years, including free travel on military planes and a monthly allowance. In return, Jeffrey had to fulfill four years of military service after graduation. He wasn't worried about that—he figured it would give him more time to think about what career he wanted to pursue *and* to save money for graduate school.

Ironically, it was my father who helped Jeffrey understand that his long-held ambition of becoming a doctor was not the best career choice for him. Jeffrey was struggling to pass organic chemistry. When my father, a doctor himself, heard that, he said, "You're the luckiest guy in the world. I make my living in a little room. And I know you—you have a much bigger horizon." His advice inspired Jeffrey to think about graduate school in international studies, a better path for him. How thrilled I would have been if my father had ever offered *me* that kind of advice and support, but sadly it was an era when the goal for a girl was just to get married.

ROTC was a brave choice for Jeffrey, considering the growing antiwar sentiment in the country. When he got back to Dartmouth, some of the guys in his fraternity asked him to use the back door of the house when he was wearing his uniform—an incredibly disrespectful attitude toward a friend who was just trying to stay in school.

My parents were uneasy about his uniform and the life that went with it. My mother was terrified that if I married Jeffrey, I'd end up being an army wife, and being in the military during Vietnam added a whole other level of concern. The death count was on the news every night, and my parents wanted to discourage me from a relationship that could lead to a future like Mrs. Garten's—a wife, waiting alone for her husband to come home from a dangerous place. They were getting a little ahead of themselves, but I knew it was on their minds.

I wasn't scared about the realities of being an army wife because I wasn't thinking about getting married at all. I was just living day-to-day, and I loved being with Jeffrey. I never for a minute thought he would do something that I didn't want him to do or didn't like. Maybe it was naïve, but knowing him now, I was totally right.

I finally convinced my mother that visiting Colonel Garten was the compassionate thing to do, and Jeffrey and I planned a day trip. When we arrived at Walter Reed, I told Jeffrey he should go in first while I waited outside. Colonel Garten sent him right back to get me, saying, "I don't want to see you, I want to see your girl!" I was thrilled to meet the man who had become such a legend in Jeffrey's descriptions, and we got along well in the short time we were together.

Back in Stamford, the summer stretched ahead, and I was counting the days until my move to Syracuse. But first, my summer job. I'd lined up a sales position at Isabel Eland, a local lingerie store. Lingerie in the 1960s was nothing like the sexy, frilly confections we know today. Undergarments—girdles and full brassieres—were so substantial that they were a form of armor. Incredibly, there were *two* Inas at the little shop, me and an older, heavyset woman who'd worked there forever. To distinguish us, the owner decided to call me "Little Ina" and her "Big Ina," which I'm sure she found unbearable.

I was the worst employee ever. Most days, I hid in a dressing room and worked on a sweater I was knitting for Jeffrey, or I spoke to him on a phone with a long cord that would get increasingly tangled as the conversation went on. I'm guessing that he could make free calls because he worked at the telephone company. We talked for *hours,* fantasizing about what life would be like when I was at college, away from the watchful eyes of my parents. When *permission* wouldn't be a word in our vocabularies. When weekends wouldn't have to end.

What was I thinking? While we were plotting our romance, my mother was hatching a plan of her own. At the end of the summer, unbeknownst to me, she pulled Jeffrey aside for a private talk. Now that I was getting ready to go to college, she "suggested" it was time for us to cool down. She told him that if we planned on seeing each other every other weekend during school, two things would happen. My grades would suffer, and he'd wreck my chances for any decent dating relationships on campus. In her words, I needed to have my chance "on the open market."

When Jeffrey told me what she'd said, I was furious that she had spoken to him, and even more outraged that she thought she could control my private life. Jeffrey was offended, too, but, ever the diplomat, he saw a reasonable way to move forward *and* a silver lining. We weren't going to stop seeing each other, but if I went on the occasional date with someone else, I'd realize that our relationship was special. Trust me, I knew that already!

Sadie, Sadie, Married Lady

I guess it's pretty telling that I don't have many memories of going to college. At Syracuse, there was none of the Ivy charm that I'd experienced at Dartmouth. My all-girl dorm, Haven Hall, was a contemporary building, curved, with a strange circular structure sticking out in the front. It looked just like a toilet bowl, which is exactly what we called it. The dorm was brand-new, so that was something, and I had a single room, which gave me privacy—but I was lonely. Thinking back now, I wonder why I chose a room all by myself, after having been confined to my room at home. It probably felt safe, but I missed that college experience of having a fun roommate. (Or did I miss the roommate from *The Shining*? I'll never know.)

And "all-girl" meant just that—no boys allowed. That wasn't a tragedy, because college men (aka the "open market") were juvenile pranksters who liked to play tricks on unsuspecting freshmen. Jeffrey took the time to write me a list of warnings based on the guys he knew at school. Dating these jokers seemed silly when I already had a grown-up boyfriend who was perfect, but I tried, just to have something to do.

It was hard for Jeffrey to come to Syracuse, because there was no good place to stay and he had to work most weekends at

Dartmouth. I didn't mind traveling to see him, but my parents discouraged trips by giving me a minuscule allowance—money, or the lack of it, was another form of parental control. I worked around the long arm of the law by finding rides from students who were heading in the direction of Hanover. My willingness to get into a random car with a stranger drove Jeffrey crazy—he lost a lot of sleep worrying about me riding in cars without snow tires, but it was worth it to have a few stolen hours together. Or I would take a Greyhound bus from Syracuse, New York, to Hanover, New Hampshire—a five-hour trip!—with a three a.m. transfer at the bus station in Albany (not pretty), arriving in Hanover at five a.m. Jeffrey would wake up and find me sitting in the cold and dark on the steps of his fraternity house.

I don't remember having any long-term plan; I was only living in the moment, a trend that would continue. When I looked back at all the letters Jeffrey wrote to me, I was surprised to see that he seemed to have a plan, which allowed me to just trip along without a care. My mother's plot to separate us had backfired bigtime, and I think she understood that there was no way to keep us apart.

I can't believe I'm opening this door, even a crack, but this story is *too* good not to share. I was at summer school in Syracuse, and Jeffrey was in a training program at Fort Devens in Massachusetts. We longed to see each other, so we arranged to meet in Albany, in the middle. Telling our parents about an unchaperoned weekend was out of the question. This was 1967, on the eve of the sexual revolution, but in their world (and honestly in ours, too), it might as well have been 1957. We thought we were clever by saying we were visiting friends in Albany on the same weekend (which should have been a dead giveaway), conveniently leaving out that we would be staying together . . . in a *motel*.

Jeffrey's favorite endearment for me was *prude*. I was only nineteen, which was *much* younger then than it is now, so it was all pretty innocent. We just wanted to spend a weekend alone, like a sleepover. Checking into the motel played like a scene from *The Graduate,* which came out that year. Rushing to get through the awkward moment of filling out the registration form, Jeffrey listed his parents' address. Then, when he returned to Fort Devens and realized he'd left his pajamas (who wears *pajamas*?!) at the motel, panic set in. He imagined the motel would find the pajamas and mail them back to his parents, who would put two and two together, and we'd be in big trouble. The next few days were tense, but luckily, the worst never happened. The pajamas were MIA, and our secret rendezvous stayed a secret. The whole episode seems beyond quaint today, but the terror of discovery was real!

In December, we planned my first trip to spend a few days with Jeffrey, his parents, and his younger brother, Alan. North Carolina—Fort Bragg actually—was warm, and so were Colonel and Mrs. Garten. I think she always wished she had a daughter, so she was instantly welcoming, wrapping me in her arms and then following me everywhere to make sure I was comfortable.

Sixteen-year-old Alan, on the other hand, had no interest in befriending his brother's girlfriend and registered instant disapproval, loud and clear—until we were saved by a game of cards.

The Garten boys had a deck that was X-rated—there's no way it belonged to their parents. Certain cards had nudes instead of the typical queen or king, and they watched my face carefully as they dealt, slyly anticipating my reaction. Eventually, a voluptuous nude turned up in my hand. Instead of being shocked or embarrassed, I started laughing and couldn't stop. Alan looked at me and decided I wasn't so bad for a girl, and we became friends.

———

One spring day in 1968, when Jeffrey was about to graduate from Dartmouth and go off to fulfill his military service, and I was heading into my final exams, we went to our favorite German restaurant in Syracuse and ordered very large, very messy sandwiches. Out of nowhere, between bites, Jeffrey said, "I think we should get married in December when I'll have some time off—and then you'll join me in North Carolina."

What? Did I hear that right? Get married? It wasn't really a traditional proposal with an engagement ring and Jeffrey down on one knee professing undying love, but *okay*! I knew how he felt, and I felt the same way. I went back to my dorm and excitedly told my friends, "I think I'm engaged?!" Then reality set in. How on earth would I tell my parents?

For years, my father had insisted that I not get married before graduating from college, and here I was, at the end of my sophomore year, about to defy him—yet again. Imagining their response, I didn't want to make that phone call now . . . or ever. But then my parents called to say they were driving to Syracuse that day. That day? They never visited me at school, and they were driving to Syracuse? In the middle of final exams? They had to be really upset, and I was pretty sure I knew why.

After we had talked about getting married, Jeffrey had called my parents to arrange a visit so he could officially ask for my hand. They had anticipated what was coming next and jumped into the car to put a stop to it. It's a long trip, and I agonized the whole time they were on the road, imagining the fireworks, the anger, the disappointment, the threats. *They're going to kill me*, I thought.

When they arrived at my dorm, they did something that really surprised me: they came into my room separately—my mother first, grim, determined, and quick to get to the point. "I think this is the worst idea," she began, her usual opening whenever I made a decision on my own. "You can't get married now. You really have to wait. You have no idea what he's going to do with his life."

I watched her and thought carefully about my answer, surprised that my first impulse was to express some compassion because she was so upset. "I'm really sorry," I said, acknowledging her feelings. Then, as difficult as it was, I had to speak the truth. "This is the first time in my life I've ever said this to you, but I really don't care what you think." It was literally the first time I'd ever defied either of my parents and stood my ground. It felt amazing! I had the power to do what was right for me, and this time, I was sure I was right.

I had never had the guts to speak that way to my mother before. What was different this time? I realized that her control over me was in the past. I legally needed her consent to get married because I wasn't twenty-one, but I quickly pointed out that if she withheld her permission, we would just wait a few months and get married right after my birthday the following February. "There's really no other option here," I finished.

She was shocked by my words, my refusal to bend to her will, as I always had in our confrontations. Silence. There was nothing left to say, so she left the room and sent in my father.

My rush of courage quickly evaporated. I was absolutely terrified. He could be violent, and he stood there long enough for me to imagine the worst. I didn't want to shrink, like Alice in Wonderland, into a little girl again, wanting his approval, which always seemed out of reach, and fearing his words, his anger.

He looked at me, then said, "I think this is the smartest thing you've ever done."

What? Did I hear that right? I remember being stunned. Just stunned. My father thought I was smart?! He had enormous respect for Jeffrey, the dream son-in-law, and Jeffrey had chosen me, so he was forced to start seeing me the way Jeffrey saw me. That moment was the beginning of a change in my relationship with my father, because for once, I'd exceeded his expectations.

Until this time, I had been, curiously, two different people. At home, I was shy and frightened, reluctant to state any opinion for fear of being harshly criticized. Punishments were meted out for infractions I didn't even understand. I stayed by myself in the safety of my room and was frankly very sad and lonely most of the time. But outside that house, I was a completely different person: confident, happy, and extremely social.

But which one of these two wildly divergent people was I? So many people set out to find a spouse who's different from their parents and end up marrying someone exactly like their parents because it's familiar and comfortable. I couldn't let that happen. I distinctly remember thinking, when I was fifteen, that if I was dating a boy who so much as raised his voice to me (let alone a hand!) the way my father did, I was gone. I chose a partner who was totally different. Only when I left my sad childhood behind and moved into a world with Jeffrey did I begin to realize that the person I was outside the house was the real me.

Finally, with my parents on board, my mother and I started to make plans for the wedding. We had six months, and the wheels were already spinning. Jeffrey was never enthusiastic about Hallmark events—even birthdays—because he didn't like to be the center of attention. He would have been happy with a small, informal wedding. But we'd won the marriage war, so we surrendered in most of the bridal battles, keeping our eye on the prize: our wedding day.

Part of that decision was practical. Jeffrey was training at Fort Sill in Oklahoma that summer and would have no time for anything else, and I was going back to Syracuse to get as many credits as possible before I transferred to a college in North Carolina after the wedding. If my mother wanted to take on the thankless job of selecting invitations; dealing with the caterer, musicians, and florists; and overseeing the countless other details that came with planning a wedding, that was fine with us.

It was a long road, filled with land mines. First, my official engagement photo, taken at Bachrach Studios and sent to *The New York Times* to announce our engagement. Then, the wedding registry, where we were supposed to sign up for all those essentials a new couple supposedly couldn't live without. I dutifully went along with the tradition, picking out china and silver and describing my choices in my letters to Jeffrey.

At the time, I thought Jeffrey would become a diplomat, so I selected china that would be appropriate for a diplomat's dinner party. Maybe I was getting a little ahead of myself, but it could have happened. I, of course, imagined setting a table in London or Paris, not realizing that the choice embassies are reserved for billionaires. We would have ended up somewhere like Outer Mongolia, where my Richard Ginori white bone china with a simple gold detail would have stayed in the box. I loved it then and I still love it today because it's classic.

Jeffrey was incredulous about my interest in all this tableware. "Can you explain something to me?" he wrote. "You said that you went looking for a silver set. Tell me more. Tell me it isn't true. We may not have enough money to eat, but we'll sure have a nice-looking coffee pot, huh? You're <u>such a girl</u>."

He countered with his own list of wedding gift essentials, and I still laugh when I think of them. At the top of his list: a filing cabinet with a locked drawer and ten-year subscriptions to *Time, Fortune, Foreign Affairs,* and *McCall's* (for me, he suggested). Then, a year's supply of tennis balls and a Dictaphone, so he could dictate letters and I could type them. (Really?)

"Does anyone give money?" he asked hopefully. Even at the tender age of twenty-two, he was planning for the future, budgeting for essentials like life insurance and rainy days, while I was obsessing about the wedding registry. PS: Fifty-six years later, nothing's changed. Jeffrey's still thinking practically and saving, and I'm still buying china!

When he heard that my mother was considering one of the local temples as a venue, he balked. "The notion of an extravagant wedding is nauseating to me . . . a huge waste of money, and for what?" he wrote.

Then, all of a sudden, Jeffrey stopped talking about the wedding, which scared me a little. Did he change his mind about marrying me? I'm a big believer in resolving a problem not by endless discussions, but sometimes just by changing my behavior. Jeffrey was anxious about getting married? Hit the brakes, stop talking about it, and let him get comfortable. It was absolutely the right approach. After I stopped bombarding him with details, he cooled off and had a better perspective. He apologized for being so grumpy, and we worked together to figure it out. We agreed that a smaller wedding at home would be preferable to a big wedding at a temple, and fate handed us a perfect location.

The previous year, when my father was in his forties, he'd had an unusual midlife crisis. Some men buy a Porsche or dive into an affair or a second marriage, but my father fell in love with a house. It was at the end of a long country road in a quiet part of Stamford and nestled on a rock cliff surrounded by forty acres of woods and a babbling stream. The house was fifties modern, with ceiling-to-floor glass walls and a gallery-like interior, all wood and open spaces. The plans for the house were a gift to the original owner from the famous architect Louis Skidmore of Skidmore, Owings & Merrill, with blueprints by Gordon Bunshaft, the firm's head architect. They had designed the iconic Lever House on Park Avenue, and this house looked like a slice of that building deposited in a beautiful setting. It was one of only two houses they ever designed—and the second was Gordon Bunshaft's own house, coincidentally built in East Hampton and later owned by Martha Stewart. It was a very cool house. My father wanted it, but it was way too expensive, and he hoped the price would eventually go down.

One day, when my parents were on vacation in the Caribbean, the real estate broker called to say that the seller had cut the price in half. In half!! My dad called his bank, arranged a mortgage, and bought the house on the spot. His dream came true, and Jeffrey and I persuaded my parents that it would be the perfect setting for a winter wedding.

I shopped for my wedding dress on my own, which strikes me as a little sad. It was just as well, because I'm sure my mother and I would have disagreed about the dress. I chose a white satin brocade gown, princess style, with fur-trimmed sleeves—very Snow Queen—and, remembering how Jeffrey loved seeing a bow in my hair, a silk tulle veil with a satin bow on the crown.

The real what-to-wear drama was all about Jeffrey. He planned on getting married in his uniform, and my mother was so opposed to the idea that, once again, she threatened that she wouldn't sign the marriage license. She was, typically, worrying about how it would look to her friends. For Jeffrey, it was a matter of principle. He was in the military, so it was unthinkable that he would dress like a civilian. His parents would have found it very strange and, more important, he couldn't imagine defying tradition just to please my mother. He stood up to her and won.

The hardest part of getting through the preparations for the wedding was being separated from Jeffrey the whole time. The smallest problems seemed bigger because we had to discuss them in letters that generally crossed in the mail.

He came home once in September, and we had the only fight we had in the six months we were engaged. In fact, we had the only fight we've had in almost sixty years. Jeffrey had it in his mind to buy me a wedding ring circled with diamonds. I thought it sounded way too extravagant and that simple gold bands would be more appropriate at this point in our lives. But I was happy to look at them, so off we went to the Forty-Seventh Street Diamond District in New York to shop for rings. When we got there, I instantly fell in love with the rings Jeffrey had imagined, but Jeffrey saw how expensive they were and decided maybe a simple gold band was perfectly fine after all. Wait a minute! What happened to my diamond ring? Jeffrey wisely suggested that we have lunch and discuss it.

I was imagining a romantic lunch at a restaurant, but instead, he took me to a walk-up pizza window. No table, no chairs, no white tablecloths, and certainly no waiters. One slice of pizza on the street was his idea of a romantic lunch? And half the pizza ended up on his sweater. *Should I be having second thoughts?*

Fortunately, the feeling passed in a flash. I wanted Jeffrey, pizza on his sweater and all, and his wonderful vision of our life together.

We went back to the jeweler and bought two lovely gold bands for the wedding. (Which, by the way, both of us wore for a couple of years, took off, and never wore again.) Life lesson—some things you think are important turn out to be not worth worrying about.

During this time, Jeffrey often wrote to me about what we'd do in the future, including one memorable (and prophetic!) letter about a trip to Paris. We had no money, so this was just wishful thinking. But he had a plan.

> Here are my plans/dreams. We go to Paris once, at least, in the next five years. We won't have much money but that will be all the fun. Maybe we could go camping. But instead of touring the Louvre, etc., I'd like to get up at 4 a.m. and walk the streets . . . down the Champs de L'Esse [*his spelling!*] while the sun comes up . . . around the markets . . . along the Seine. That's us . . . not the fancy restaurants, etc.
>
> Next time we go, we'll just live in some small apartment for about two weeks . . .
>
> Next time—I'm older . . . you're not.
>
> Next time—maybe we'll have some money, and then we'll want to do only the things we did when we didn't have any.
>
> I'm so excited about this idea. You're going to make my whole life so exciting—

He was going to make *my* life so exciting!

The wedding was set for Sunday, December 22, in the late afternoon. The caterers took over the house while I went to my parents' bedroom to get dressed. One of the catering assistants came in, complimented my gown, and asked if my name was Irene. I said "Yes!" *Wait a minute! That's not right!* I was so nervous that I didn't even remember my own name!

Finally, the big moment.

I put on my veil and picked up my bouquet of white sweetheart roses and stephanotis. My father took my arm and escorted me down the aisle that led from the master bedroom, through the living room, to the sunporch, where the ceremony would take place. Dad was his usual volatile self. Twenty minutes before the wedding, he had exploded—gone absolutely berserk—when the tent guy told him they hadn't brought a heater . . . in freezing December. Dad had carried on until he was assured one was on the way. Now he smiled at the guests and whispered jokes in my ear the whole time we walked.

I tried not to show that I was annoyed by his antics, which seemed inappropriate during this special moment. Instead, I focused on Jeffrey, who looked so distinguished in the uniform that had caused such a fuss, and he watched my every move.

Then it was just the two of us, bride and groom, impossibly young but so certain about what we were doing, about the vows we would take, about the crazy adventure that was about to begin with the words "I do"!

At one point during the ceremony, I looked out the wall of glass and saw snow falling, covering the trees. It was magical, like something out of a fairy tale. The guests who had to drive home probably didn't share my enthusiasm for the sudden storm, but it was so beautiful.

We had champagne and hors d'oeuvres with our guests in the (heated!) tent outside the house, while inside, the caterers removed the chairs from the ceremony and set up tables for dinner. After the wedding, as the woods filled with snow, one of the parking attendants approached my father and said nervously, "Dr. Rosenberg, the snow is so deep we can't get the cars out." My father, who I'd *never* heard say a swear word in his life, said, "Fuck it! Give them more champagne!" I think it was the perfect sentiment for how deliriously happy he felt that day. Happy that I was married, and honestly, relieved that Jeffrey was the one who had to worry about me from now on. *More champagne!*

One of my favorite moments was captured in a photograph. I'm dancing with my father, movie star handsome in his tuxedo, and he's looking at me with love and pride. As we twirled and dipped, I felt that he was starting to see me, *really* see me, in a way he hadn't before.

Lovely as the wedding was, Jeffrey and I couldn't wait to get out of there and be alone, and no amount of snow was going to stop us. I changed into my going-away outfit, a Calvin Klein powder-pink coat and the first dress Calvin Klein ever designed—in chocolate-brown wool—plus a brown mink pillbox hat (very sixties and very Jackie Kennedy), matching shoes, purse, gloves, and a corsage. We waved goodbye and jumped into a car with friends who were driving us to New York for our wedding night at the Plaza Hotel before we left on our honeymoon.

We were excited about going to the Bahamas the next day, a wedding gift from Jeffrey's parents. But, as Jeffrey confessed to me years later, one terrifying thought crossed his mind when he looked at me sitting in that car: *Oh my God, I'm responsible for this person. I have to make sure she keeps breathing!* I imagine it's what first-time parents think when they look at their newborn baby. I was just living in the moment, happier than I'd ever been.

That Girl

Honeymoon in the Bahamas . . . warm beaches, tall drinks with umbrellas, sunsets, and long, romantic evenings. The perfect start for a perfect marriage. That's what we expected when we boarded our flight to Nassau. It was still snowing in New York, so we bundled up in our heaviest clothes and packed our bathing suits and everything else we needed for the vacation. Big mistake. We arrived, but our luggage didn't. Jeffrey immediately found the airport manager—it was a tiny place at the time—and explained to him that we would be there only a few days and we had nothing but the wool clothes on our backs. Help!

The manager assured him that this happened all the time and our bags would follow on the next flight. We checked into our hotel, looked longingly at the beach, and waited patiently.

For the next flight . . .

And the next flight . . .

And the flight after that . . .

No bags. No bathing suits. No beach.

The next morning, Jeffrey was a man on a mission. He went back to the airport, cornered the manager, and tried to make him understand the urgency of our situation—this was our honeymoon, and he was on a short-term pass from gruesome jungle training. The clock was ticking, time was running out, and he was getting mad.

"I don't want you to take this personally," Jeffrey said quietly, "but if our luggage isn't at the hotel by noon, I may have to burn down this airport. I've just been to paratrooper and ranger school, so don't think I don't know what I'm talking about."

It's hard to imagine Jeffrey, the gentlest man in the world, saying anything like that, but he was *really* mad.

The manager looked at this young soldier who was clearly desperate—on his honeymoon, no less—and pulled out his wallet and started counting bills, offering Jeffrey $300 to go out and buy some clothes and whatever else we needed. Jeffrey pointed out that we would spend it right away. What would happen if the luggage showed up? We didn't have any money and could never afford to pay it back.

The man, eager to see the last of Jeffrey, told him not to worry about it, that we should spend the money and have a good time.

Jeffrey raced back to the hotel to give me the good news. *We're rich!* We jumped on the bed and threw the cash up in the air. Before it even hit the ground, the phone rang. Our bags had arrived and were on their way up to the room.

Well, that nice man did say to spend the money, and Jeffrey had an idea.

My father always said there were two things he would never buy for me: pearls and cashmere. According to him, that would be something special to look forward to when my husband bought them for me. (Apparently, it never occurred to him that I might be able to buy them for myself, but it *was* the sixties.) Two days into the marriage, Jeffrey was taking his new role very seriously. He disappeared with the cash and came back with a surprise, a pink cashmere sweater set, a popular resort look, and pearl earrings— I still don't even know how he did that for $300!

The honeymoon went by too quickly, and soon it was time to head back to our new reality, which was a little unusual for newly-weds. Jeffrey reported to the base to continue his jungle training, and I went back to Syracuse to take my finals. How strange to be a married woman, back in my old dorm room, surrounded by students who were pulling all-nighters! The last thing I felt like doing was studying.

But passing my exams was the least of my problems. Back in the fall, when it had started to get cold, a friend had told me that her father, a furrier, would give me a great deal on a fur blanket (made from the leftover bits and pieces of the fur coats he sold), which I apparently had decided I couldn't live without in freezing Syracuse. I had placed an order and promptly forgotten about it because I didn't have to pay for it until delivery (talk about living in the moment?!).

When I got back to school, the blanket was waiting for me, along with the bill—it was close to the $100 Jeffrey had given me to spend for the month that I was at school. In those days, husbands generally managed the family finances because they were, as we quaintly called them, the breadwinners. There was no way I could burn through all my money on the very first day! Jeffrey would think I was so irresponsible! I had to find some way to pay for that blanket. I came up with an *I Love Lucy* solution that turned out to be my first foray into the food business.

It was finals week in the dorm. Everyone was cramming for exams and pulling all-nighters. I went to the nearest Dunkin' Donuts and bought dozens of doughnuts in every flavor. Then I went door-to-door in the dorm, selling them individually (at a significant markup) to all the students who were desperate for sugar. When I ran out of doughnuts, I bought more and sold them to my hungry customers. In between, I studied for my own exams, but I made enough money to pay my debt, and I learned something about unit pricing and profit, which I filed away for the future. (Not to mention, I could never look at a doughnut ever again!)

My next destination was Fayetteville, North Carolina, where I joined Jeffrey at Fort Bragg. Our first "home" was in the bachelor officers' quarters on the base, and it was the most revolting place I'd ever seen. The sheets looked like they hadn't been changed since the last person had stayed there, maybe even the person before that. I slept in my clothes, refused to touch anything, and vowed to get the hell out of there as soon as possible. Admittedly, I'm a bit of a germaphobe, but this was *dirty*. Maybe this marriage thing wasn't going to work out so well?

I met with a real estate agent the next morning and rented the first place I saw, which may have been a little hasty. Jeffrey came over later and took one look at the dark, dingy rooms and shook his head, predicting we'd be out of there fast. My answer was curtains! "Curtains and a deep cleaning will make this place really nice," I promised. I spent the next three weeks scrubbing, until I literally threw in the towel and admitted I'd made a terrible mistake.

We paid the rent through the end of the month, lost our deposit, and bolted, settling into a beautiful garden apartment with a brand-new kitchen. The rooms were airy, with lots of windows, great light, and a washer and dryer. It was a blank slate, and I remember standing in the apartment, realizing that for the very first time, I was free to turn it into whatever I wanted; my parents had no control over me and they couldn't tell me what to do. After all my mother's negativity, I could design the rooms, cook anything I wanted, throw parties, and make a home for us.

The funny thing is that we were probably on a very tight budget, but I never felt financially restricted. I could always find something that I liked and that we could afford. Luckily, I knew how to sew, and I was too young and inexperienced to be afraid of mistakes. Like the rug in the living room: I picked one that had a million colors, thinking it would go with everything. It went with nothing. That rug's superpower was to make every stick of furniture look bad. Lesson learned.

We bought a few pieces of furniture, but we also borrowed some from the army inventory that was available to military families, with everything from tables to framed photographs. Like most of my contemporaries in the late sixties, I was enamored of anything Scandinavian—Marimekko, Dansk—to the point where Jeffrey suggested it would be cheaper to send me to Sweden to shop. In the end, it all came together in some crazy, mismatched way, and we loved it because it was ours. I actually still have a spatula from our first kitchen.

We quickly settled into our young marrieds' routine. I kissed Jeffrey goodbye at five a.m., when he left for the base. His uniforms were professionally dry-cleaned and pressed to perfection, with so much starch in the pants that he had to roll them on a hanger to make them soft enough to wear. They could have walked out the door on their own!

What did I do? Besides going to college, there was dinner to prepare every night—we certainly couldn't afford to go to a restaurant—which meant coming up with a menu, shopping at the base, and then teaching myself how to cook. I had to learn everything. My bible at the time was Craig Claiborne's *New York Times Cookbook,* and I immediately started making his recipes. We loved his chili, but Jeffrey begged me to stop making it because he ate so much he would make himself sick.

One day, Jeffrey called from the base to say he was bringing a friend home for lunch. *Lunch? Lunch? I have to make lunch, too?*

I ran to the store and got the ingredients to make a big gooey lasagna, a nice green salad, and, for dessert, ice cream sundaes covered with hot fudge, whipped cream, and nuts. Double whammy! Jeffrey and his friend ate every bite and dragged themselves back to the office, trying to stay awake for the afternoon. Oops! As they say, sometimes actions speak louder than words, and that was definitely the last time Jeffrey asked if he could bring a friend home for lunch!

Like most young couples, we were eager to host our first grown-up party. We invited about twenty people who didn't know each other (bad idea!) to come for brunch. It was so awkward! Everyone sat around in a big circle in the living room, saying very little. To make things worse, I had decided to make an omelet for each person, which of course had to be prepared one at a time, so I was stuck in the kitchen for the entire party (although I don't think I missed much), while Jeffrey was in the living room trying desperately to keep the conversation interesting. Total disaster! I think it took us a year to get up the courage to have another party, but at least I learned what *not* to do.

I was supposed to continue college at North Carolina State University, but my first term got off to a rocky start when I tried to register for classes. The process was so frustrating—trying to match the right course to the right time—that I told Jeffrey I'd had enough of school. I just didn't want to do it anymore. He listened to me and calmly said, "Okay. Forget about college. Don't go."

I was shocked because I had been expecting the harshly critical response I would have gotten from my parents if I had dared to suggest I didn't want to finish school. Instead, Jeffrey simply threw the ball back in my court. "Fine! Don't go to college." In a flash, I understood that this was *my* decision, not anyone else's, and in that moment, I realized that I actually wanted to finish college. And for the first time in my life, someone believed in me and knew I would make the right decision.

This is when Jeffrey started "bringing me up," the way a good parent would have done. Sometimes that "parenting" was annoying, especially when he pestered me about studying, which he did constantly. One day, I was alone in the bedroom we used as an office, and he noticed that I'd been quiet for a long time. Jeffrey thought, *Oh my God, I've broken her,* figuring that he'd put too much pressure on me to study. He came in to see how I was doing. Startled, I put down the book I was "studying," and its cover slipped off. He saw that I'd hidden a cookbook under a textbook jacket so I wouldn't get "caught" while I sat at my desk happily reading recipes. That's why I was so quiet! It was my small—and I must say *very* creative—way of rebelling.

I'll never forget the day when Jeffrey came home unexpectedly and found me sitting in the living room in front of the television at eleven o'clock in the morning. Ironically, I was watching *That Girl,* the Marlo Thomas show about an independent young woman making a life for herself in New York City. It was considered quite shocking at the time that a single woman lived on her own and that she had a "career" and a boyfriend who came to her apartment unchaperoned. Jeffrey looked at me for a moment and said, "You need to figure out what to do with your life or you won't be happy."

He wasn't being mean or calling me lazy. He knew I had other ways to occupy myself—school, friends, dinner parties! He was telling me that I was too smart not to do something with my life, which no one had ever said to me before. I thought getting married was what I was "supposed" to do, and I had done it. Instead, Jeffrey was inviting me to think about the future because he knew that at some point, I would want more for myself. I often think that Jeffrey was the first feminist I knew; he believed women had as much potential as men and I had a responsibility to myself to fulfill mine.

At first, I was shocked because, after getting married, I had stopped thinking about "doing" anything or making big, long-term choices about a career. I used to talk about being an architect or a real estate developer. Why did marriage dim those ambitions? The problem in our case was that we were in a holding pattern until Jeffrey got out of the army, which was years away. But he was right. It wouldn't hurt me to start planning, and clearly, I needed some motivation.

Like, for example, when he persuaded me to take a really difficult history class. Knowing that I was fiercely competitive, Jeffrey suggested that we both sign up for the class—it was offered in the evening, after he finished work—and promised that if I got an A, he'd teach me how to play squash, something I'd always wanted to do. What he failed to tell me was that he'd found out that the professor had *never* given an A to anyone in the history of the class. I studied harder than I'd ever studied before because I wanted to beat him. I got an A, Jeffrey got a B+, and we were off to the squash court.

Or so we thought. It turned out that the squash courts were designed to ensure that women couldn't play. The architects had made the entrance to the courts through the men's locker room so there was no way for a woman to access them. This was a time when women faced barriers everywhere, which was why Gloria Steinem and other feminists were asking important questions. Why weren't women allowed in a school, a bank, a club, or even a squash court? I wanted to do what I wanted to do without any barriers standing in my way.

After all my hard work, nothing was going to keep me from playing squash.

We figured out a way to sneak me into the men's locker room so I could access the court, and I ended up loving the game. But there would be more barriers ahead, some bigger than others, and the thing about me is that I see a barrier as a challenge rather than a stop sign.

Whenever we drove to the base from our apartment, we passed a small private airport. I was intrigued because one of my friends at Syracuse was an aerospace engineer, and I thought being a pilot was cool. As I watched the planes flying in and out, I decided I wanted to get my pilot's license. I marched into the terminal to find out about taking flying lessons. "I'm really sorry," the startled person at the desk told me, "but we don't have anybody who'll teach a girl how to fly." Really? Had he ever heard of Amelia Earhart?

I stood there, stubbornly refusing to take no for an answer. When they realized I wasn't going away, they found an open-minded instructor in the next town over who would come give me lessons.

This was one of the moments that I learned to appreciate later in my life—an example of my belief in trying lots of things to see if they feel right. I had no idea what flying a plane would be like, but I wanted to try. In some ways, it was like driving a car, just a little more complicated and much more dangerous. If something goes wrong with your car, you can just pull over to the side of the road and wait for the tow truck to rescue you. Not so much with an airplane—you needed to know what to do in an emergency. My instructor would do things like turn off the engine midflight (yikes!) so I'd know what to do if the engine failed, or he would have me fly using just the instruments (no peeking out the window) so I'd know what to do if I ended up in a passing cloud. My first solo flight was exciting but also terrifying!

There were some mishaps along the way (which no one wants in an airplane!). One time when I was landing solo, I asked for permission to land (so far so good) and landed beautifully. I was very pleased with myself, but unfortunately, I forgot to ask for permission to taxi to the terminal. I made a sharp right turn (without looking first, which is like driving a car and not looking when you turn), and there, in the middle of the taxiway, was a HUGE helicopter, just hanging out there with its rotor whirring. I realized that I wasn't going to be able to stop in time, even if I was STANDING on the brakes! Fortunately, the helicopter pilot saw me and swooped up just in time for me to taxi UNDER the helicopter like a stunt in an action movie, except this was the real thing. All I could hear was the humiliating sound of the tower telling the helicopter pilot in a disgusted tone of voice, "Student pilot!" (I'm surprised he didn't say "Girl pilot," but I'm sure that's what he was thinking!)

Soon Jeffrey realized he might end up in a plane with me at the controls. He decided that he didn't want to just sit there, not knowing what to do in an emergency, so he signed up for flying lessons, too. His one problem was that he had a hard time reading maps. I mean, Jeffrey is really smart, but he could barely unfold the map.

When it came time for his first solo flight, he had to fly to Charlotte and back in one day, but without a map, that's an impossible thing to do. As always, he came up with an ingenious workaround. He picked a gorgeous, cloudless day, executed a perfect takeoff from Fayetteville, and flew so low that he was able to follow Interstate 95 and read the road signs all the way to the airport in Charlotte. He could have been driving a car. Still reading the signs, he took a right turn on I-74, landed in Charlotte, then flew the reverse trip over the same highway back to Fayetteville.

We never ended up flying anywhere together, which was probably a good thing for everyone else in the air. And like many things I've undertaken in my life, once I tried flying, I decided I wasn't passionate about it, so I left my flying days behind me in North Carolina. But I'm so glad I tried.

After I gave up flying, I decided to get a job after school, first at a women's clothing store called the Prissy Hen. The first day, I worked from four thirty to six p.m., and I was so excruciatingly bored that when I went home that night, I told Jeffrey I couldn't spend another minute at the Prissy Hen (which I couldn't even say with a straight face), so I ended up working there for all of an hour and a half.

My next job was at a local bookstore. The owner was a retired naval officer—I think he was an admiral—who ran the place like a warship. On the first day, he presented every employee with an SOP, the store's standard operating procedure, and we had to memorize it. It wasn't a bad idea to set standards and practices for employees so they would know how to handle various situations with customers (and it was something I did later at Barefoot Contessa). But this was like the United States Navy's *Bluejacket's Manual,* with rigid rules for absolutely everything. The place was small, only about a thousand square feet, with a few employees, yet when the admiral wanted to communicate something to the staff, he'd circulate a memo, which everyone (all four of us) had to sign, indicating that we'd read it. At least we didn't have to salute and say, "Yes, sir!"

I stacked books, tracked inventory, and tried to keep up with the admiral's never-ending demands. The best thing about the job was meeting my friend Carolyn. We started working on the same day and quickly discovered that we had a lot in common—we both had husbands at Fort Bragg, we loved to cook, and we enjoyed exploring the area together. At work, we chatted constantly, the only sparks of life in that dour place. The admiral eyed us disapprovingly as if we were misbehaving toddlers.

One day, when yet another annoying memo came around, I was shocked to read that it was about me. I'd been fired! Fired, just like that, no explanation, for all (well, the other three people) to see. I wasn't devastated by the news—it was like being thrown out of class for talking too much. "I guess he didn't find our conversations as interesting as we did?" I told Carolyn, who'd somehow escaped the guillotine. But I was appalled by the way it was delivered, abruptly, publicly, and with absolutely no consideration for my feelings.

It was a good experience, though, because years later, when I became the boss, I knew how to be a better one. If I had a problem with an employee, first we'd talk about it privately to see if we could fix it. If there wasn't a solution, and firing was the only option, I'd take the time to explain why, so they might know how to approach the next job differently or find a job that better suited their interests. People usually thanked me for firing them! Afterward, I would call the rest of my staff together and explain why the person was fired. I did this for two reasons: first, to show them that I wasn't being arbitrary, there was a specific problem; and second, to clarify that the employee's behavior wasn't okay. Surprisingly, although I was concerned that everyone would be upset with me for firing their coworker, they always agreed with me. Each time, I found out that the staff was as annoyed by the bad behavior as I was. Lesson learned.

Our holding-pattern approach to life continued. After spending eighteen months at Fort Bragg, Jeffrey, a paratrooper and then a Green Beret, was stationed overseas for a one-year assignment in Thailand. We were relieved that he wasn't deployed to Vietnam, but I was devastated by the thought of being separated for so long. Unfortunately, there was no exotic destination in my future. My plan was to move in with my parents in Stamford and finish college at a local university.

My Green Beret husband

The Body Shop
Doesn't Do Car Repairs??

Why didn't it occur to me to go to a different place? Maybe find a job in New York, or anywhere else, and rent an apartment? Have an adventure? It's just amazing to me now that my one thought was to move home, to go straight from living in my own house to living with my parents again, an arrangement I didn't even like the first time around. I think I didn't see myself as independent. I was somebody's wife or daughter, not a woman who could live on her own, despite Marlo Thomas's example. And given our limited income, we needed to save money, not find new ways to spend it. I wasn't happy about my situation, but I didn't think of another solution.

We packed up the things we wanted to keep (not the multi-colored rug), and just before Jeffrey left, I hid some surprises in his suitcase. I buried candy in his socks and tucked a desk calendar under his uniforms, so he could count the days (months, actually) until we would see each other again.

Then I *cried* for days, until I forced myself to get up and put one foot in front of the other and head back home. I tried to work up some enthusiasm for an existence that was all too familiar, and not in a good way. My mother was still very judgmental, my father mercurial, but I deflected or ignored their disapproval when it came my way and spent more long, lonely hours in my room.

My brother, Ken, rarely came home while he was at college, and he spent the summer after graduation in Palo Alto, California, where he saw—and was inspired by—young people living communally. When he moved to Boston for medical school, he and his girlfriend bought an eight-bedroom house that they ran communally, sharing expenses with housemates. He was political (a member of SDS, Students for a Democratic Society, at Dartmouth) and wanted to change the world, but I think he was searching for the same thing I wanted after growing up feeling so lonely and isolated—community, companionship, and a more nurturing environment.

I saw friends occasionally, although most of the people I knew had moved away, and I tried to keep busy with outings to museums, the opera, the philharmonic—*anything* that would distract me. And I read—and reread—Jeffrey's letters from the other side of the world, where his days played out in a place I couldn't see, where he was living in a "hootch," eating strange foods, and meeting new people.

My one goal that year was simply to graduate from college. I was an economics major and registered for classes in biology, French, and philosophy—an ambitious schedule for someone who always found a way to avoid schoolwork. I also signed up for a business class, which was based not on theories but on actual case studies. I was shocked that I had finally found something in school that inspired me. We were taught business through studying actual business problems, an approach that changed the way I looked at the subject.

Instead of dry facts and statistics, there were detailed stories about real-life companies caught up in challenging situations. I was using the same part of my brain that powered my high school science projects. Whether I was analyzing production issues at

Boeing or predicting consumer behavior in agricultural markets, the process was the same: observe, test, and evaluate effectiveness and results. Flash forward to the future: when food became my business, I used this exact methodology to grow Barefoot Contessa, even to test recipes, experimenting over and over again until I found the perfect combination of ingredients to create the taste I wanted.

I knew I was the kind of person who jumped into situations—"leap before you look" seemed to be my standard operating procedure, and it was doubtful I would ever change. But I was learning that once I landed, I just might have the analytical skills to make it work—whatever "it" was. At this point in my life, I had no idea how I could use these skills in the real world or at a real job. But I was exercising intellectual muscles and figuring out my strengths and weaknesses, which was a good start.

Meanwhile, Jeffrey continued to entertain me with long letters about his adventures. He was recounting once-in-a-lifetime experiences—living in the shadow of a mountain that was home to tigers, teaching English to Thai children, exploring Bangkok in his free time—while I was just getting through the day.

Telephone calls were rare because the circuits were always busy. When we did manage to speak, it was hard to have a conversation because there was an annoying delay during international calls. I'd say something, then I'd have to wait for Jeffrey's response. By the time he answered, I'd moved on to the next topic. There was too much to say in too little time, which was frustrating for both of us. Still, it was wonderful just to hear his voice.

What I really missed was cooking for Jeffrey. When we were in college, or he was training somewhere in America, I could send him his favorite oatmeal cookies and brownies. But Thailand was so far away that most foods would be inedible by the time they got there. (There was no FedEx in 1970.) I needed something that was delicious *and* indestructible. The solution was a word I thought I'd never say—fruitcake! Turns out fruitcake can survive for days, weeks, even months. Like landfill, you can't kill it. In December, I found a recipe full of fruit, coconut, pecans, almonds, and cognac in my trusty Craig Claiborne cookbook, baked it, and shipped it to him. He loved it (at least he said he did!), and the thought of him enjoying my cooking on the other side of the world made the lonely holiday season more bearable.

After five months of painful separation—missed anniversary, missed birthdays, missed everything—we decided to meet in Tokyo for a vacation. I think planning the trip was the most exciting part. Whenever I felt depressed about my living situation or overwhelmed by school (I was determined to graduate the following May, so I kept adding classes to my schedule), I had something to look forward to in March—my first reunion with Jeffrey.

Finally, the advantage of being an army wife. See the world! At the end of March, I met Jeffrey in Tokyo, and it took about a second and a half for us to forget that we had been apart. We checked into the Palace Hotel, which was a beautiful combination of East-meets-West architecture, and immediately started exploring the city. I don't have vivid memories of the food, probably because of a funny quirk of the seventies. The restaurants considered to be the "best" in every city were always French, the fancy Le Cordon Bleu kind, with a cuisine heavily dependent on elaborate recipes with lots of butter and cream. This was true in Mexico, where I vacationed with my parents; in Bangkok, where Jeffrey occasionally went out for dinner; and now in Tokyo. Travelers weren't encouraged to eat local, the way they are today, so it was possible to visit a place and never taste anything regional. I doubt that I had a single piece of sushi the whole time I was in Japan.

We spent two weeks together, and at the end of the trip, I decided that as soon as I graduated from college in May, I'd move to Bangkok to be closer to Jeffrey for the rest of his stay in Thailand.

Easier said than done. First, I had to graduate, which meant powering through the final weeks of school. Then, Jeffrey and I had to figure out how to get me to Bangkok and where I would live once I arrived. I was told that "dependents" weren't allowed to come to Thailand, but there is nothing like a barrier to trigger my rebellious streak—the army couldn't stop me from going to Bangkok, right? I had no idea what I would do or where I would live; I just needed to be in the same country as Jeffrey. I must have gained a lot of confidence over the past year, because the same young woman who thought it was a good idea to move home with her parents felt perfectly comfortable with the thought of flying halfway around the world and living on her own in Southeast Asia!

It was a pretty radical idea at the time. One of my friends toyed with the idea of traveling with me, and she checked with the Dartmouth Travel Bureau to see if they could help with the arrangements. The response was that the bureau didn't have any *objection* to our traveling to Thailand without our husbands. I'm sure they thought it was incredibly open-minded to green-light a trip for two unaccompanied women. Now it seems outrageous to me that anyone thought we needed their permission!

My friend decided to stay home, so I was on my own. I graduated at the end of May and felt incredibly relieved and excited when I dressed in my cap and gown and collected my diploma. Finally, school was behind me! I think I jumped on the next flight to Thailand. It was possible to find a cheap ticket for the international flight, but it bought me a long trip that involved switching planes and an overnight layover in Belgium. In my excitement,

I'd neglected to plan how or where I would spend the night between flights. Fortunately, I sat next to a friendly girl on the plane who said I could crash in her hotel room. My immediate response was "Great!"—never thinking about serial killers, sex trafficking, kidney theft, or any of the other scenarios that might stop a sane traveler from accepting an invitation from a total stranger. It was fine; a few hours in a hotel and I was on my way.

Jeffrey picked me up at the airport and announced that we had plans that very night: the Dartmouth Club was hosting a dinner for alumni in Bangkok. I may have had second thoughts about getting off an airplane and going to an event, but it turned out to be a really good decision. I sat next to a charming man who was the head of Citibank in Bangkok. When he heard that I was planning on living in a hotel and seeing Jeffrey on weekends, he stepped in with an incredible invitation. "You know what," he said. "My wife and I have a huge house with a big staff to take care of us and our three children. Why don't you just stay with us?"

Seriously? I'd been in Thailand only a few hours and I already felt comfortable and secure.

Maybe a little too secure. A few days later, I decided I would take a bus to visit Jeffrey, three hours north of Bangkok in the middle of nowhere on the Thai/Burmese border. There was no hope of communicating with anyone on that bus. Thai is a tonal language—the same grouping of sounds with a different tone has a completely different meaning, so it's not like I could pick up a word here and there and start speaking. All I could do was smile, nod, and hope for the best.

I was literally the only Westerner on the bus, which was filled with women chewing betel nuts that turned their mouths bright red (think Bloody Mary in *South Pacific*!), with chickens and ducks and other livestock in baskets tied to the roof. I wasn't nervous or worried, just blindly confident that I would get off in the right place and find Jeffrey. What was I thinking? I had no way to understand what anyone was saying, no cell phone (because they hadn't been invented yet), and yet no fear of ending up stranded in the wrong village and never being seen again.

Like a cat with nine lives, I reached my destination, even though I couldn't even pronounce the name of the village he was living in. Somehow, the bus driver knew when to tell me to get off the bus, and suddenly a little kid appeared and grabbed my luggage. I thought he was running away with it, but he led me to a car and motioned for me to get in. The driver didn't say a word—he just looked at me and took me to the only other Americans in town. And there was Jeffrey. I can't even imagine how that worked out okay!

The Pentagon encouraged Jeffrey to think about a career in the military, which was flattering, but we were ready for civilian life. Jeffrey's deferred enrollment at Johns Hopkins School of Advanced International Studies was scheduled for the fall of 1972. With only six months of service left, he didn't have time to begin anything serious or long-term, so he requested an administrative job in Colorado. The best part about spending the winter in Colorado was that we'd be able to ski.

We returned from Thailand; packed up our English Rover, which we'd left in Connecticut; and headed west. Driving cross-country may have been overly ambitious. The car was so full we barely had room to sit, not to mention my parents had given us a houseplant we had to take along for the ride and somehow keep alive. It was the longest road trip I'd ever taken, and no matter how many miles we covered, we always seemed to be in Kansas, surrounded by endless fields. The car broke down in St. Louis, where the only foreign car they'd ever seen was a Volkswagen, so we waited for days—without a car!—for the replacement part for the Rover to be airmailed from London.

I was going crazy in that car. At one point, I opened the door and threatened to jump out while Jeffrey was still driving. We finally got to a Holiday Inn at the end of the Kansas highway, and the only room they had left was . . . the bridal suite. I told Jeffrey that I was divorcing him if he didn't book that room, so that's where we spent the night.

Finally, we arrived in Colorado Springs to a bright-blue sky and snow on the ground in September. Life was going to be just fine. My friend Carolyn from Fort Bragg and her husband were living in nearby Breckenridge, a ski resort, which meant we could plan playdates. Carolyn and I fed the ducks at the Broadmoor Hotel, played bridge, and started cooking together, competing to see who could make the best quiches and pâtés, the signature recipes of the early seventies. She didn't have a dishwasher, so when we cooked at her place on weekends, we just packed up the dirty dishes in a box, brought them to our apartment, and loaded them in our dishwasher, which I thought was an ingenious solution. (It probably would have been easier to just wash them by hand!) We felt so sophisticated when we learned how to brew drip coffee, and we drank bottomless cups while we discussed provocative new books, like Kate Millett's *Sexual Politics*.

Eventually, I did have to find a job, so I went to an employment agency to see what was available. They pulled out some file cards listing secretarial positions; the first paid $250 a week, the second $275 a week, and then, "Oh wait, this one pays five hundred a week!" "I want that job," I said immediately. I didn't ask any questions. They gave me the address of the Body Shop, an office in a strip mall, and I felt like I'd won the lottery when I was hired on the spot. I assumed the Body Shop was an auto repair place.

It was mostly clerical work—I had to answer the phone, keep the books, and make out the payroll, which seemed simple enough until I saw the first name on the list of employees, "Boom Boom" something. *Oh my God,* I thought. The Body Shop wasn't a business that had anything to do with car repair—it was the back office for the strip club down the block!

My boss asked me to place an ad in the newspaper for "models"—nude models, he explained. "But don't write that," he quickly added. When women started calling about the ad, I'd whisper, "You know this is for nude modeling, right?" trying to warn them. Most of them just hung up on me, but one woman said, "Honey, I wasn't born yesterday!" (She got the job.)

Unfortunately, at some point, the police showed up, and my boss ducked out the back door, saying, "Don't tell them I'm here." That seemed like a cue for my exit from the Body Shop, so two weeks later, I walked away from Boom Boom, the nude "models," and my big salary.

My next job was far more respectable but not nearly as colorful. The employment agency that found me the job at the Body Shop hired me to be their receptionist. There was absolutely nothing to do, so my new boss and I played chess all day. I did have to place "help wanted" ads in the local paper, and I remember coming across an ad for a store that sold musical instruments looking for someone to "display organs." I didn't think anyone was going to answer that ad!

Our stay in Colorado Springs was a long, lovely vacation in a beautiful place. The only issue was our timing, which was a little off. There was a gap between when Jeffrey finished his military service at the end of April and when graduate school started in the fall. We were saying goodbye to the army, but we had no idea what to do until school started.

The fun-loving newlyweds were about to become nomads!

Two for the Road

Where would we live from May through August? What a good question! We dismissed any number of options—there wasn't time to get established in a new location, we didn't have enough money to start renting an apartment in Washington, and there was no way (yes, I'll say it, *no way in hell*) we were going to move in with my parents . . . again.

That left one completely wild and crazy idea, which, of course, immediately became our first choice.

We'd go to Europe! The dollar was strong, we had no responsibilities until the fall, and we loved to travel together. Jeffrey took a long, hard look at our tiny savings account and calculated that we could stay in Europe for four months IF we kept to a budget of five dollars a day. I know that sounds insane, but there was actually a very popular book at the time, Arthur Frommer's *Europe on 5 Dollars a Day,* that told us exactly how to do it. Ironically, the little paperback cost about $3.50, which was most of a full day's expenses, but worth it.

Jeffrey, the master planner, figured out some of the major expenses in advance. Flying to Europe was pretty cheap. He found an airline that offered ninety-nine-dollar round-trip tickets from New York to Frankfurt that were technically for students, but he was going to graduate school, so we made the cut. Finding a way to live abroad for all that time was another story. Hotels were out of the question; even the cheap ones with the bathroom down the hall were way beyond our means. The only way we could swing it was by camping our way through Europe, which actually sounded like fun!

Jeffrey found a great deal on a car, a purchase/buyback arrangement where we could buy the car in Paris, then sell it back to the dealer at the end of the trip for $500 less than the purchase price. Arrangements in place, we flew into Frankfurt, toting our bags, tennis rackets, a camping stove, and a very small, extremely bright orange tent. We took the train from Frankfurt to Paris, where we picked up our cherry-red Renault 4, one of the very first hatchbacks, with the gearshift on the dashboard and a removable seat in the back. For the first time in our lives, we were free as birds! We could go anywhere, see anything, stay as long as we liked, leave at five in the morning, and eat a croissant any time of the day. No parents, no teachers, and no military rules. And I would have my best buddy with me the whole time. I was as happy as I'd ever been.

I think we were shocked (*How did we pull this off?!*) and nervous (*What do we do next?*) but definitely excited when we loaded the car and took our positions in the front seat—Jeffrey, the driver, and me, the navigator and reader of the maps (as I've mentioned, not Jeffrey's strong point!) and guidebooks. For the next four months, our little Renault would be our chariot, our home on wheels, our everything. The "plan" was to not have a plan—to travel like real Europeans, moving from country to country, campsite to campsite, whenever we pleased. Military life, with its regimens and tours of duty, was in the rearview mirror. Ahead, open roads and endless possibilities.

I think what I loved most, aside from Jeffrey's constant company and undivided attention, was that there were no straight lines between where we were and where we wanted to be. Our route was dictated by whimsy, not logic. Money wasn't really an issue because frankly, we didn't have any. What we had in abundance was time—time to wander, time to get lost, time to waste. We knew it was a rare opportunity to have no agenda or anything we *had* to do. Our only responsibility was to explore and have a good time. And we knew we'd be really good at that.

Where did we go from Paris? We started the car and headed north to Amsterdam, a very popular destination in the seventies. No, we weren't going for the drugs. I wanted to see the Van Goghs and an exhibit of drawings by Matisse (my favorite) at the Kröller-Müller Museum. It wasn't so far, about three hundred miles, like driving from New York to Vermont. That was the other great thing about traveling in Europe. The distance between countries was so short that we could start out in France and end up in the Netherlands later that day.

At some point during the drive, we realized we wouldn't be able to camp that first night on the road, so *just this once* we broke our own rule and decided to stay in a hotel in Amsterdam. The precious sum of ten dollars (two days' budget!) bought us a small, dank room in a hotel basement—it was so dark that I couldn't see what bit me in the middle of the night. I'm still hoping it was a spider and nothing worse! One bite was enough to convince me that I needed a sleeping bag to protect me from other creepy-crawlies that might see me as a tasty meal. Jeffrey was hardier—he was fine with an air mattress and a blanket. I needed a padded fortress.

We woke up the next morning and went directly to a camping store to buy a sleeping bag. For the next four months, even on the hottest nights—and Europe was *historically* hot that summer—Jeffrey slept next to a puffy khaki bag with two eyes peeking out at the top. It was hard to tell there was a girl under all that wrapping. Not so romantic, but safe from biting bugs!

For our first night of camping, we drove to the North Sea coast in Holland, a landscape that was cold, wild, and windswept in early April. All the other campers were safely tucked into heated caravans on wheels that looked like little houses with porches. But we had to brave the fierce winds and pouring rain and figure out how to put together that damn orange tent. Not knowing whether to laugh or cry, we got it assembled by reading the directions with a flashlight in the dark and climbed inside. Safe! But not for long. A few hours later, the whole tent came crashing down on top of us and we crawled out of the mess and went to sleep in the car.

Following a roundabout route, we headed for the romantic-sounding Isle of Skye in Scotland, which in fact felt like the end of the world. Darkness fell, and the road was eerily empty. I searched my map, but there didn't seem to be any campsites in the area, so we just pulled over by the side of the road and set up our tent in a nearby grassy area. Dinner would have to be crackers and cheese from my little tent "larder." With nothing else to do, we tucked ourselves in and went to sleep.

The sun came up *very* early in Skye, and by four thirty a.m. the tent was boiling hot and glowing like a space orb. Then we heard strange noises coming from outside. A chorus of "baaa, baaa, baaa." We peeked through the opening and saw what we'd missed the night before. We were in a field, and our tent was surrounded by a flock of very curious—and very loud—sheep. They watched with great interest as we dismantled the tent, packed up the car, and made our getaway. After some sightseeing in Edinburgh, we headed south and took a ferry from Dover, England (think white cliffs), to Belgium (think frites!).

After Brussels, we drove to Normandy, just a few hours south. The next part of the trip was the beginning of something magical, the adventure we could never have imagined when we sat at our kitchen table in Colorado Springs, studying our travel books. When I think of it, our deep dive into France was a *Wizard of Oz* moment, especially for me: the black-and-white screen burst into glorious Technicolor. The weather was better, that's for sure. And wherever we looked, there was something beautiful to see. The roads were lined with rows of trees—chestnut, plane, elm, and ash—planted by Napoleon to shade his soldiers from the sun during their long marches. Behind the trees, we caught glimpses of ancient stone farm buildings and houses that ranged from Norman Tudor to classic French country.

Who knows what was inside these old places? Probably crumbling walls and bad plumbing. But outside, there were tall, thin cypress pines, short, sculpted boxwoods, and dense plantings of lavender and rosemary. And the flowers! Roses, poppies, jasmine, and sunflowers, right out of an impressionist painting. Pea pebble walkways and bleached stone walls. The gardens made such an impression on the *young* me that, decades later, the *older* me tried to re-create some of that magic in my garden in East Hampton.

On the road, even the infamous roundabouts that popped up every so many miles seemed charming to us. In the States, rotaries, as we call them, usually provoke squealing brakes, honking horns, and the occasional rude hand gesture, because nobody understands who has the right-of-way. But in France, these little traffic circles are a reminder that life is not about straight lines or the shortest distance between two points. *Slow down,* they seemed to say, *you can take a little twirl and still get exactly where you're going.* Such a nice approach to life.

We settled into a leisurely routine, riding with the radio tuned to local stations playing the latest pop hits, usually in French, occasionally in English. Jeffrey and I had studied French in school, so we were comfortable with the language; I wouldn't say we were fluent, but we could certainly fake it! *Mais oui! Deux croissants, s'il vous plaît!*

Our two biggest decisions every day? Where to sleep and what to eat. How wonderful was that?! The sleeping part was easy. No more hotels for us, not on our budget. For better or for worse, we were officially happy campers. A word about campsites, our home away from home: In France, "camping" didn't mean pulling into a clearing in the woods and pitching a tent. When we looked at our maps, we saw campsites everywhere, and they were rated according to their amenities. High-end campsites, the ones with four stars, offered specialty food stores, restaurants, bars, pools, tennis courts, even beauty salons, kind of like DIY resorts. The ones on the low end (our range) still had nice bathrooms, showers with lots of hot water, laundromats, and places to buy food, and they usually cost the equivalent of a dollar a day.

We weren't the only thrifty travelers in Europe during the spring and summer of 1972. A record-breaking thirty million vacationers had spent their holidays at campsites the previous summer, whether in tents or more structured caravans, because it was so much cheaper than staying in a hotel. European families booked reservations for weeks at a time, typically the whole month of August. Experienced campers set up huge tents with portable kitchens and even porches with awnings. If they didn't have their own equipment, they could rent the whole setup. The campers, often regulars who came back year after year with families and groups of friends, had a real sense of community, like the vacationers at bungalow colonies in the Catskills. We rarely spent more than two nights in the same place, so we weren't exactly insiders, but it was hard to be an outsider because everything was so close.

The toughest part of adjusting to life at a campsite was suspending our American standards of cleanliness. I suppose we were lucky to have bathrooms at all, but I was not happy about using public showers. I was in and out in a flash, soaped, rinsed, dried, and ready to go. Then we had to wash our clothes. We'd packed so little that we spent a lot of time in laundromats, a process that became even more complicated when I insisted on washing my heavy sleeping bag.

We tried to power through these housekeeping chores so we could concentrate on the fun of exploring. Our newfound passion was driving to various towns and villages to visit the open-air markets where real French people shopped for their food. On certain days of the week, starting very early in the morning, local vendors set up stalls and tables in a designated area, creating a sprawling outdoor market. I'd never seen anything like it.

In the 1970s at home, you could find carrots and celery in the produce department, but four different varieties of strawberries, each with its own season? Not a chance. Bread came in plastic bags with twist ties, and the closest thing to freshly baked rolls started out in pop-open cardboard cylinders in the fridge. The variety of products in France was astonishing. Displays of fresh cheese—cow, goat, sheep, blue, brie, double crème, triple crème, and ones I'd never tasted or even heard of, usually made and sold by the farmer who actually kept the cows, the goats, and the sheep. This was the original farm-to-table food that inspired Alice Waters to create Chez Panisse and what we now think of as California cuisine. I'd never even tasted cheese made with unpasteurized milk, so the difference between authentic French cheese and the waxy orange stuff we had at home was a total revelation.

Olives—green, black, brown, and deep purple, briny and garnished with garlic, lemon, and slivers of red peppers. Pâté—every kind imaginable, from the classic liver I made with Carolyn in

Colorado, to duck, wild boar, and venison. And the charcuterie! Ham studded with rosemary; garlicky saucisson, sold by the *tranche,* or slice. Not a piece of plastic wrap anywhere, and best of all, we could ask for a taste of anything, so we felt like we'd had a meal before we even sat down for lunch.

Butcher stalls offered fresh cuts of beef, lamb, pork, and poultry, along with wild game and meats we couldn't identify—and probably didn't want to know. But for us, with our limited "kitchen" of one skillet and a gas camping stove, rotisserie chicken, or poulet rôti, was the most enticing choice. Somewhere in every French market was a stall with gorgeous chickens roasting on a spit, caramelized to a deep, golden brown and glossy with drippings falling onto roasted potatoes below. Once again, we had Napoleon to thank. Apparently, he popularized this particular preparation when he was marching with his soldiers and insisted on having a steady supply of fowl cooked on a spit.

Moving through the market, we saw fresh fish, heads and all, on beds of ice, sitting next to piles of oysters, mussels, tiny clams, shrimp, and snails in their shells. There were local olive oils presented like fine wines, honey from nearby hives, and spices from distant lands. My taste buds were on high alert, especially when we came to the rainbow of seasonal produce stacked on tables, nothing like the vegetables in the supermarkets at home.

No anemic tomatoes sealed in little green plastic trays in *these* markets! Instead, tomatoes in the brightest shades of red, yellow, and orange, fresh from the vine; green and white asparagus; purple eggplant; ruby radishes; and deep orange and purple carrots, soil included. Vibrant colors were everywhere, as far as the eye could see. Even the lowly potatoes were freshly dug and looked like little jewels.

Then, the fruit, which arrived at market according to the calendar, because if it wasn't in season, it wasn't there. What I noticed first was the fragrance of each fruit at its peak moment. In the late spring, the Gariguette strawberries, exploding with intense berry flavor. In the summer, peaches, dripping with juice at first bite and tasting like the best peach jam; plums; melons, including the syrupy-sweet ones from Cavaillon; figs; and cherries.

And the beating heart of every place in France, even the smallest village, was the boulangerie, with its racks of freshly baked bread, rolls, and croissants. They're easy to find because your nose will lead the way. That's how we ended up at Poilâne bakery, on rue du Cherche-Midi, during our brief stop in Paris. This famous street is lined with luxury boutiques, but we were drawn to a small, family-owned bakery, stocked with the most beautiful loaves made with a sourdough starter and fresh from an ancient oven. The large round ones were marked with a gracefully scripted "P" for *Poilâne,* like small works of art. And wow, were they delicious!

At the boulangeries in Provence, we fell in love with the baguette, the crusty, elongated loaf made from only four basic ingredients: wheat flour, water, yeast, and salt. Turns out the baguette has a storied past, and according to folklore, Napoleon was involved in this, too. Supposedly, he was the mastermind who commissioned this particular shape for his soldiers, so they could tuck it into their pants, like a sword. It seems incredible that the same man who was busy planting trees, eating rotisserie chicken, and conquering the world also had time to invent a loaf of bread.

A more believable explanation is that the baguette debuted in 1919, after a new labor law prohibited bakers from working between the hours of ten p.m. and four a.m., presumably to give them time to sleep. The problem was that if bakers wanted to have bread to sell to their early-morning customers, they had to come up with a loaf they could bake quickly. The fast-cooking baguette was the solution, and it became so popular that, along with the Eiffel Tower and the beret, it's probably one of the first things we think of when we think of France. We didn't know the baguette's history at the time, but we knew it was really good, and we were happy to make it our daily bread.

This was a new way to shop for us, picking up this and that every day—whatever was fresh, delicious, and cheap, which was everything. A meal could be some fruit; a ripe cheese, sometimes stinky, sometimes nutty or sweet; and, of course, a rotisserie chicken. I think that's when a perfectly roasted chicken became our version of Proust's madeleine—the food that could instantly transport us to a happy memory—and it is still Jeffrey's favorite meal today.

Another vivid memory . . . the sandwiches. In the United States, a sandwich is two slices of bread from a plastic bag (no flavor at all) and as much roast beef or turkey as you can pile between the slices. Instead, the French take a length of a crusty baguette, one thin slice of delicious ham or pâté, maybe a little cheese, maybe a little butter or Dijon mustard, and *voilà!* The best sandwich you ever ate. The texture, the flavors—the delicacy of it all is perfect. I wish I could remember the names of the places where we stopped for a snack or a coffee, but we could literally go anywhere—a market stall, one of a dozen little shops, or a concession at a gas station—and the food was always delicious.

Even exploring an ordinary French supermarket was an adventure. I swear it was possible to get a whole Christmas dinner in a single can or jar. Beef pot-au-feu with four vegetables, blanquette of veal in a sauce with mushrooms and onions . . . just pop the lid and heat. I particularly remember heating up a jar of cassoulet on my camping stove; at home it would have taken me a day to prepare, and here it was all done and beyond delicious. (I later learned that French housewives always kept a jar of cassoulet in the pantry, just in case.) There was boxed milk, miraculously with no refrigeration needed. And a big assortment of flavored yogurts, which were just beginning to show up in American stores.

We drank wine, although we didn't know a thing about it. We couldn't tell the difference between a Bordeaux and a Burgundy, but it didn't matter. In France, we were surrounded by vineyards, and the best and cheapest wines were the house wines, better than anything we ever drank at home.

Our experiences at the street markets taught me everything I needed to know about the importance of really good ingredients. Our meals that summer couldn't have been simpler or more casual, like a never-ending picnic. But each element was fresh and flavorful, and that's also when I began to understand that presentation was important, too.

At one point, I was feeling so European that I bought a colorful piece of fabric at a street market to use as a tablecloth. We took out the back seat of the car and set up a kind of tailgating "dining room." When I laid out our croissant and coffee on the cloth, I wanted the backdrop to be as pretty as the food. Jeffrey still talks about how beautiful that simple breakfast looked on the "tablecloth," which was really just a remnant I found at the market.

We don't have many photographs of the trip, but one that survived shows me cooking in the tent. I'm sitting cross-legged, my long hair (very seventies) parted and tucked behind my ears, while I stir the pan on the camping stove, making fondue. Everything I needed—something wrapped in wax paper, probably from the street market; a bottle of oil; a jar of pepper; and our "pantry," a Coca-Cola carton filled with other essentials—was within reach, although frankly, everything is within reach in a tent that small. How crazy is it that Jeffrey chose to take a picture at this very moment—me, my shoes tossed aside, practically barefoot, smiling over a stove! I'd always liked cooking, but now I was falling in love.

We settled into a routine, driving, talking, and occasionally reading the *International Herald Tribune* to keep up with the news, but mostly we were in our own little world. We stopped at American Express offices to change money and pick up our mail, the best way to communicate with family and friends while we were on the road. I can't remember how the letters from home found us—it was like magic. One day, I got a letter from my mother that included a newspaper clipping describing a cooking class being offered at a hotel in Le Havre, Normandy.

We actually happened to be in Le Havre at that very moment! I needed a pot for cooking on my camping stove, so first I stopped in a hardware store and bought the pot, and then I went to this grand French hotel, pot in hand, and asked about the cooking class in my less-than-perfect French. The man at the desk didn't understand fully and was just horrified that this crazy American had read the article, gotten on a plane, and flown to Le Havre— with a pot!—ready to take the class! "Madame," he said warily, "the classes don't start for a month." I walked away, still clutching my pot, disappointed that my first French cooking class wasn't meant to be.

I missed out on that experience, but there was a better one right at the next campsite. We were staying near Mont-Saint-Michel, the famous island and medieval abbey in Normandy. When we arrived, the French woman who ran the campsite looked at us sympathetically, probably thinking (correctly) that we were hungry. She said that she was making coq au vin for her husband and asked if we would like some. I'm not even sure I knew what coq au vin was, but the aroma coming from her little stove was so seductive that we instantly accepted her invitation.

It was as if the world stopped still. I was completely blown away by how delicious it was, because it tasted even better than it smelled. The first bite delivered an explosion of flavor—tender chicken with onions and slivers of mushrooms in a sauce, somehow simple and complex at the same time, with hints of wine, cognac, and fresh thyme. I always thought classic French food had to be fancy haute cuisine, with complicated, time-consuming recipes and hard-to-get ingredients. But this meal, prepared in a kitchen by a woman who was simply making that night's dinner, was authentic French cooking at its best. Not at all fussy, just fresh and delicious. I wanted to cook like *that*, and I made up my mind that I would teach myself how to do it as soon as I got home. Years later, I discovered that Julia Child had a similar moment eating sole meunière—sole in butter sauce—also in Normandy, and that's when she decided to learn all about French cooking. I totally understand what happened to her, because the same thing happened to me.

We slowly made our way across France, stopping in Saint-Tropez, the playground for the rich and beautiful, with their famous "Saint-Tropez tans." Okay, I'll admit it, we just wanted to see the nude beach. It was a bit of an eye-opener, but not in the way we expected. The truth is that every beach in France qualifies as "nude" because women of all ages, including grandmothers, are comfortable going topless. There was nothing risqué about it, just another day at the beach, and we moved on.

We drove on the road nearest the shore, and at one point we spotted a restaurant on a stone terrace right on the beach, so close that we could see a big family, or large group of friends, dining by the water. They were all dressed in white, sitting at a long table covered with platters of food and wine bottles. A Sunday lunch in the perfect setting, huge white umbrellas flapping in the breeze shading the table, and the blue sea beyond, just like in a French film. It was incredibly beautiful, and even though it passed by in a flash, the image made a deep impression on me. The simplicity, the harmony with nature, the informality. And the people, so relaxed and comfortable, having a wonderful time. We've been to the South of France many times since then, and whenever we're on that road, we always slow down, searching for that remembered spot.

While we were speeding through the Côte d'Azur, we were *this close* to Plascassier, the town in Grasse where Julia Child had her summer home. Years later, when I read her book *My Life in France,* I discovered that she was there at that very moment—sitting in the shade of an olive tree with James Beard! Listening to the birds, smelling the orange and yellow roses, and, of course, cooking. I laughed when I came to her rapturous account of having lunch at the restaurant in the Nice airport. The meal, wine, and service were all perfect, she said. Clearly, we shared the same love of French food, wherever we found it, even at an airport. It's fun to imagine that we might have passed each other on the road that summer.

Jeffrey indulged me by making a quick detour to Cap d'Antibes so I could see the legendary Hôtel du Cap-Eden-Roc. I can't even imagine how I'd heard of it, maybe from reading F. Scott Fitzgerald or travel magazines. We decided to do a drive-by—checking in was definitely not an option at $100 a night, cash only! Our Renault seemed to get smaller as we drove down the long road lined with manicured lawns and tall palms and pines. Then the hotel itself: an imposing white château straight out of a fairy tale. "I'd really rather stay here the next time we're in Provence," joked the twenty-three-year-old whose current home was a four-foot-high orange tent. A girl can dream, right?

(Flash forward—it took me forty-five years to get there, but I did! Some dreams really do come true, and staying at Eden-Roc with Jeffrey was even better than I imagined—simple, yet utterly elegant, in that classic French way.)

On to Monaco and Monte Carlo. Incredibly, the place where Princess Grace lived in a castle and James Bond gambled at his favorite casino actually had a campsite packed with tents. And I mean packed! It was so tiny, like everything else in the storybook principality, that the tent poles overlapped, leaving barely enough room to walk. We were used to roughing it, but this was way too cramped for us. We visited the cliffside Jardin Exotique to see the amazing cactus imported from Mexico and Africa, and the stunning view of Monte Carlo below, then headed a few inches east to Italy.

At this point, we had a foolproof system in place whenever we arrived in a new location. We'd find the center of town—"centre-ville" in French—get our bearings, absorb a little local color, buy food, then search for a nearby campsite. We expected to do the same in Italy. The border between France and Italy is practically invisible: if you blink, you'll miss it. But it truly is another country, and once we crossed the border, our French, which had gotten really good over the summer, was absolutely useless. English was no better. Other than waving our hands and raising our voices, like caricatures of clueless tourists, we had no way to communicate with the Italians.

My first goal was to drive to Milan to see the famous opera house La Scala. How hard could that be? I knew it was in the center of the city, so I stopped people to ask, "Centro?" which is center in Italian, but I was clearly pronouncing it wrong. No one had any idea what I was talking about. That's because the word is pronounced chentro. Then we tried to get an espresso and panini, and that wasn't any more successful. It was clearly our problem that we didn't speak Italian, but it made our stay in Italy very frustrating. At a certain point, we decided to throw in the towel, make a left turn, and head for Switzerland.

Like magic, we were in Davos, in the Alps, where it was incredibly cold, considering it was July. Worse still, it actually started snowing. Our campsite was right next to a stream where we had to wash our dishes after meals. This was real down-and-dirty camping, not the glamping that is popular today. The water was so frigid that I broke one of our drinking glasses—a tragedy because we had only two—which didn't bode well for the temperature in the great outdoors that night.

We did the only sensible thing and headed straight to a camping store to buy a little gas heater for the tent—but it cost thirty-five dollars! With our budget, we had to make a very hard choice: buy the heater and go home a week early, or walk away from it and freeze. It's amazing to me now that thirty-five dollars was way beyond our budget. But who cared? We were having the time of our lives, and so we'd just have to snuggle up a little more against the cold. We didn't buy the heater and, somehow, teeth clenched and bodies shivering, we made it through the night . . . and the rest of our trip.

Inevitably, our final days flew by way too fast, and then it was time to go home. The thought of leaving Europe made me so sad. I would miss everything, except maybe the laundromats and the public showers. "Can't we go home, wash our clothes, take a shower, and then come right back?" I teased Jeffrey. He felt the same way. But it was time to do everything in reverse. After our last night of camping, we said goodbye to the orange tent (I was totally fine with that), gave all our gear to a very grateful couple at the campsite, returned the car to the dealer in Paris, took the train to Frankfurt, and flew to New York.

When I look back, I see the luckiest couple in the world. We were never sick. We were never bored. We never had a meal we didn't love. And neither of us recalls a single bad day, which is pretty amazing considering that we were together nonstop.

During the pandemic, when we couldn't go out, Stephen Colbert asked me how I felt about spending so much time in the house with Jeffrey. "You know what?" I told him. "Jeffrey and I spent four months in a little Day-Glo orange tent and we had a ball. Having a whole house to ourselves is a luxury!"

I didn't know it at the time, but our trip through Europe was so much more than a dream vacation. It was an experience that changed the course of my life.

Coq au Vin

SERVES 6

Over the years I've tried many times to make a good coq au vin, the renowned French chicken stew with red wine, but with disappointing results. My television producer Olivia Grove one day told me, "Well, it's just beef bourguignon with chicken," and I thought, "So it is!" With that in mind, I adapted my old recipe for beef and came up with an easy chicken version that's such a satisfying winter dinner. Usually the chicken cooks for hours and is dry and stringy, but I found that after only thirty to forty minutes in the oven, the chicken is perfectly cooked and still tender and juicy.

Good olive oil
8 ounces good bacon or pancetta, diced
2 (3- to 4-pound) chickens, each cut into 8 serving pieces
Kosher salt and freshly ground black pepper
1 pound carrots, cut diagonally into 1-inch pieces
2 yellow onions, sliced
2 teaspoons chopped garlic (2 cloves)
¼ cup Cognac or good brandy
1 (750-ml) bottle good dry red wine such as Burgundy

2 cups chicken stock, preferably homemade
1 bunch fresh thyme sprigs
4 tablespoons (½ stick) unsalted butter, at room temperature, divided
3 tablespoons all-purpose flour
1 pound frozen small whole onions
1 pound porcini or cremini mushrooms, stems removed and thickly sliced

Preheat the oven to 275 degrees.

Heat 1 tablespoon olive oil in a large Dutch oven over medium heat. Add the bacon and cook for 8 to 10 minutes, until lightly browned. Remove the bacon to a plate with a slotted spoon.

Meanwhile, pat the chicken dry with paper towels. Liberally sprinkle the chicken on both sides with salt and pepper. After the bacon is removed, add a few of the chicken pieces in a single layer and brown for about 5 minutes, turning to brown evenly. Remove the chicken pieces to the plate with the bacon and continue to add the chicken in batches until all the chicken is browned. Set aside.

Add the carrots, onions, 1 tablespoon salt, and 2 teaspoons pepper to the pot and cook over medium heat for 10 to 12 minutes, stirring occasionally, until the onions are lightly browned. Add the garlic and cook for 1 more minute. Add the Cognac, *stand back!*, and carefully ignite with a match to burn off the alcohol. Put the bacon, chicken, and any juices that collect on the plate into the pot. Add the wine, chicken stock, and thyme sprigs and bring to a boil. Cover the pot with a tight-fitting lid and place in the oven for 30 to 40 minutes, until the chicken is just no longer pink. Remove from the oven and place on top of the stove.

Mash 2 tablespoons of the butter and the flour together in a small bowl and stir the paste into the stew. Add the frozen onions. In a medium sauté pan, melt the remaining 2 tablespoons butter and cook the mushrooms over medium-low heat for 5 to 10 minutes, until browned. Add to the stew. Bring the stew to a simmer and cook for another 10 minutes. Season to taste. Serve hot.

"It's That Crazy Ina Garten!"

We packed our belongings and moved to Washington, DC. We were finally starting our lives! We would make a home for ourselves there for at least two years while Jeffrey was in graduate school, an eternity after being in motion for so long. After living in that tent, our average-sized apartment felt like a palace, and it had a small balcony with a gorgeous view of Capitol Hill. Jeffrey was officially a student, and my days of part-time jobs at stores like the Prissy Hen (and the infamous strip club) were behind me. Thanks to a friend's father, I started working at a real, nine-to-five job at the impressive-sounding Federal Power Commission. I was a young professional. I woke up; drank my coffee; dressed in my very adult blouse, skirt, and stockings; and went off to the office with my briefcase. And did what?

I can't remember. I don't want to remember. The job was so bureaucratic and boring that I suppressed the details. I was so deeply miserable that the high point of my day was when Jeffrey took pity on me and walked all the way across town to our offices in the middle of nowhere, in the sweltering Washington heat, to buy me lunch at Arby's.

But an oversize roast beef sandwich was just a temporary fix. What I really needed was a better job. After a mind-numbing year, I jumped at the chance to be an analyst at NASDAQ. Suddenly, I was Ina Garten, girl investigator, sniffing out fraud in the private sector. Brokerage houses were my beat. If NASDAQ got a tip about something fishy, my team was dispatched to examine the books. To this day, I have no idea what I was looking for, and I probably wouldn't have known it if it reached out and smacked me in the head—fraud can be really hard to uncover and even harder to prove. Bernie Madoff was the chair of NASDAQ, and he fooled the SEC for *decades*! But the job's saving grace was my coworkers, who were smart and funny.

Work was work—there were good days and bad days. Whatever happened at the office, I left it all behind when I came home to my kitchen, where I tried to re-create the incredible meals I'd fallen in love with in France. Long before *Julie & Julia,* there was *Ina* and Julia—me and my copy of *Mastering the Art of French Cooking.* Casserole-Roasted Chicken with Tarragon, Boeuf à la Bourguignonne, Marinated Leg of Lamb. I might have drawn the line at Goose with Prune and Foie Gras Stuffing, mostly because I couldn't possibly afford the ingredients. But I felt like we lived like kings when I cooked. I wouldn't pick up a chicken at the grocery store; like the French, I'd go to the butcher first and then a specialty produce store for the vegetables. You could do that on a government salary, and I felt like I could buy almost anything I wanted.

I saved the more complicated recipes for weekends, when I had more time. Each one was an adventure—a chance to meet new ingredients, learn a technique, or solve a problem. And when I finished, Jeffrey and I—and our friends—sat down for a delicious meal.

What a nice life we had, exploring Washington, usually on foot; seeing plays at the Arena Stage theater, which was right around the corner; and meeting other people who, like us, were starting their careers. I can't imagine I made more than $15,000 a year, and Jeffrey was a student, so he didn't have any income. How did we even live on that? But once again, I don't remember feeling like I couldn't afford the things I needed. Or maybe it was that I never wanted what I couldn't afford.

When it comes to money, I do this calculation in my head: I know that I can spend up to X amount of dollars without worrying about it. In the beginning, it was probably only five dollars. Anything more than that, I had to decide what to give up if I wanted to buy it. But even as our income increased, I made that same calculation. Could I afford it? What would I have to give up? The number may have changed over the years, but my formula is still the same.

My philosophy about money stems from my childhood. When I was growing up, my mother was one of those rabid bargain hunters who always shopped at discount stores and made decisions based on "such a good price!" instead of quality. I hated that system because everything was second-rate . . . and usually ugly. I valued things that were beautiful *and* had quality. If I could afford it, great! If I couldn't afford it, that was okay, too. I wouldn't even buy a pencil that I thought was cheap or ugly. I'd rather just wait until I could afford a good one.

We happily became a two-income family when Jeffrey graduated and literally talked his way into a job at the White House, where he worked at the Council on International Economic Policy. Around that time, he heard from a friend that there was a job opening at OMB, the White House Office of Management and Budget. I jumped on the opportunity and, in 1974, started working in the legislative office of OMB. For the first time, I felt that my work was important. My department analyzed pending legislation and recommended that the president sign or veto a bill.

Pretty heady stuff, knowing that I was part of a team working in the White House and my memos were going directly to President Ford.

The issues were big, like the campaign finance reform bill that placed limits on private and corporate contributions. Everyone in my office was so excited when it passed with bipartisan support—nobody thought it would—and President Ford signed the bill. Then I experienced the reality of politics. Within what seemed like minutes, high-end donors figured out a way to get around the new law by setting up PACs (political action committees), so they could send endless piles of money to the PACs, which would in turn give the money to the candidate of their choice, making the legislation completely worthless. Everyone knew which PAC was contributing to which candidate, so nothing had changed. My guess is that everyone knew that in advance except me. Politicians could brag that they had passed campaign finance reform and know that oceans of money would continue to flow into their coffers (and their votes would continue to be compromised by that money). That was Washington: Whac-A-Mole and move on to the next mole.

I remember another time when I tried to save the government $20 billion a year by simply transferring a nuclear fuel project from the public sector to the private. A great idea, until a very powerful senator in South Carolina, where enriched uranium just happened to be produced, did his damnedest to make sure it didn't come up for a vote. This turned into a dance we did every single year. We'd take enriched uranium out of the budget, and he'd put it right back in. Nothing would really change about uranium enrichment—the same company the government hired to do the job would have continued to run the plant. All the same people who were working there would still be working there. The only two things that would have changed were that the government wouldn't have had the enormous expense and the senator from South Carolina would have lost his power over the project.

The big-picture issues were interesting, and there was a great sense of urgency when we stayed all night at the office to get every detail right before sending legislation, or a budget, off to the White House. But after that, the slow-moving process was an obstacle course lined with glue, and I found that deeply frustrating.

Because my day job didn't satisfy my creative energy, I spent my evenings and weekends doing other things that made me happy and satisfied my need to develop my own skills. First and foremost, cooking was my after-hours therapy, and because *that* wasn't enough for me to do (really?), I decided to buy an old house and renovate it. And for some reason, I decided *that wasn't enough,* so I also enrolled in the graduate MBA program at George Washington University. Looking back now, I can't imagine how I did all that, but clearly, I was searching for a career path besides the government.

There was another issue, and that was the dynamic of my relationship with Jeffrey. I've said before that Jeffrey "brought me up," as my parents had done such a dreadful job. They had made me feel worthless and belittled, and Jeffrey had given me confidence and taught me how to be strong in the world. I was so grateful to him for that. But there was the sense in our marriage that he was the parent, and I was the child.

Then, when I went out into the world and started working, the dynamic shifted, and our roles became "man" and "wife." At our wedding, and most weddings at the time, the last words were, "I pronounce you man and wife," which set up inequitable roles for the couple at the starting gate. Now *I* was the wife, expected to take charge of anything that had to do with the household. After a long day at the office, I made dinner, took care of the laundry, and did countless other chores, and I began to resent it. I didn't like that it was assumed I would make dinner, nor did I like that it was assumed Jeffrey would manage our finances and pay the bills. I thought these classic gender roles were annoying and unfair.

I wasn't alone. Women everywhere were rethinking their roles and responsibilities. Yes, we had new opportunities in the 1970s, but it began to dawn on us that we were expected to add them to whatever we did in our traditional roles. It wasn't having it all, it was *doing* it all.

I tried changing my behavior in small ways, hoping Jeffrey would get the message. I stopped taking out the trash and emptying the dishwasher, but he didn't seem to pick up the cues. And when we talked about it, he didn't seem to hear what I was saying. Jeffrey had grown up in a very traditional home, and it was in his DNA to see himself as the "head" of the family, like his father. To be fair, that's how most men were at the time. After all, who wouldn't like to come home to a beautifully prepared dinner and a well-kept house? If I were a husband, I might have felt that way too. Jeffrey was incredibly caring and wonderful in so many other ways, and, as I've said, feminist in how he championed my greater ambitions, but the quotidian problems had no apparent solution. I'd just have to live with them until I figured it out.

We'd been renting apartments for a few years, and when we realized we would be staying in Washington for a while, we decided it was time for a real house. It would be a stretch financially, but we had good jobs and expected our income to grow. We found an old row house off Dupont Circle and went to the bank to apply for a mortgage.

Two Washington policy wonks with solid jobs in the White House would seem to be ideal candidates for a loan, or so we thought. But the banker took a quick look at our application and told Jeffrey (he refused to even look at me!) that we didn't have enough income for the loan we needed. Jeffrey pointed out that our combined incomes were more than enough. "Oh, we don't count her income," the banker explained, as if I weren't sitting right there. "She's just going to get pregnant and quit her job, so we only consider *your* income."

Wait, what? Did this man sleep through Gloria Steinem, the Equal Rights Amendment, and second-wave feminism? How dare he say that? I wanted to tell him that what he said was offensive and my body was none of his business. But we really wanted the mortgage, so I simply assured him I was not quitting my job and my income was secure. No matter my protests, when it came to borrowing money, I was worthless. "You actually don't even exist on paper," the banker told me. "You have no credit history." (All our cards were in Jeffrey's name.) "There's nothing we can do."

We were both shocked. Later, we found out that some banks actually required married women to submit a "baby letter," signed by their doctor, promising they would not get pregnant if they wanted to be considered for a mortgage. Really? Even in 1974, this was borderline medieval, but it was not even an option at our bank, which quickly became *not* our bank. How was it possible that someone who worked in the White House couldn't get a mortgage? Even worse, I didn't exist? I had an office—and a brief-case! I was good and mad and determined not to let this petty banker stop me. Barriers, of course, only make me more determined.

There was one thing I could fix immediately. I went home from that meeting, cut up all our credit cards, and applied for new ones in my name—my name only. Now, sadly, Jeffrey didn't exist!

Fortunately for us, Jeffrey's father knew someone at a bank

who gave us not only a mortgage but also the down payment. At last we were homeowners, so proud and excited to have the keys to our shingled row house. We raced there to celebrate after the closing and were greeted by an elderly woman who lived next door. I thought she was coming to say hello. Instead, she looked incredulously at our wreck of a house and said, "I just wanted to see who was so sick in the head that they would pay forty-nine thousand dollars for *this*." Welcome to the neighborhood!

Did I say we were proud and excited? Maybe more like naïve and inexperienced but full of enthusiasm. Our house had been built in 1909 and was full of charming original details, but it needed a major renovation. It was less "home sweet home" and more *The Money Pit*.

The first problem was that we couldn't afford to live somewhere else during the renovation, so I decided to fix up the bedroom before we started so we could have a refuge from the mess. It was the era of blue-and-white Japanese prints, so I chose a pretty blue-and-white wallpaper with cherry blossoms, which I decided to hang myself. I painted the ceiling and the trim—so far, so good—and then hung the wallpaper. When I was done and stood back to admire my work, I realized that I'd hung the entire room of wallpaper upside down! Oops. Sadly, we couldn't afford to buy a second round of wallpaper, so when I woke up every morning, I was confronted with cherry trees whose branches gracefully curved down instead of up.

We hired a contractor, who immediately went to work on the rest of the house, ripping out the kitchen and the bathroom—in fact, our ONLY bathroom, and of course, our only kitchen—on a Friday afternoon. "We'll put the bathroom and kitchen back on Monday," the contractor promised.

Later that weekend, when we opened our Sunday *Washington Post*, we saw a terrifying headline. Our contractor had been arrested for torching a restaurant he owned for the insurance money. Arson was one thing, but leaving us without a kitchen and bathroom? Now, *that's* criminal! What in the world were we going to do without a kitchen or a bathroom while we found a new contractor? Fortunately, health clubs were new in Washington, and they were all offering a free week's membership so you could see if you liked them before signing up for the year. I'm not proud of this, but for the next four months—the time it took to find a new contractor and finish the construction—we went from one health club to the next, arriving with a towel and a toothbrush to use the bathroom and the shower. They all offered a tour of the facilities, but I don't think we ever actually used any of the equipment. For meals, we had to resort to deli takeout, and we had a pretty nasty bucket under the sink for wastewater. Amazingly, we did make it through the four months without getting a divorce.

Eventually, we started putting the house back together, including some details like a mirrored fireplace that I'd like to forget. But my obsession was the kitchen. It was small and had to be totally gutted. I'd stand there and think to myself, *Okay, how do I make a cup of coffee? What do I need to reach to do that? What's the best arrangement for the sink, stove, and refrigerator? Is anything obstructed?* I wanted to think through how I would actually cook in that kitchen. It wasn't only about the décor or the look of it, although that's important too. The funny thing is, I intuitively arrived at the classic triangle I use today, with the sink, stove, and refrigerator arranged so you can move easily from one to the other, with counter space in between.

Having a better kitchen and our first real dining room meant that I could host dinner parties. Like the little girl with the pink tea set, entertaining became my creative outlet, the thing I obsessed about at three in the morning. I loved the whole process of coming up with a menu, shopping for ingredients, and cooking.

I would never make something for the first time for guests. That would be too scary! I'd make it for Jeffrey, then I'd probably make it again, and by the time Saturday night came around, I was cooking that one dish like a pro, confident that it would be delicious.

I'd learned my lesson the hard way in North Carolina, when we hosted our overly ambitious omelet debacle. It's best to plan a menu that can be almost completely prepared before the guests arrive instead of laboring like a short-order cook. And small, intimate parties are so much more satisfying than big ones.

By the time we were in Washington with my first real kitchen and dining room, I had learned a lot about entertaining, but I was still making complicated dinners from Julia Child's books, like roast leg of lamb and tomatoes stuffed with duxelles (finely minced mushrooms). I would go to work during the day, come home and cook dinner, and prep something for the weekend party. Finally, Saturday night would come, and I'd work myself to the bone preparing for the party, serving the guests, and entertaining everyone until I was totally exhausted. On Sunday, I'd spend the day lying on the sofa, vowing never to have a dinner party again. But by the time I went back to work on Monday, I'd have forgotten about how hard it was and would immediately start to plan a party for the next Saturday night. I'd find some recipe I *had* to try and throw myself into the frenzy of planning a dinner party and testing the recipe, and the insane cycle would start again. I just couldn't help myself.

I spent years this way, obsessing over the most complicated Julia Child recipes, until an unlikely dinner at a friend's house opened my eyes to a different way of entertaining. Dick Erb was a colleague of Jeffrey's at the White House, and we would occasionally play tennis together. One day, Dick invited us to dinner. It was sweet of him to invite us, but other than restaurant chefs,

I didn't know one man who could cook. This was decades before Bobby Flay and Jacques Pépin were cooking on TV or writing cookbooks. Maybe we should have a snack before we go, I suggested to Jeffrey, anticipating a few polite bites and a main course made with Campbell's Cream of Mushroom Soup.

Wow, was I wrong! The first course was perfectly sautéed shrimp with hints of butter and garlic, followed by an entire roasted filet of beef, with potatoes and vegetables, each cooked to perfection. I also remember a loaf of warm crusty bread, and at this point, I wouldn't have been surprised if Dick had baked it himself. Then there was dessert—fresh orange sections fanned in a syrup flavored with Grand Marnier. The meal was simple, with a wonderful balance of flavors, textures, and colors. Amazingly, Dick didn't look the least bit exhausted from the preparations—he was enjoying the party as much as we were.

Something clicked that night. Why was I cooking elaborate meals that made me feel like I was training for the Olympics, when simple food, perfectly prepared and beautifully served, delighted the guests and didn't make the host feel like killing themselves afterward? Successful entertaining didn't have to be about proving I could master a four-page recipe that had ingredients that were recipes in themselves. A party was about connecting with your friends and having a good time; food designed to impress was not just beside the point—I was beginning to realize that it was actually counterproductive. A simple dinner with delicious food was the best way to have a good party.

While I was changing the way I cooked, I also started thinking about how I wanted to present food at a dinner party. The customary way was to serve the main course on a platter and the side dishes in separate bowls. The guests could help themselves and pass the bowl to the next person. Perfectly fine, but it did nothing to make the food look appealing, and there were a lot of half-eaten bowls of food strewn around my beautifully set table.

Jeffrey and I often took weekend trips to New York, and one of my favorite stores was Bailey-Huebner in the Street of Shops at Henri Bendel on Fifty-Seventh Street. Lee Bailey was an incredibly talented man—a photographer, cook, and great host—who could make a hunk of cornbread look like the only thing you ever wanted to eat and set a table with napkins made out of blue-and-white ticking that felt like they had just come fresh out of the dryer. It was so casual and yet so sophisticated, all at the same time. I'd walk into his shop and feel the urge to throw away everything I owned so I could replace it with the perfect white pitcher, wooden salad bowl, or silver cake stand.

The object he sold that made the biggest impression on me was the stack of big white oval restaurant platters. I bought one and lugged it home on the train because I knew instinctively what a difference it would make. First, the food would look better on white than on a platter in a color or busy pattern. The food would stand out, not the platter. Second, because the platter was much bigger than the small bowls I scattered around the table, I could fill one platter with, say, a filet of beef down the middle and roasted potatoes down one side and roasted cherry tomatoes down the other side, and it would look like a party. It was such a genius way to serve a dinner! Dick Erb had changed the way I cook forever, and now Lee Bailey, who later became a friend, was changing how I served food. They both had the same message—use good ingredients and serve them as simply as possible. It felt so right to me.

Around this time, real estate became my second obsession, after cooking. When I was growing up, my father invested in apartment buildings, and sometimes he'd ask me to talk through a deal with him—how to finance it, how to negotiate. It was one of the few topics we actually discussed, and I loved working out a deal with him. Our house was starting to feel a little small, so there was a practical reason for looking at real estate, but I also loved the experience of walking into a new place and imagining the possibilities. I started looking at the listings of houses for sale in Washington, then I'd contact the agent to make an appointment to see a house. I must have done it a lot, because one day when I called about a listing on Capitol Hill, the agent put me on hold—or thought she put me on hold!—and I heard her yell across the office, "It's that crazy Ina Garten on the line!"

Hmm . . . was I crazy? (Maybe.)

One Sunday afternoon, Jeffrey and I were taking a walk along the beautiful Embassy Row, not far from where we lived (in decidedly *not* Embassy Row). We happened to pass a gorgeous historic town house with an open house starting right then. I said, "Let's just go in and see it," thinking it would be fun to have a quick look. Once inside, I realized it had amazing bones—four stories, eight fireplaces, bedrooms everywhere, a huge double living room (with two fireplaces!) looking out on a beautiful private garden, and lots of room to build the kitchen of my dreams.

I told Jeffrey that I *had* to have that house, calculating we could sell our row house and get a new mortgage. He probably, like the realtor on Capitol Hill, thought I was crazy, but he only asked one smart question—"Can we sell it for what we bought it for?" YES!! We literally raced home to get our checkbook and I did something no one did at that time—I offered $1,000 more than the asking price to be sure I'd get it. I knew that would seal the deal—nobody ever offered *more* than the asking price; they always offered less. It worked! It should have been overwhelming, but I was just too excited to notice!

First, I had to find an architect. I read a newspaper article about George Hartman of Hartman-Cox that described the firm as "one of the few bright spots on the generally dull Washington architecture scene." I loved his work and hired him to draw up the plans. But when we submitted them to a contractor, the contractor said the renovation was going to cost even more than the price of the whole house! Jeffrey and I went for a long walk and discussed what to do. We were in over our heads, not sure how we'd even make the next mortgage payment, let alone pay for a massive renovation. The answer was that we had to sell the house, and there may have been a tear or two, but we made the decision together. I learned my first big real estate lesson: it's good to reach for something aspirational but not *totally* beyond your budget!

As we walked back into our little clapboard house near Dupont Circle, the phone was ringing. It was someone who had offered full price on the Embassy Row house (but not $1,000 more). They'd been watching the house and saw that nothing was happening (tell me about it!) so they got our number from the realtor. Would we be interested in selling it to them? Jeffrey, the future investment banker, said, "Absolutely not! But if you would like to come see it, I'll be happy to show it to you." He met the couple at the house; they walked upstairs, then came back down and said, "If it makes any difference, we don't care what the price is!" And Jeffrey wisely said, "I think we have the makings of a deal!"

Jeffrey had to go off on a monthlong trip for the State Department, so I worked out the details. I totaled all the bills, added on $5,000 for my trouble, and sold the albatross—along with George Hartman's gorgeous architectural plans!—to the nice couple, who proceeded to build my dream house. By the time Jeffrey got home from his trip, the house was gone. I'd paid all the bills and bought myself a very nice fur coat with the money left over. Not exactly the outcome I'd expected, but I would learn from the mistake.

The first house was too small, the second one was too big, but the next house was just right. Developers were transforming a neglected block of beautiful but dilapidated brick row houses on Pennsylvania Avenue halfway between the White House and Georgetown. After my Embassy Row caper, I decided my budget was best served by buying real estate in up-and-coming areas rather than fancy established ones.

One Christmas Eve, a realtor showed me the model house for an entire block of renovations, and it was love at first sight. It was a three-story brick town house with a skylight at the top and an atrium cut through its center, so the rooms were filled with light. And best of all, it had a gorgeous brand-new kitchen with a dreamy, windowed alcove for a breakfast table. I made an offer on the spot but was told that they couldn't sell the model because they needed to show it in order to sell all the other houses they were preparing to renovate.

Remember that when someone says no to me, it gets my creative juices going, and I love to find a solution that works for everyone? In negotiations, as I learned from my dad, it's important to figure out what each person needs to make the deal work for *them*, and interestingly, it's often not about the price; it's about something else entirely. In this case, the sellers needed to show the model, so I told them if they sold the house to us, they could continue to use it for showings, and it might actually show better because it would be beautifully furnished. That did it! We shook hands, and soon after that night before Christmas, the house was ours.

But now I'd promised to furnish it beautifully! I called an interior decorator whose work I liked (it was very exciting to hire my first interior decorator!), who did a very seventies design, with gray carpeted platforms and colorful architectural Knoll furniture from the fifties. I loved it—it was simple and modern. The furniture and design proposal—for the entire house—was $5,000, which I thought was totally reasonable. Jeffrey, on the other hand, said, "Five thousand dollars! I'm not spending five thousand dollars on furniture!" (By now, I should have anticipated this, but I'm always the optimist.) When he looked at me incredulously, I said quietly, "But it's my hobby," which weirdly made sense to him, and he immediately agreed to do it. To this day, whenever I want to take on a new project, he still teases me about it, knowing I will always get the best of him. "I suppose this is your hobby, too?" he'll ask. Such a good sport!

I called it a hobby. Now I see it as more of a metaphor. Whenever I took on the renovation of a house, I was proving to myself that I was capable and that change was possible. I ended up with a beautiful setting for more dinner parties with ever-expanding guest lists. Clearly, all my energy was going into anything that didn't involve my day job. I wanted to feel engaged and excited by my work, to experience the rush of adrenaline that almost never happened at the office, where the vibe was more like . . . *Am I dead yet? How many times can I possibly submit the same legislation or nuclear energy budget and have nothing happen? Why can't I do this differently?*

I tried, but nothing seemed to work. My business school classes at George Washington were at night, after a long day at the OMB, and I quickly realized that they were the opposite of the ones I'd loved in college. The professors took a dull, textbook approach that made every minute seem like an hour, maybe two. I wasn't ready to admit I'd made a mistake, so the teenager in me found a work-around. When Jeffrey dropped me off at school at night, I'd wave goodbye, walk into the building . . . and then walk right out the back door to study on my own in the library or meet a friend for coffee. Later, when he picked me up and sweetly asked how class was, I'd say fine and leave it at that. I didn't feel good about my deception—I was wasting money and time—but I didn't know what else to do.

How long could I keep up this race to nowhere? I was turning thirty and still trying to figure out who I wanted to be when I grew up.

Then I picked up a book that was sitting in my library: Gail Sheehy's *Passages*. I'd read it in my twenties, when it was a big bestseller, but I just couldn't connect with it then. This time, I understood what Sheehy was talking about—me! Her research found that women who grew up in the 1950s, before women had some independence, didn't have female role models to look up to, so they chose to be like the men they admired most.

That's exactly what I was doing! I wanted to grow up to be Jeffrey, by going into government and enrolling in graduate school. But I wasn't Jeffrey. He's a true intellectual who likes big ideas and theoretical problems. Throw in historical context and global consequences, and he's on fire. But I like rolling up my sleeves and solving a small problem I can wrap my arms around, like preparing a great dinner party or renovating a house. Thanks to Gail Sheehy, I understood that I needed to figure out who I was separately from who Jeffrey was.

Don't worry, *Passages* assured me, your twenties are the time when you master what you think you're *supposed* to do. But in your thirties, when you've figured out what you like and don't like, and you're more confident, you can move on to what you really *want* to do, which might be totally different.

It was so reassuring to know that I wasn't alone, that other women were experiencing the same confusion, making the same mistakes, and choosing to make big changes when they hit thirty.

More important, I realized that I hadn't been wasting my time when I worked at jobs that were so unsatisfying. I was simply doing research, and now I just needed to decide my path forward.

My experience in government made me feel secure about my abilities. I knew I could do the job and get promoted to a more important position at the OMB or another government agency. But I didn't want that job. That was somebody else's dream, not mine, and the "security" of a good job doesn't make me feel calm; it makes me anxious.

My challenge was to find a job that offered structure, but a structure that *I* created. I'm a terrible employee because I hate being told what to do—that's what my life was like growing up! Instead, I wanted to do something with my hands, be creative, and be responsible for the choices and results, *results* being the key word here. I needed to be my own boss—to make decisions and see where they would take me. Maybe real estate? Or cooking?

As Gail Sheehy's book predicted, my true *Passages* moment began two months after I turned thirty, when I looked at the Business Opportunities section of *The New York Times*. Was the universe calling when I spotted that tiny advertisement for a "Catering, Gourmet Foods, and Cheese Shoppe" in the Hamptons? Or when Diana Stratta (the owner of Barefoot Contessa) accepted my impulsive offer to buy her business? Maybe. I'm a big believer in serendipity. But responding to that ad was a logical next step for me at that moment. I'd spent so much time figuring out what I didn't want to do that I was eager to trade the safe and familiar for the exciting unknown: Barefoot Contessa, with its quirky name and thrilling, if risky, possibilities.

Buying the store was my answer to the question the teenage me didn't dare ask when my father demanded to know what I'd accomplished that day. At the time, I wondered why doing what you loved couldn't be an accomplishment. Now food and cooking—my hobby, my escape, my obsession, and definitely what I loved doing—was about to become my business and, if all went well, my accomplishment.

It was definitely an *"Oh shit!"* moment for someone who had no clue how to begin. But the adrenaline I'd longed for was pumping through my veins. I couldn't wait to get started.

---

* *TOMATES À LA PROVENÇALE*

[Tomatoes Stuffed with Bread Crumbs, Herbs, and Garlic]

One of the most savory ways of serving tomatoes is *à la provençale.* These tomatoes go well with many things—steaks, chops, roast beef, lamb, roast or broiled chicken, broiled mackerel, tuna, sardines, herring, or swordfish. They may also be a hot hors d'oeuvre, or accompany egg dishes.

For 6 people

Preheat oven to 400 degrees.

6 firm, ripe, red tomatoes about 3 inches in diameter
Salt and pepper

Remove the stems, and cut the tomatoes in half crosswise. Gently press out the juice and seeds. Sprinkle the halves lightly with salt and pepper.

1 to 2 cloves mashed garlic
3 Tb minced shallots or green onions
4 Tb minced fresh basil and parsley, or parsley only
⅛ tsp thyme
¼ tsp salt
Big pinch of pepper
¼ cup olive oil
½ cup crumbs from fresh white bread with body
A shallow, oiled roasting pan just large enough to hold the tomatoes easily in one layer

Blend all the ingredients to the left in a mixing bowl. Correct seasoning. Fill each tomato half with a spoonful or two of the mixture. Sprinkle with a few drops of olive oil. Arrange the tomatoes in the roasting pan; do not crowd them.

(*) May be prepared ahead to this point.

Shortly before you are ready to serve, place them in the upper third of the preheated oven and bake for 10 to 15 minutes, or until the tomatoes are tender but hold their shape, and the bread crumb filling has browned lightly.

Mastering the Art of French Cooking by Julia Child

Starting from Scratch

Seven weeks after Diana accepted my offer, we were on the road, speeding to Westhampton. I'm tempted to say, "How easy was that?" but it wasn't easy at all. Leaving OMB and saying goodbye to friends. Finalizing the contract, which meant going against the advice of my father and his accountant, who raised every possible roadblock to this "you think it's a good idea but it's not" plan. At one point, my parents were so desperate to save me from becoming a shopkeeper that they offered to pay for me to go back to school to study architecture. Momentarily curious, I made an appointment at an architecture school and somehow ended up meeting with the dean.

He was incredibly arrogant and dismissive when he learned I was interested in doing urban renovations of old buildings rather than building model cities. He asked extremely condescending questions. "Do you even know any architects? Have you heard of Frank Lloyd Wright?" Unbelievable. What an ass. I had gotten married in a mid-century modern glass house in the woods designed by Louis Skidmore! I was incredibly offended at the time, but now I wish I could write him a thank-you note for convincing me that I *never* wanted to be an architect, not if it meant spending another minute with a windbag like him! Next stop: Westhampton Beach.

We ran into our first problem about a minute after we arrived, when we pulled up to the house we'd rented, which was just a few blocks from the store so I could walk to work. Our plan was to make a quick stop, drop off our stuff, and meet Diana at Barefoot Contessa. But when we opened the door to our lovely house, we were surprised to find another entire family in residence. Somehow, the rental had been double-booked, and a dentist, his wife, and their two young children had already moved into what we thought was *our* summer place. Did the real estate agent think we wouldn't notice there was someone else living in the house?

However it happened, we were heading into Memorial Day weekend in the Hamptons, and finding another rental on such short notice was NOT an option. Fortunately, the other family was understanding. They were there only on weekends, and I was going to be at the store full time, working my ass off. Miraculously, we agreed to share the house and split the rent.

Day one, lesson one: flexibility is *really* important in business.

Our unusual living arrangement sounded like it might be the premise of a bad sitcom, but it worked out perfectly. The family was nice, and they usually went back to Manhattan on weekdays, when I might have been home for a few minutes or more. On weekends, as I predicted, I'd come home, take a shower, change my clothes, and run right back to the store, so we never got in each other's way.

Problem solved, I went to meet Diana. I opened the door to Barefoot Contessa (now my door!). Then I felt a rush of panic. I didn't know anything. I didn't even know what I didn't know! Fortunately, the more rational me had prepared for this moment. Wisely, the deal I made with Diana was that she would stay with me for a month and we wouldn't even tell anyone that I was the new owner, giving me time to work by her side while I figured it all out. I had made brownies for six friends, but I'd never baked *a hundred* brownies. *Where should I buy bagels? What about cheese? When is Camembert ripe? How do I slice smoked salmon? How do I operate the cash register?* Just a few of the things I had to learn . . . *and fast!* Diana was a wonderful teacher, and I managed to get through the first day without having a total meltdown.

That night, she was showing me how to cash out the registers, and I remember that the total income was eighty-seven dollars. That was before expenses like food, rent, and salaries. Jeffrey was there trying to help, and he calculated eighty-seven dollars times the number of days in the summer, looked at me sadly, and said, "I don't think you're going to make it here," meaning, what happened to the "unlimited potential" and "gross over six figures in summer alone" the *New York Times* ad had promised? But I was undaunted. This was where I wanted to be, and I was determined to make it work.

That was the Thursday before Memorial Day weekend. Because we were new to the Hamptons, we had no idea what happens on *Friday* of Memorial Day weekend, when a sleepy little beach village turns into Times Square. The customers started lining up before we opened, ready to kick off the summer by treating themselves to pastries, bagels, and smoked salmon first thing in the morning. By the time we closed that night at ten p.m., the shelves were literally empty. Empty. Diana had purchased conservatively because she was worried about spending too much money when she knew I'd be responsible for the bills. Everything she had bought for the entire weekend was gone. Gone. Oh my God, how were we going to get through the rest of the weekend with no food?! Now I was starting to panic.

Melinda, our cook, could make anything (which was fortunate because I had no idea how to prepare food in the quantities we needed), but she had finished her shift and gone home, so we were on our own. Diana came to the rescue with a plan. She turned to me and said, "You and I are going to the grocery store to buy flour, sugar, and everything we need to bake and cook—*all night!*" She turned to Jeffrey and said, "There is a nice Danish bakery in the nearby town, Center Moriches, and they open at eight a.m." (We opened at nine a.m.) "Why don't you go there and buy some croissants and muffins and we'll sell them when we open tomorrow morning?" And then Diana and I got busy making salads, dinners, cakes, pies, and anything we could think of to sell the next day.

On Saturday morning, Jeffrey drove his little robin's-egg-blue Fiat two-seater sports car to the bakery, and he was the first one standing at the door when it opened. He looked at the baked goods, thought they looked delicious, and said to the women behind the counter, "I'll take everything in the bakery!"

"What? Everything?"

"Yes, everything."

The look on their faces!

One of the women immediately said, "We can't do that!"

The other asked, "Why not?"

"Because we'll have nothing left to sell."

"Well, then we could go to the beach!"

Suddenly, selling everything to Jeffrey sounded like a really good idea, and they quickly packed up all the baked goods.

Jeffrey put the top down on that little two-seater sports car, loading the bags and boxes into every possible space. When he was finished, he raised the top and squeezed himself behind the wheel. He made it to Westhampton just in time for the Saturday madness, when a fresh batch of vacationers came in and cleaned us out again. The next day, Jeffrey went back to the bakery in Center Moriches, and when the saleswoman looked aghast at him, he nodded and said, "Yes, everything!" By Monday, Diana and I had figured out how to make enough muffins and croissants, so he didn't have to go back to Center Moriches. I've always had this horrible thought that on Monday, the bakers decided they would make twice as much for Jeffrey *and* the store, and then he didn't show up! I'm so sorry!

Late Sunday night, after we had just closed and we were wondering how we were going to stock the store for the next day, someone knocked on the door. "Do you have any cakes left?" the man asked. "No, I'm really sorry," I told him. "We're totally cleaned out—well, except for one incredibly expensive chocolate cheesecake, but we sell that by the inch, not by the cake." "Great!" he said, peeling twenty-dollar bills out of his wallet. "I'll take the whole thing." *Wow*, I thought, *this might be a really hard job, but at least I'm doing it in the right town!* Jeffrey and I looked at each other. Maybe, just maybe, I *was* going to make it!

But I truly wasn't thinking about money. The weekend had been a trial by fire, a blur of baking, selling, solving problems, and making mistakes. Diana and I worked twenty-to-twenty-two-hour days all weekend. We would go home, take a shower, and come back and bake some more. I was exhausted but so exhilarated. But there was a moment when I said to Jeffrey, "This is truly the stupidest thing I've ever done. I had no idea how hard this would be." And Jeffrey, *being the totally supportive husband he always is,* said, "If you could learn the business in a week, you'd be bored in two weeks." (Boy, did he know me!) Challenging work was exactly what I needed.

After that first weekend, Jeffrey went back to Washington—he still had a "real" job working for the secretary of state—so I had a little time to take a closer look at my new home. Barefoot

Contessa was right in the middle of Main Street, which was only a few blocks long, where everything was very casual and beachy. I learned that each town in the Hamptons has its own vibe. There was a saying that Southampton is old money, East Hampton is new money, and Westhampton is funny money. It really was a sort of Studio 54 environment, with its own disco, Club Marakesh, and flashy Ferraris parked everywhere, with a mix of young people in the fashion industry and families with kids. It was fun but also very casual. I loved it! For me, it couldn't have been more different from Washington, where everyone was young and working for the government in buttoned-up coats and ties. This beach town had so much more style and energy, and I was so happy to trade high heels, silk shirts, and issue papers for a pair of comfortable sneakers and a store that felt like a party. Barefoot Contessa was literally and figuratively the center of town, and everyone met there to pick up a coffee or lunch and sit outside to watch the world go by.

The store was very small—only about four hundred square feet. In fact, the kitchen was so tiny that it barely fit Melinda, who baked in the ovens in the kitchen and cooked everything else on the stove in the main part of the store, filling Barefoot Contessa with the tantalizing smell of whatever she was making. Our customers felt the way I did the first time I walked into the store and inhaled the intoxicating aroma of warm chocolate chip cookies. Like they'd come home.

The rest of the staff Diana had hired was young, beautiful, and really smart. Unlike now, when kids want to have a summer adventure like Outward Bound, in 1978, young people came to the beach with their parents and looked for a summer job. If it worked out, they came back the next summer, and most of the people Diana hired stayed for years.

Thirteen-year-old Shawn Warren and the teenage Esterling sisters, Lee and Sarah, had worked at Barefoot Contessa the previous summer, so they actually had more experience than I did! They were confident and completely at home in the store. Shawn loved working behind the counter and could charm even the surliest customer. Lee and Sarah could do anything: pack food, prepare special orders, whatever came up. All three were smart and gorgeous and spoke fluent French and delighted in carrying on rapid-fire conversations that no one else could understand. They could have been Mean Girls but instead, they were very sweet with customers and me. Instead of resenting the change in ownership, they were genuinely interested in helping me wrap my arms around this new business.

This was the first time in my life I was a boss—with a team!—and I was a little nervous. But I had learned about having employees by *being* an employee. I just had to ask myself how I'd like to be treated, then treat the people who worked for me exactly the same way. I wanted to show the girls that I was going to work just as hard—maybe twice as hard—as I expected them to work.

But I also wanted the store to be a place where we had fun, where there was energy, laughter, and good times—the kind of place that made you want to come to work in the morning. I certainly felt that way. I even wanted to come to work in the middle of the night! Why waste time sleeping when there was so much to learn and so many cakes to bake?

I think I proved that point one Sunday morning, when Sarah came in early to start packaging salads. She stepped behind the counter to reach for the plastic containers and found me, curled up on the bottom shelf, sound asleep. I was too tired to go home, so I had cleared a space, wrapped myself in a sweater, and went to "bed." It was that kind of job. You had to give it your all.

By the time Diana left at the end of June, I was on steadier ground. I had mastered slicing salmon, probably massacring a few innocent fish before I got it right. I had connected with the best suppliers and was experimenting just the tiniest bit with the menu. I had decided to keep everything set up the way Diana had it until I understood the business. The summer was too short and I was too inexperienced to do a major overhaul.

Occasionally, I'd slip in a new dish just to see what happened. I was crazy about Scandinavian food in 1978, so I made something called Beet and Herring Salad, which doesn't sound the least bit appetizing to me now. It sat there all day, shunned, the loneliest food in the refrigerated case. The same thing happened when I made a fancy dish—Veal with Morels—and watched while absolutely no one bought it. I was lucky that I made my mistakes in a small store, where the quantities were modest and inexpensive. We could all just eat the mistakes for lunch (well, maybe except that herring salad).

I figured out pretty quickly that people didn't want fancy restaurant food at home: they wanted the best home cooking without the trouble of making it at home. Roast chicken, poached salmon, chicken salad, potato salad, coleslaw, all prepared with the freshest ingredients—that's what sold. My rule was that I didn't sell anything I didn't love, so it had to pass my taste test first.

I also learned that customers responded to how the food was displayed. A big white platter (think Lee Bailey) with beautiful roasted chickens arranged on a bed of fresh herbs looked gorgeous, but I was surprised to see that it didn't sell. Didn't people want roast chicken? I took that platter back to the kitchen, ditched the fresh herbs, and put each chicken in one of those red-and-white checked paper containers that you'd get french fries in—and we sold them all in twenty minutes! The paper containers screamed, "Put me on a picnic table!" "Take me to the beach!" "Eat me with your hands!" Suddenly they were accessible, and we sold chickens that way for the rest of the summer.

Apparently, *I* needed a little help with *my* presentation, too. At some point during the summer, I realized my customers were treating me the way they treated everyone else who worked at the store—I was just the "girl" behind the counter—and frankly it annoyed me. I was the owner, and although we had never made a big deal about the fact when Diana was still there, I wanted to subtly communicate authority, and I had an idea.

My uniform was a flouncy white cotton midi skirt paired with a white top—clean, casual, and beachy, and a happy change from the stuffy business outfits I had to wear in Washington. But I wanted to look like the woman in charge, so I needed something that made me look like the owner. I walked across the street to Joan Boyce Jewelry and bought myself the biggest gold necklace I'd ever seen. (That's how I remember it, although I looked at it recently and was shocked to see it's just a tiny little thing.) When I came back into the store, customers started asking, "Is this your store? It's wonderful!" and treating me totally differently. I love when changing your behavior—in this case, how I dressed— changes everything without your saying a word. It's a lesson that I've used many times in my life.

I also thought seriously about changing the name of the store. Barefoot Contessa meant something to Diana—she's Italian, and when she was a little girl, her family called her that after the famous Humphrey Bogart and Ava Gardner movie—but not only did it have nothing to do with me, it didn't say what or where the store was, as I thought a store name should. I decided I would change it the next summer. As the summer progressed, however, I realized it was perfect. *Barefoot* suggests a casual, beachy vibe, and *Contessa* is elegant—earthy and elegant—just what I would want a specialty food store to feel like. So Barefoot Contessa it stayed, and I'm so glad it did! There was a period when customers would actually call me "Contessa," a far cry from my Russian peasant roots!

We steeled ourselves for July Fourth weekend, the red-hot center of the summer feeding frenzy. Jeffrey was already complaining that he never saw me anymore (which was sadly true!) because I was working constantly. But I imagine it's like having a new baby—I wanted to be at the store all the time. A few days before the holiday, he stopped by the store. At the same time, a man walked up to the counter and said, "I'd like you to cater a party for me this weekend." CATERING? I told him that I was sorry, I didn't do catering. He said it again, deaf to my polite refusals.

Finally, he moved a little closer to the counter and said, "You don't understand. I want all the smoked salmon and caviar you have in the store, and *I don't care what it costs.*"

I glanced at Jeffrey, and he was nodding as if to say "Do it!" (So much for a chance to spend more time together.) *This guy doesn't care what it costs? I guess I just became a caterer.*

I asked the kids at Barefoot to be waiters, planned a lavish buffet, and set it all up at his flashy apartment on the beach. I had to run back to the store to close up for the night, but I promised I'd be right back and told the young girls how I wanted things done. When I returned, I was shocked by what I saw. My beautiful platters piled high with food were completely untouched. No one had eaten anything—not a single bite. *I'm finished in this town,* I thought. *No one wants to eat the food we prepared.* That's when I discovered the secret world of Westhampton. After the party was over, I found out the host was the biggest drug dealer in town. The guests at his party were there for something, but it definitely wasn't the food!

The next day, he asked me to come by to pick up the rentals and settle the bill. When I showed up, the host—who looked like he was having a BIG morning-after—said he would like to tip me and asked if I could come back to his bedroom. What? I followed him (pretty stupid, I now realize), and he asked if I wanted some "blow." I thought, *You want me to do what?* I thought *he* was tipping *me*, and it sounded like this was the wrong way around, until I realized that "blow" was cocaine. Hmm. I remember going back to the store to slice some smoked salmon that morning—and I sliced it *really fast!* And I also realized that when you're catering a party in Westhampton, you need to know who the customer is. I never made that mistake again.

My second catering job seemed to be more conventional but was a nail-biter in its own way. A very good customer asked me to do a dinner party for thirty people. What should she serve? she wondered. The summer of 1978 was all about poached salmon. Suddenly, it was everywhere, as if it had gotten a publicist, and it seemed a perfect choice for a summer dinner at the beach. I didn't have a fish poacher, but my mother told me I could "poach" a fish in the oven by wrapping it in foil, pouring the poaching liquid into the foil, closing it tightly, and baking it on a sheet pan. The crazy thing was that I had actually never done it before this party, and I was so terrified that I brought Julia Child's *Mastering the Art of French Cooking* with me in the car, in case I needed help. How many "caterers" show up carrying a cookbook?

I thought I'd be tucked away in the kitchen, separate from the rest of the party, free to figure it out. But it turned out that the house had an open plan, so the kitchen was center stage and I was the main attraction! I might have gotten used to the guests watching me cook until I ran into a problem and wanted to hide. For a big house, the kitchen had a teeny-tiny oven, so small that the salmon, which suddenly looked like Moby Dick, didn't fit. I quickly cut it into two pieces, figuring I'd reassemble the cooked fish and cover it with cucumber slices to hide the scar.

I turned the oven to 350 degrees, in went the fish, and I prayed for the best. But when I opened the oven an hour later to take it out, the salmon was stone cold, sitting there like a slab of sushi. The oven was too small, and the fish filled it completely, so the heat couldn't circulate. The dinner hour was approaching. I was desperate—no, terrified—so I took the nuclear option. I cranked that tiny oven up to 500 degrees, slammed the door closed, and prayed it wouldn't catch fire or explode. Fortunately, the fish gods were with me. I opened the door and the salmon was poached to perfection! Whew! Crisis averted! I remember thinking, when the hostess commented on how calm I was making dinner for thirty people, *You should only know!* (And she never did!)

Every day at Barefoot Contessa was different. It usually began with a visit from a wonderful man who always came just as we opened to buy smoked salmon and bagels for breakfast and a slice of Westphalian ham for his dog, Charlie. One customer would buy ten pounds of grilled lemon chicken every Sunday, and when I got up the nerve to ask who was eating all that grilled chicken, I found out that it was her cat! Some days involved a trip to the emergency room when one of the girls inevitably ignored my instructions and sliced her thumb cutting a bagel, which was almost a rite of passage. Or it could be a long and uneventful but wonderful day of preparing food, chatting with customers, and watching them sit outside at the small tables in front of the store, enjoying a salad or a coffee with a friend.

But there was one really, really hard day each week. Every Wednesday, I would rent a station wagon and drive to New York City to buy many of the specialty foods we sold at the store—imported cheeses, specialty nuts, smoked fish, smoked meats, caviar, whatever wasn't available locally, which was basically everything. On the way home, I would stop at a huge grocery store and buy all the flour, sugar, eggs, and butter for baking. It was a long day.

I learned the drill from Diana: rent a station wagon on Tuesday night and drive to the city at three a.m. on Wednesday. There, I raced from supplier to supplier, picking up food and dropping off checks. Traffic was a nightmare, *parking* was impossible, but the suppliers were wonderful. Alleva Dairy, the oldest cheese shop in America, where they made fresh and smoked mozzarella in the basement; Voilà Bakeries, where the buttery scent of croissants was better than any perfume; Bazzini for nuts; Raffetto's for fresh pasta: New York was a giant smorgasbord of the best foods. When I finished making my rounds, I drove back to Westhampton, usually during rush hour, to restock the store at midnight. It was a twenty-one-hour day, and this was all before I started cooking for the first wave of hungry weekenders who arrived on Thursday. It was exhausting, but I loved connecting with all these small producers who made extraordinary handmade products for me to sell. And just when I recovered, it seemed as though it was time to do it all over again the next Wednesday!

I loved my routine, even when I had to drop everything to play den mother to my team of volatile teenagers. I was in a perfect position to listen to their problems because I was older, with a slightly wiser perspective, but younger than their parents, so I could certainly relate. Whenever one of the girls broke up with a boyfriend or had a fight with Mom, I'd walk her across the street to a nearby dock, a pretty place with boats, to talk her down from the cliff. First, there were tears, then we'd find something to laugh about, and soon all was well and she'd be back helping customers in the store in no time.

The truth was I needed someone to walk *me* to the dock. But the only person I could talk to about this problem was myself, and I was avoiding that conversation. My summer of bliss was a different experience for Jeffrey, who probably felt that he was watching a speeding train pass right by him. He tried to be helpful when he came to Westhampton on weekends, but there wasn't much he could do. He was traveling all that way, leaving his own high-pressure job, to do what? Hang around and watch me go crazy running Barefoot?

He definitely had more important things to do. One day when he was visiting, the phone rang at the store and the employee who answered yelled for Jeffrey. When he asked who it was, she said, "I don't know. It's some secretary."

That "secretary" was Jeffrey's boss, Secretary of State Cyrus Vance, and he took the call behind the counter, spitting distance from the customers lined up for lunch.

I knew Jeffrey was happy that I was happy, and our attitude at the beginning of the summer was, *We've been married for ten years; we'll figure this out.* But I suspected that he saw Barefoot Contessa as my summer job and thought that when the store closed in September, we'd go back to our old life in Washington . . . and the old roles that went with it. I'd be the wife, responsible for everything domestic, and Jeffrey would be the "man" who helped occasionally. It wasn't the stupid chores that bothered me; it was the feeling that I wasn't an equal partner in our marriage.

I couldn't let that happen.

When I bought Barefoot Contessa, I shattered our traditional roles—took a baseball bat to them and left them in pieces. While I was still cooking, cleaning, shopping, managing, and so on, at the store, I was doing it as a businesswoman, not a wife. My responsibilities made it impossible for me to even think about anything else. There was no expectation about who got home from work first and what they should do, because I never got home from work!

The other problem was that when Jeffrey came on weekends, he was a distraction. I didn't pay enough attention to him, I'm absolutely sure about that. I feel terrible whenever I think about it. I just wanted everyone to leave me alone so I could concentrate on the store. I wanted to spend all my time working, learning, and making the store better. I needed to concentrate on Barefoot Contessa and nothing else, because I could easily fall on my face. Jeffrey was fully formed and living the life he wanted to live. I wasn't, and I wouldn't be able to figure out who I was or what I wanted unless I was on my own. I needed that freedom.

I thought about it a lot, and at my lowest point, I wondered if the only answer would be to get a divorce. I knew I was getting ahead of myself, but the upside of divorce was getting a lot of attention that year after the release of Paul Mazursky's blockbuster movie *An Unmarried Woman*. The heroine, played by Jill Clayburgh, discovers that there is life (and Alan Bates—because this was the *Hollywood* version) after her marriage ends suddenly. The movie suggested that divorce could be a positive move, a new beginning, and a pathway to independence. I wanted all of that, but I loved Jeffrey and didn't want to shock—or hurt—him, so I'd start by suggesting we pause for a separation.

Sometime in the middle of the summer, we went for a walk on the beach. It was the hardest thing I ever did, but I found the courage to start the painful conversation. Haltingly, I told him that I needed to be on my own. I didn't say whether it was for now . . . or forever. He listened quietly, thinking about my words and processing their meaning. In true Jeffrey form, he said, "If you feel like you need to be on your own, you need to do it." He made it even more painful for me because he was so damn understanding! He packed his bag and went home to Washington with no plan to come back.

We'd been apart when Jeffrey was in the military, but this was different. I'd asked the only man I'd ever loved for a separation, knowing that I was taking a terrible risk. I needed to find myself, but was I really ready to lose him in the process? Who was I without Jeffrey? I was about to find out. In my head, I was convinced there was no other way to move forward. But in my heart . . . well, I couldn't even go there. I buried my emotions and threw myself into my work.

And just like that, I was alone.

Photograph by Tom Eckerle

1,000 Baguettes and the Business End of a Gun

For the rest of the summer, I focused on the store and catering, catering and the store. I'd made a few friends in town and had an occasional minute for a social life. But the only heat I felt on my face was at the oven, never on a sunny beach. I didn't care, because there was no other place I wanted to be, and when I was busy, for the first time, I didn't have to worry about whether Jeffrey was happy.

Nothing prepared me for the bittersweet reality of Labor Day, when everyone goes home and beach businesses close for the winter. We packed up the food, cleaned the store, and said our goodbyes. Melinda was moving to Woodstock, Vermont, so eventually I'd have to find a new chef, which was nerve-racking. The girls in the front of the store went back to college, promising to come back next summer. When I turned off the lights and locked the door, it hit me that I was truly on my own, and on top of that, I was homeless. I had to find a place to live and figure out what I was going to do for the next eight months while the store was closed for the winter.

I had made enough money to live on a budget, but I was going to have to be careful. Was I free or was I completely unmoored? A little of both, but considering this was the first time in my life that I had no one to depend on, no one to care what I did, no friends nearby—they were in Washington—and I was alone in New York City, where I'd never lived before . . . it was quickly becoming apparent to me that it was more the latter than the former.

These decisions were big, terrifying firsts for me. I had gone straight from my parents' house to my life with Jeffrey. Now, even though I was thirty, I was like a naïve college graduate, facing important choices on my own. It was a painful but necessary process. I went to New York to look for an apartment and immediately learned some tough lessons. I had to choose between a nice apartment in a dodgy neighborhood and a crappy apartment in a good neighborhood. The real estate market in New York City was very hot at the time. If I wasn't the first person standing at the door when an apartment became available, I didn't get it, so I had to move fast.

I finally found a dingy little apartment in Greenwich Village, where I wanted to live. It was small, hot, and empty, and I literally didn't know what to do with myself. I couldn't sleep at night, then I couldn't get out of bed in the morning. There was no reason to get up. I had no purpose. I had no space to cook in that terrible kitchen. I can't even remember what the kitchen looked like, but I know I was never tempted to use it. The worst part was that I was so completely alone. And to make it even more painful, Jeffrey—still my best friend—came to New York to help me get the apartment set up. He bought me a stereo system and a rug for the living room. I thought, *Am I crazy? He's the sweetest man in the world!* But I remained convinced that I needed to figure out who I was on my own before I could be an equal partner with him. And frankly, he needed to do the same thing.

One day, Jeffrey called to check in. "What's going on?" I went directly from "hello" to a total meltdown. When I got to the part about not being able to get out of bed, he spoke calmly and reassuringly. "Why don't you take a taxi to Grand Central station and catch the next train to Washington. I'll pick you up at the other end. I'm going on a six-week round-the-world trip for the State Department. Your friends are here. Your support system is here. Just stay in our house, where you'll be comfortable, and I'll see you when I get back."

I cry just thinking about his tenderness and concern when I needed it most.

I did exactly what he suggested. Jeffrey met me at the station, and when we got to our house, we sat together on the steps outside, reluctant to go in because we were caught between two worlds: the way it used to be when we were Ina and Jeffrey, and the sad way it was now. A painful limbo.

Jeffrey broke the uncomfortable silence with a question. "What can I do to change your mind?"

He asked so hopefully, not understanding that I doubted we could make our relationship work, and that we might be heading for divorce. Not because I didn't love him—I loved him so much—but because I just couldn't live with him in a traditional "man and wife" relationship, which seemed to be what he wanted. Maybe I should have had more confidence in Jeffrey, but I'd never been through something like this before, so I didn't know what was possible.

Let me be clear. Jeffrey hadn't done anything wrong. He was just doing what every man before him had done. But we were living in a new era, and that behavior wasn't okay with me anymore. *I* had changed. I felt differently about myself. My summer at Barefoot Contessa showed me who I really was, and even though many of my experiences at the store and when I was on my own in New York had been a trial by fire, I came out of the challenging times feeling stronger and more secure, and, for the first time, I had a real sense of my identity. I couldn't go back to the way we were, when my sense of self was so dependent on being his wife.

What could he do to change my mind? I answered him, knowing the stakes were high. Still, I tried.

"The only chance of this working is if you go to a therapist," I told him. I hoped that if he discussed our situation with a professional, he'd see me differently, not as a child or as a wife but as a partner whose voice was as important as his.

He shocked me by agreeing instantly, promising to go as soon as he got back from his trip.

But I was betting all or nothing. "That'll be too late," I said, certain a six-week wait would be the beginning of the end. "You have to start right now."

"I'll go tomorrow," he promised.

And he did.

It was incredible. On his way to his flight in New York, Jeffrey stopped in Connecticut to talk to the therapist who'd treated my family over the years and knew us all very well.

I felt a rush of conflicting emotions. *What if it doesn't help?* But the more I thought about it, I realized that Jeffrey's willingness to see the therapist was as significant as anything that might happen during their session. He was *that* determined to convince me he was serious about making our marriage work. If he could change a little and I could change a little, we could meet in the middle and start again.

Six weeks passed. I was comfortable in Washington and used the time to connect with friends and recover from the breakneck pace of the summer. In the kitchen of our old house, I tested new recipes for the store for next summer, talked to suppliers about buying new products, and scoured catalogs for the best smoked salmon and Parmesan cheese.

When it was time for Jeffrey to come back from his trip, we met in Palm Springs, California, away from any distractions, to see if we could make this work. I had no idea what to expect. A honeymoon or scorched earth? We were facing a critical moment, and it could go either way. I was terrified but determined.

It was amazing! We talked, we listened, and more important, we *heard* each other when we aired our concerns. I wasn't the only one who thought it would be liberating to throw out the old gender roles and start again. Jeffrey admitted that he wanted a job where he traveled for work but always felt that he should stay home because he was the *husband* and had to be responsible for me. He understood—maybe for the first time—that he didn't have to feel that way anymore. I had pecked my way out of my shell and was a fully formed, independent person. I could breathe on my own. Moving forward, we could be equals who took care of each other. It wouldn't happen overnight, but if we worked toward the same goal, we could change things together.

I remember thinking, *Oh my God, this is the most wonderful man! I'm falling in love with someone who just happens to be my husband.*

The Palm Springs summit was the beginning of the rest of our lives. A therapist many years later told me her theory of marriage. When you're young, you marry someone who has the qualities you wish you had. In my case, I was drawn to Jeffrey because he was smart and serious. He was a "grown-up." He did the same thing, seeing me as someone who was always fun and happy—the life of the party. As you grow older, one of two things happens. Either you start to find those differences increasingly annoying and you grow apart, or—and this is what was happening to us— you gradually become more like each other, even as you remain who you are. With time, Jeffrey became lighter, while I became more serious without losing my sense of fun. Eventually, we found our balance.

We'd resolved the big problems; now we had to figure out the practical choices. In the spirit of starting over, we decided that Jeffrey would move to New York City. There might have been a complication when, for a hot minute during our separation, Jeffrey got it into his head that he wanted to find a job in the private sector, specifically in international agriculture, and work in a modern glass high-rise in Chicago (really?), the total opposite of his Washington experience. He found a huge firm headquartered there and started looking for a connection, landing a meeting with Nat Samuels, a partner at Lehman Brothers in New York and, more important to Jeffrey, a board member at the international agriculture company he was targeting.

Nat Samuels listened patiently as Jeffrey went on and on about his interest in food chains and farming. Confused, Nat finally managed to get a word in. "Why do you keep talking to me about agriculture?" he asked. When Jeffrey explained that he was hoping to get a job at the company in Chicago, Nat let loose. "You don't want to work there! They eat lunch at eleven o'clock in the morning and they wear string ties. You want to work here, at Lehman Brothers!"

And that's exactly how Jeffrey ended up with a terrific new job as an investment banker in New York City. Phew!

We sold our house in Washington to a friend from the State Department and got ready to move. When I say "move," what I really mean is that we got rid of absolutely everything except two suitcases of clothes. We just took all our stuff—furniture, art, skis, boots, books, wedding gifts we never used, literally everything we owned—and moved it from the house to the sidewalk in front of the house. We were looking for a fresh start in New York, and this felt so cleansing. Expensive, maybe, but very cathartic, and Jeffrey was going to be an investment banker, so I figured we could afford the luxury of starting over. People in the neighborhood watched eagerly, waiting for the next drop. There's probably a deep psychological reason for our impulsive way of leaving the past behind. Whatever our motivation, it made moving really easy!

Our new home was the top two floors of a beautiful Greenwich Village town house. The building was historic, but the apartment had been completely renovated, so the space was a blend of old and new, with gorgeous wide-planked wood floors and a fabulous kitchen that would double as my winter office. When I wasn't happily installed there—studying my expanding collection of cookbooks; trying new recipes; playing with my new favorite toy, a Cuisinart food processor; and planning for my second summer at the store—I was out on the streets of Manhattan experiencing the food renaissance that was happening all around me.

For decades, the best restaurants in New York served classic French cuisine prepared by classically trained French chefs. Le Pavillon and Le Cirque were formal places frequented by high society, businessmen with expense accounts, and people celebrating special occasions. André Soltner's Lutèce had an atmosphere that was a little warmer *if* you could ever score a reservation. Jeffrey and I managed to eat there once, on my birthday. I remember being totally intimidated by the enormous wine list, which looked like the *Encyclopædia Britannica*. Jeffrey handed it to me, shocking the waiter because the MAN always ordered the wine. I flipped through page after page until I finally found two bottles that were under $100 and randomly chose one. When the waiter left, Jeffrey asked if I'd picked red or white. I had to admit I had no idea! That's how little I knew about wine—dining at these places felt like taking a test you couldn't possibly pass.

Around the same time, Alice Waters at Chez Panisse in Berkeley, California, was changing all that. She ignited a restaurant revolution when she—an American woman who hadn't been formally trained—prepared food that was seasonal and locally sourced (what we now call "farm to table"), in a charmingly homey setting. Her first menu didn't conform to the old notions of haute cuisine: instead of Timbale de Crabmeat Newburg or Ris de Veau Meunière, she served mesclun salad with house pâté, seared duck breast with green olives, and a simple plum tart topped with homemade ice cream. No Soufflé Tous Parfums or Cerises Jubilé here!

Suddenly, it was acceptable, maybe even desirable, to be untrained, to be intuitive in the kitchen, which was very good news for me, since I had never seen the inside of a cooking school.

The most exciting part of being in New York City was the opportunity to visit the specialty food stores. The golden age of prepared foods started in the 1970s, parallel to the women's movement. Women were going to work, but at the end of the day, they still had to put dinner on the table. The solution was *really* good takeout. At a specialty food store, it was possible to pick up a delicious meal, made from fresh ingredients, on the way home from the office, and by 1979, every neighborhood in New York had one.

Downtown, Dean & DeLuca imported goat cheese, sun-dried tomatoes, and ingredients that nobody knew about. On the Upper West Side, Sheila Lukins and Julee Rosso of the Silver Palate worked magic with raspberry vinegar and made Chicken Marbella the "must-serve" dish for every dinner party. At E.A.T. on the Upper East Side, Eli Zabar prepared the most delicious takeout salads, dinners, cheeses, and baked goods, and later he started baking his own bread, which was a revolution in itself. There was

a store called Fay and Allen's Foodworks, which dazzled customers with a five-foot display of fresh caviar and 160 cheeses. At
Word of Mouth, Eileen Weinberg and Christi Finch made quiches
with unusual ingredients, memorably eggplant with a whisper of
dill and a mustard glaze, and cold pasta salads that nobody had
done before, like tortellini, ham, green and red peppers, and salsa
verde. Unlike the old deli stuff, it was fresh and appealing, just as
easy to serve but a thousand times better.

Good food was everywhere! Even Macy's and Bloomingdale's
celebrated food with European-style food emporiums and first-
class restaurants. There was the kind of buzz you'd feel at a great
party. "I have met more people at Bloomingdale's than I have at
any singles bar on the Upper East Side," one customer told a reporter.

Eating became a sport and food a passion, leading Gael Greene,
New York magazine's "Insatiable Critic," to coin the word *foodie*.
Gourmets were selective, maybe finicky. But foodies just loved
food. They were adventurous, always on the hunt for new taste
sensations.

There I was, at the center of a business that was becoming very
exciting. I tasted my way around town, exploring new imported
ingredients, adding curry to chicken salad and sun-dried tomatoes to pasta salads. Everything was fresh and colorful, and burst-
ing with flavor. You could make a classic dish like roast chicken,
but you could also bring new flavors like fennel and olives to it.
All of a sudden, food wasn't about following a classic Julia Child
or James Beard recipe; the only limit to what you could cook was
your imagination, and inspiration was everywhere. At the same
time, I wanted to improve my cooking skills, so I signed up for a
cooking class, probably expecting a quick review of the basics, but
I got so much more.

My teacher, Lydie Marshall, grew up in France and moved to America when she was a teenager. She loved to cook but studied Romance languages in college and at graduate school, until she came across a line written by Jean-Paul Sartre. He said that it was bad faith to do something you know you're not good at, and good faith to do the thing you're best at doing. That's when she changed her life and started cooking professionally, so we had that wonderful philosophy in common.

Lydie had a professional kitchen in the basement of her Greenwich Village brownstone, just a few blocks from my apartment. I would walk over in the evening and feel as if I had been transported to Provence. My classmates and I prepared five recipes, not fancy, but really good country French cooking. I learned so much about seasoning and maintaining a balance of flavor. Then, when we'd finished cooking, we'd sit down and eat our work. Pissaladière, lemon tarts with puff pastry and paper-thin lemons sliced on top . . . I was in heaven! I think I took the class three times (with a different menu each time); I was like a sponge soaking up all of Lydie's knowledge, and maybe a little of her country French style. This was the essence of what I love—elegant and earthy food.

One of my jobs that winter was to find a new chef for Barefoot Contessa. I frankly had no idea how to even interview a chef, let alone decide who would be the best candidate. I put an ad in the local paper (remember "help wanted" ads?), and an elegant European woman showed up. We talked a little (I loved her sensibility and style), and then I asked if she would cook something for me. She kindly suggested that I come to her house the next day and said she would make me lunch. Really? How lovely was that?

I will never ever forget that lunch. It was one of the truly serendipitous meetings of my life. The woman was Anna Pump; her lunch was the first frittata I ever ate, and it was delicious; and her apple tart was out of this world. She was the only person I interviewed, and I hired her on the spot. Not only did Anna and I work together that summer at Barefoot Contessa, but we became very close friends. Anna taught me many things about food and presentation that are still with me today.

For example, one day during Anna's first summer with me, a customer asked for a cheese platter, and since it required no cooking, I decided to make it myself rather than bother Anna. I piled all kinds of things on that platter that might go with cheese, and it must have looked like a dog's breakfast. Anna very quietly walked over to me and said, "Now take everything off that platter, put a large bunch of grapes in the middle, put the cheeses back around the grapes, then a few groupings of strawberries and crackers, and then *stop* yourself." Anna taught me that often, "less is more," and quality is everything.

Barefoot Contessa's second summer was nothing like the first, in all the best ways. This time, Westhampton felt like an old friend. I started my tradition of hand delivering the first muffin of the season to Gloria, the plump older woman who owned the candy and newspaper store next door and was a fixture in Westhampton. I thought she was ancient, but she was probably the age I am now. Gloria always sat behind the counter with her dog, and whenever he needed to "exercise," she walked him down the front steps of the store and then back up, and that was it. She was delighted to see the muffin and always said, "Oh, this will go right to my hips!"

The town was full of characters and contrasts. The old-fashioned grocery across the street was owned by the Weixelbaums (they took the train to Westhampton in the early 1900s and liked it so much that they never left). The servers stood behind the counter, waiting to take your order. When you told them you needed Hell-mann's mayonnaise and white bread, they'd go back to the stock-room to get it. It was right out of Mayberry. On the other hand, at the other end of Main Street, Club Marakesh attracted a hot young disco crowd, wearing spiked heels and dripping in Rolexes. They danced and did God knows what else until four a.m., just when Dave's Bun 'n' Burger opened for breakfast.

This time, I felt prepared and excited, ready to refresh Barefoot Contessa with ideas I'd developed over the winter. I ordered new T-shirts and spanking white aprons for the staff. Shawn Warren and Lee and Sarah Esterling were back, and I hired Martine Sharp to join them. (This was the most educated retail team on earth— they went to Williams, Yale, and Wellesley, respectively. I wasn't even sure if I was up to their standard!) Anna Pump ran our tiny kitchen in the back, while I took care of the front of the "house."

One thing I learned, and continue to learn every day, is that the food we enjoy most connects to our deepest memories of when we felt happy, comfortable, nurtured. It could be something from childhood (definitely not my childhood—my mother, who was a trained nutritionist, never served anything remotely comforting!) or a taste that somehow made us feel good, even if we didn't know why. I wanted to re-create those nostalgic sensations, with fresher ingredients, and make them even better than remembered.

Our pan-fried onion dip is a perfect example. In the 1950s, we called it California Dip, and it was omnipresent at rec room par-ties because it was so easy to make: just a package of Lipton onion soup mix with two cups of sour cream, served with a bottomless bowl of potato chips. It was addictive, but who knows what was in it? *But,* I thought, *what if the onions were fresh instead of de-hydrated, cooked over low heat until they caramelized to a golden brown, and mixed with sour cream, cream cheese, mayonnaise, and a dash of cayenne pepper?* It's familiar, but it tastes so much better than you remember.

Or what about chicken salad? Why is it always so *beige*? I started with grilled lemon chicken and added raw sugar snap peas, julienned red and yellow bell peppers, freshly squeezed lemon juice, and good California olive oil. The colors were bright, the ingredients were fresh, and the lemon juice gave it all an "edge" that made everything taste better.

The time I had spent roaming Manhattan's specialty food stores also gave me a better understanding of how to make Barefoot Contessa more welcoming. I never liked the places that made you feel like the person who'd crashed the party, where the staff was snooty or dismissive, or where the merchandise was so staged that it screamed *"Don't touch."* Anna taught me to stock the shelves and then remove one item so it's not so perfect. That way, customers don't subliminally feel that they're ruining the display by taking something off the shelf. I wanted the store to say, *"Please touch!"* and *"Please taste!"* Basically, I wanted everyone to feel right at home.

I thought about every part of an interaction with customers. For example, we greeted them by name, if we knew them, and if we didn't, we'd find out and remember it for next time. It was forbidden to say, "May I help you?" because they knew we were there to help them, and I felt there was a subtle reluctance for the customer to say, "Now you can help me," after they'd earlier said, "No." We never asked, "Is that all?" but rather "What else can I get you?," like we had all the time in the world for them. It was because it was all new to me that I could think it through: *How would I like to be treated as a customer?*

I loved our return policy. Usually, when you return something to a store, you get some kind of resistance. I thought this was an opportunity to be different. Every person in the store knew what to do if someone returned any product. First, you got your money back, no questions asked. Once you had your money in your hand, we'd ask what you didn't like about the product. Finally, based on the answer—you don't like a dense chocolate cake, or the cake you got was overbaked—you got something free, such as a different chocolate cake or a new cake that wasn't overbaked. People were stunned! A serious problem turned into a happy customer for life, and the cost to us was minimal.

That summer was crazy busy, so busy that we didn't even have a minute to count the cash in the register at the end of each day. We opened at nine a.m. and closed at ten p.m., when I was too exhausted to breathe, let alone "cash out" the register. Instead, I would stuff all the bills into bank bags and bring them to the night drop at the bank at the end of the street each day. On Mondays, Sarah and I would take one of those private rooms at the bank where you can open your box of valuables, and we would spend the entire day counting cash as if we had just robbed a bank. One day, when I decided to run out to get us coffee, Sarah said, "You're going to leave me here alone with all this cash?"

I looked at her incredulously. "You work in the store. If I didn't trust you with the cash, I'd be in real trouble!"

There were a few "oh shit" disasters we managed to avoid or fix. One evening, Shawn was getting ready to clean the frozen yogurt machine. It was a nasty job that involved filling a bucket with water mixed with a splash of bleach and pumping it through the system. I was talking to a customer when Shawn walked by, and I got a whiff of ammonia. "Shawn, what's in that bucket?" I asked. She said, "Oh, I couldn't find any bleach, so I put some ammonia in it." Luckily, I stopped her, and we didn't kill any customers that day with deadly fumes. Who knew you could kill people in a specialty food store?!

Frozen yogurt may have been the hottest food of the seventies, as the ad for the store I *didn't* buy promised, but that damn machine was the source of many headaches. To clean it, someone (and that "someone" was often me) had to stand on a ladder and drain the old yogurt into a bucket. One memorable day, the bucket tipped over, leaving poor Sarah standing in a pool of goop—yogurt everywhere. Our collective sense of humor kicked in and we laughed hysterically as we cleaned. But that was the last straw. Barefoot Contessa would not be selling frozen yogurt anymore. Some decisions aren't made the way they teach you in business school!

Then there was the time a customer came in to pick up a birthday cake she'd ordered. I called out to Anna in the back, "Is that chocolate cake ready?" The words were barely out of my mouth when I saw Anna drop the box holding the cake. Thank God the customer couldn't see her gorgeous chocolate cake, broken in half in the box. Anna quickly put it back together, smoothed the cracks with fresh icing, and presented it as if nothing had happened.

Sometimes I was the culprit. One night, as Anna was leaving the store, she put a dozen carrot cakes in the oven and asked me to take them out in exactly one hour. I said, "Sure," then completely forgot about them and went home . . . until I woke up in a panic at four o'clock in the morning with one thought: *Anna's cakes!* I felt so terrible that I ran back to Barefoot, tossed the charred cakes and the ruined pans in the trash, and made them all over again, which was even harder than it sounds.

First, I had to scrub and trim the carrots, then the recipe called for grating them by hand on a metal box grater, enough for *twelve* cakes. At five a.m. (which felt like the middle of the night in cake time), it was a struggle to keep my knuckles out of harm's way. But this arduous step, I learned, was critical to making a perfect carrot cake.

Several years later, I had a really good baker who kept having problems with the carrot cake. She'd bake a large batch, and they would collapse as soon as they came out of the oven. I thought the problem might be how she was handling the flour. In a commercial setting, you can't take the time to sift all that flour before measuring, so it has to be weighed on a scale or aerated in the bin. The flour was right, but the next batch of cakes also collapsed and ended up in the trash.

Finally, I asked the baker if I could watch her prepare the batter. And there it was! She had decided to save time by grating the carrots in the food processor, but they came out much wetter that way and made the cake soggy, which caused it to fall in the middle. The solution was to add a little flour to the wetter carrots, and we never had a problem again.

I had a much stickier situation with a bread baker. This was the early eighties, when it was very unusual for a store to bake its own bread. In fact, I had placed French deck ovens in the window of the store so people could watch the bread being made.

Right before the season started, a nice young man came in looking for a job as a baker. He told me that he'd been baking all his life, and in fact, his father was a bread baker. I took him at his word and hired him.

That nice young baker may have been able to make traditional loaves of white bread, but it turned out that he had *never* made baguettes, and he made the worst ones I'd ever eaten. Baguettes need to be light and airy on the inside, with a crisp and flavorful crust. He was using my recipe, but his baguettes were somehow soft and tough at the same time—and they had no crust! What was he doing wrong? The detective in me (or maybe the scientist) was called into action.

Bread baking depends on kneading the dough to develop the

gluten, the protein in wheat flour that creates the structure of the bread. Gluten is tough—almost every cake recipe says, "Add the flour and mix only until combined," because you don't want to "develop the gluten" or the cake will become tough. That sounds logical, right? So to my mind, since his bread was too tough, clearly he was overkneading the dough and creating too much structure.

I suggested that he knead the dough less. To my surprise, the baguettes were still tough. Now I was getting worried. The summer crowds would descend on us soon, and the baguettes were inedible. I decided I needed to do the same thing with the bread baker I'd done with the woman who made the carrot cakes—come in at three a.m. and watch him bake to find out what was going wrong. I suggested that he knead the bread even less. This time, the baguettes were even tougher!

Intrigued, I called in the cavalry. I phoned Anna Pump, who had given me the recipe, and she explained the paradox of gluten in bread. Yes, gluten is a tough substance, and it creates the structure of bread. But the *more* you knead the dough, the better the structure you create to trap the carbon dioxide given off by the yeast, so the bread becomes lighter—exactly the opposite of what I was doing! Mystery solved, the baker and I made delicious, light and crispy baguettes together. Unfortunately, he couldn't master the process on his own (and I wasn't about to come in at three every morning!), so I had to let him go.

I didn't know what I was going to do. Just at that moment, a Swedish girl walked in and said she was looking for a job. I asked her if she had ever baked bread. "No," she replied. "Would you like to learn?" I asked. "Yes!" she said enthusiastically. "Perfect! You're hired!" Her name was Heidi, and I taught her how to make gorgeous baguettes. She baked a thousand of them every single day, and they were gone by three p.m. I have to admit she was incredibly beautiful, and the fact that the ovens were in the window may have helped.

This is a roundabout way of saying that what I learned in my tiny kitchen at the first Barefoot Contessa became more important as my business expanded. I had to hire and train a whole new kitchen and catering staff every year, and do it quickly and expertly. I had to really know how to cook and bake and solve any problems that might come up along the way. Even when I had a bigger and bigger staff, I was always hands-on in the kitchen. If someone couldn't come to work one day, I always knew I could jump in and do their job.

But my worst experience that second summer, hands down (or hands up, as it turned out), happened on the streets of New York when I was doing one of my food runs. By that time, Wednesday was my least favorite day of the week, when I saddled up the rented station wagon and raced from supplier to supplier, picking up food for the weekend. The crime rate in the city was off the charts, especially in the edgier neighborhoods. I was in a parking space, getting ready to go to my next stop, a restaurant supply store on the Bowery. I had to pick up some equipment there, so my purse was bulging with an envelope filled with $2,000 in big bills. Suddenly, I noticed a man approaching my car. This happened all the time, and it was usually someone wanting to wash my windows with a dirty rag. Not this time.

The man pulled out a gun and demanded fifty dollars. Trying to stay cool and thinking this is how people get themselves killed, I slipped my hand into the envelope, hoping he couldn't see, thinking, *Please let it be a fifty, not a hundred!* It was! I handed it to him. He looked at it and said, "Give me twenty-five more." Did he think I was a bank? There is no such thing as a twenty-five-dollar bill—and all I had anyway were fifties and hundreds—but I didn't tell him that because he was waving the business end of a gun at me. I looked him straight in the eye, and with a tone of ultimate authority, I said to him, "I'm not giving you twenty-five dollars, I'm giving you fifty, and then you're going to leave!!" Thankfully, he did! I have no idea if that was the smartest thing I've ever done or the stupidest, but happily, I'm here to tell the tale. I promised myself that day that I would find another way to handle the weekly shopping trip to New York.

Every business owner worries about cash flow and the most important obligation of all: meeting the payroll. I had never had a problem until the one time I did. I looked at the numbers and realized I was in trouble. Our income was down that week, but our expenses were the same—a classic problem for small businesses—and I just didn't have the money to pay my employees. I simply couldn't figure out what to do about it. The thought of letting them down, even for a week, was devastating to me. I kept running the numbers in my head, trying to come up with a solution. Jeffrey noticed that I seemed preoccupied and asked if I was anxious about something. When I confessed I didn't have the money for payroll, he listened, then said quietly, "Let me see what I can work out."

Jeffrey loved working at Lehman Brothers, but that didn't stop him from making the very drastic move of going to the office and asking if he quit his job, could he have the money in his retirement account? The answer was yes, but they thought it was crazy to quit for that reason (as did I!) and offered him a loan. Crisis averted. But I'll never forget that Jeffrey was willing to sacrifice everything to help me out of a bind, like something out of one of those wonderful O. Henry stories.

As the summer ended, I felt that Barefoot had really become

the heartbeat of the town. People came to the store to buy food, yes, but also to see who was there, and they'd end up hanging out at a table in front of the store with a coffee and a friend. One day, a man popped in and asked if anyone had a guitar. Amused, I explained that we were a food store—no musical instruments here—but he insisted that someone had told him that if *anyone* could find him a guitar, it would be Ina Garten. *Really?* I didn't think anyone even knew who I was! Well, it turned out the man asking for a guitar was Peter Yarrow of Peter, Paul and Mary, so I asked if anyone shopping at that moment had a guitar. Yes! A customer ran home quickly to get one, then Peter sat outside, playing the guitar and singing for us.

I looked around at the gathering crowd, listening so happily, and thought, *Oh my God, this is so much better than writing nuclear energy budgets for the government!* I had a job I loved and a real community in a beautiful resort town. There were days when I thought I'd made the stupidest decision in the world, and there were days that were fun. I had jumped off a cliff not knowing where I was going to land, and here I was, sitting outside my own store, making my own decisions, hiring people I loved to work with, and as though that wasn't enough, Peter Yarrow had come to sing for us. I felt that my work was satisfying and that it actually mattered to the people in the village. We had created a happy place where people wanted to be.

A lot of celebrities spent time in the Hamptons, and several came to the store. I was never starstruck until the day I looked out the window and saw a familiar—no, an *iconic*—woman walking down the street. Long, swinging hair, aviator glasses . . . "Oh my God, that's Gloria Steinem!" I announced to the girls in the store. When their response was, "Who's that?" I knew what I had to do.

I shudder to think that I did this, but I did. I ran outside and stopped her. "I'm so sorry," I apologized, horrified even in the moment that I had the nerve to do this. "Would you mind coming in for a minute? I have all these young women who work for me, and they need to know who changed their lives." She may have thought I was crazy, but she graciously followed me to the store. I told the girls what she'd done—that she advanced feminism, campaigned for the Equal Rights Amendment, founded *Ms.* magazine. "Your mothers didn't know that they had options. *I* didn't know. Gloria Steinem changed all of that," I explained, wanting them to know what a difference she'd made in the lives they could lead, in the choices they could make. I would have given her anything in the store, but all she'd accept was a cup of coffee. I've never forgotten that encounter, and I believe the young women who were there that day remember it, too.

I was in a really good place. I loved what I was doing, we were making some money, and Anna and I started talking about forming a business partnership at Barefoot Contessa. We drew up a contract, and just as we were about to sign it, she came to me, distraught. "I have a serious problem," she said. "And I'm afraid you'll never speak to me again."

Loaves & Fishes, a fabulous specialty food store in Bridgehampton owned by Devon Fredericks and Susan Costner, was for sale, and Anna wanted to buy it. Anna was important to me, so I didn't have a moment's hesitation in supporting her. In fact, I was sure we could support each other. "This is great," I said. "Let's share everything! We can pool all our recipes and suppliers. If I need help with the baguettes, I'll ask you, and if you run out of shopping bags, you can ask me. We can pool the resources of Barefoot Contessa and Loaves & Fishes, and we'll both win."

She thought it was a great idea, and that's exactly what we did. She bought Loaves & Fishes, and she also wrote many wonderful cookbooks that I use all the time. We even did catering jobs together in the winter. We were friends and "partners in crime" for the rest of her life.

Anna and I were dear friends, but I now realize that we would have been horrible business partners. I'm impulsive. If I have an idea, I want to do it right now. When it occurred to me that it might be a good idea to sell coffee at Barefoot, I immediately called the supplier, ordered twelve twenty-pound canvas bags of beans, and put them out to see what would happen. If it worked (it did!), fine. If not, I was willing to take the risk, and I'd just end up with a lot of coffee to drink.

When Anna was thinking about selling coffee in her store, it took her years to make up her mind. She was cautious—that was her nature. One way wasn't better than the other—both Barefoot Contessa and Loaves & Fishes thrived—but our styles were completely different and ultimately incompatible, so we dodged a bullet by *not* becoming business partners. As Jeffrey says, "You never know your good breaks from your bad ones."

I'm a big believer in collaboration, in playing nicely with others. I think it makes everyone better because we can learn from each other. Business doesn't have to be cutthroat and isolating. It's much more fun and productive to exchange ideas, to be genuinely curious about how other people do things, to be generous, and to root for a competitor's success. I chose to work in food because I wanted a life filled with good times and meaningful connections with friends like Anna, Eli Zabar, Devon Fredericks, George Germon and Johanne Killeen, and later Sarah Leah Chase, Danny Meyer, Erin French, Missy Robbins, Bobby Flay, Michael Symon, and others who shared my passions for both food and business.

Losing Anna as a partner was a disappointment, but I knew I'd figure it out. I settled into a pleasant rhythm—winters catering parties in New York, crazy exhausting summers in Westhampton.

Jeffrey and I bought a loft on lower Fifth Avenue, where I built a huge kitchen to work in. Then, during Barefoot Contessa's third summer, I was blindsided by a completely unexpected problem. When I was buying the store, my father had told me to pay attention to the lease assignment. The what? I had bought Barefoot Contessa—meaning the name, the business, and its holdings—but I was also leasing the building. Actually, Diana held the lease, and, it turned out, she didn't actually have the right to assign it to me without the landlord's knowledge.

At the time, I didn't understand the importance of assignment versus sublease, but now that I am a landlord, I know that it makes all the difference in the world. Without his knowledge, the landlord now had a tenant he had never met and didn't know, and one he'd had no say in giving a lease to. Oh, and by the way, a tenant who had very little retail experience. Let's just say, he wasn't happy.

Sam, the owner of the building, lived in Miami, so it took him a while to figure out that Diana was no longer running the store. Because Diana never had the right to reassign her lease in the first place, essentially, I was a squatter. I asked Sam for a new lease, but he was understandably annoyed that we'd violated the existing lease, so he decided to play hardball. I could have the lease, but I wouldn't be allowed to keep tables and chairs outside.

That wasn't an option. The store was set back from the street, so the outdoor seating area was key to our success—it instantly signaled that Barefoot Contessa was a place where customers could buy food and hang out with friends. I flew to Miami to meet with him, hoping I could charm him into changing his mind. But he wouldn't budge, and neither could I. I knew his restrictions would be *very* bad for business. I needed a new location . . . and I needed it fast.

The good news was that the huge old-fashioned grocery store

owned by the Weixelbaums across the street was for sale, and I had a million ideas for how to turn the historic building into the food market of my dreams. We'd modernize with white walls, shiny floors, new lighting, and an industrial kitchen, and keep touches from the past by using the original wainscoting from the former market for the counters.

The bad news was that Jeffrey and I didn't have two dimes to put together and couldn't afford to buy it *or* come up with $150,000 to do a gut renovation.

Lucky for me, a local man wanted to buy the market as an investment, and he offered me a ridiculously favorable lease of $25,000 a year for ten years. *That* I could afford, because I knew the new store would be profitable. And given the numbers, I realized that if he ever wanted to sell the building during that time, he'd have to sell it to me, because anyone else would be stuck with a tenant with a very low rent for a very long time. If all went well, I could be in a position to buy the building in a few years.

That left the problem of the renovation, which was my responsibility. My plan was to apply for a business loan at our local bank, but I suspected I was doomed because no one in their right mind would give me the $150,000 I needed with no collateral to offer except maybe my bicycle.

Jeffrey stepped in with a solution from a very unlikely source. He had been reading *The Power Broker,* Robert Caro's brilliant biography of the legendary Robert Moses, the public official who transformed the infrastructure of New York by building bridges, tunnels, highways, and parks. Moses was highly creative (another way of saying "fast and loose"!) when it came to financing his projects. He wanted to build the Long Island Expressway, which was sixty-six miles long, almost the entire length of Long Island. He knew he wouldn't get all the funds he needed from the state legislature, so he'd routinely underestimate the cost, get started, then go back and say it was going to cost twice as much. The state couldn't walk away from a project that was half-built, so in the end, he got the money he needed. "You can't make an omelet without breaking some eggs," he'd say to justify his financial sleight of hand.

Following Moses's lead, I asked the bank for $75,000 (half of what I needed), and the loan was approved. We started demolition during the winter, and at the point of no return, I went back to the bank and asked for the rest of the money. Smart, if embarrassingly devious, but I figured the end, like Moses's omelet, would justify the means. Except there was a problem. For that kind of loan, the bank president John Kanas *himself* would have to approve the additional money, and he was on vacation for the next three days. *Oh my God, if this doesn't work, I'm in deep trouble,* I thought. The anxiety was overwhelming.

Three days of hell and uncertainty. Three days of worrying that I would be stuck with a wreck of a building that I could never turn into a store and a $75,000 loan to repay, with no store and no income. Three days of kicking myself for thinking I could play high-stakes poker. Jeffrey was in New York and I was too nervous to be alone, so I camped out in Anna's guest room, hiding underneath the covers like a frightened child. She brought me tea and toast, the only thing I could eat, while I imagined the very worst. Many tears were shed.

Finally, the big meeting. I walked the banker through the demolished building and described my plans . . . the counters here, the bakery there, the kitchen in the back. He listened, then smiled at me and asked me what I did before I got into the food business. I told him that I used to work on nuclear energy policy at the White House. Then I asked what *he* did before he went into banking.

"I was a second-grade teacher," he laughed. "Loan approved!"

He walked away, giving me a hundred and fifty thousand reasons to love Westhampton and North Fork Bank.

I thought that losing the lease on the little Barefoot Contessa was a disaster, the worst thing that ever happened to me. In the end, it was the best thing, because it forced me to move to the building across the street, which turned out to be fabulous for my business. "You never know your good breaks from your bad ones!"

Anna and her Frittata recipe from The Loaves and Fishes Cookbook

FRESH BASIL FRITTATA

Traditionally, frittatas are started on the stove in a frying pan, then transferred to the broiler. We've come up with this way to cook frittata that places the whole meal in the oven, so that no one needs to watch over it. We have so much basil growing in our garden behind Loaves and Fishes that this seemed the most natural "pie without a crust" to make.

¾ cup unbleached white flour
1½ teaspoons baking powder
15 eggs
1 cup (2 sticks) butter, melted
3 cups ricotta cheese
1½ pounds Gruyère cheese, grated
¾ teaspoon salt
1 teaspoon ground black pepper
1¼ cups chopped basil

Preheat the oven to 350°F.

Place the flour, baking powder, eggs, and butter in the bowl of an electric mixer and blend well. Add the ricotta, Gruyère, salt, pepper, and basil. Mix enough to blend.

Pour onto a buttered 12-by-17-inch baking sheet with 1-inch raised edge. Bake 40 minutes, or until the frittata is set and browned. Serve at room temperature.

Yields: 10 to 12 servings
Preparation time: 1 hour

The Loaves and Fishes Cookbook by Anna Pump

Photograph by Tom Eckerle

Tokyo, How Hard Could That Be?

The new Barefoot Contessa was four thousand square feet, which was almost ten times the size of the old store! Wonderful in some ways, challenging in others. I remember reading an article about how people congregate, learning that they do exactly the opposite of what you'd expect. If two friends run into each other on a busy street, you'd think they would duck into a quiet alcove to talk. Instead, they move right in the middle of a crowd, because people want to be with other people. Therefore, I always felt that a store should be slightly smaller than you'd expect so it always feels busy, no matter how many people are shopping. Now I had taken on a much larger store, and I was worried that no matter how many people were in it, it would feel empty. I needed to figure out how to give the store a buzz, make it feel crowded yet intimate and with lots of energy. People wouldn't be aware of why it felt good to be there, but they would be drawn to the store because it just felt like a happy place.

I divided the space into sections to re-create the shopping experience I loved at Faneuil Hall in Boston. When customers walked in the front door of my new store, they'd enter a vibrant food emporium. Barefoot Contessa would be the "anchor," with our bakery ovens and bread-making counter, the "Sandwich Box" (coffee and croissants in the morning, sandwiches and picnic baskets at lunch), and refrigerator cases filled with prepared foods. I leased the rest of the space to my favorite food boutiques: a farm stand stocked with produce, Votucci's fresh pasta and sauces, David's Cookies pumping sugar into the air, and Sweet Temptations candies and ice cream.

Sarah, who knew how to do everything at this point, became manager of the store, and Martine, who had worked for me the previous summer, was the head chef. Later, I encouraged Martine to set up Ribs! Ribs! Ribs!, a rotisserie with racks of sizzling chickens, just like in France, plus barbecue ribs, so she could learn about running her own business. My little sorority of workers exploded into a staff of thirty, then fifty, most of them teenagers. The new Barefoot was crazy busy from the very first day, with lines everywhere, even when we stayed open until midnight on weekends.

I hired Martine's friend Hunt MacWilliams to work at the bakery counter, and he kept us howling with his funny stories, especially one about the time he measured Cary Grant for new pants (he was a teenager working at a Westhampton men's shop) but had absolutely no idea who the incredibly famous actor was. The joke was on Hunt at Barefoot Contessa when a customer came in and said he wanted lox. New to the Jewish term for smoked salmon, Hunt politely directed the very surprised man to the hardware store down the street. "They sell locks," he promised.

But my best hire, and the gift that kept on giving, was Tedd Libath. As Tedd likes to say, it all started with a fib. Earlier that winter, Anna Pump and I were baking cakes and delivering them to restaurants and specialty food stores in Manhattan. I finally decided I couldn't make that trip one more time and advertised for an experienced driver who was familiar with New York City. Tedd answered the ad, and when I asked him if he knew his way around the city, he said, "Like the back of my hand!" Turns out the only thing he knew about New York City was that it was west of Westhampton. He; his wife, Barbara; and their three children had just moved to the Hamptons from upstate New York!

That didn't stop Tedd. He could figure out anything. One day, he was driving a van filled with Barefoot Contessa cakes to deliver to stores in New York City when he got caught in a sudden snowstorm. He called me from the road, and I told him not to worry—just bring the cakes home to his family. He laughed and thought, *Seriously, fifty cakes?* He couldn't eat them, and he certainly wasn't going to throw them away, so he spent the next two hours skidding around his neighborhood in the worst weather, determined to find good homes for those cakes. That was so Tedd.

During the summer, when he took over my weekly food runs, he turned a job I hated into an epicurean adventure—a gourmet food tour of the best suppliers in New York. At that place on North Moore Street, he'd buy a sliver of goose liver pâté for himself and anticipate how it would pair with a glass of Moët & Chandon brut when he got home (Tedd had been in the wine business before he moved to the Hamptons, so he knew his stuff). Or he'd stop for lunch at the Greek food truck parked next to our biggest wholesaler because they made a "killer" gyro. The suppliers loved him. If I forgot to leave him the envelope of checks to pay for everything, as I sometimes did, they'd wave a hand at Tedd and say, "Pay me next time!"

Tedd wanted his children to see the world outside the Hamptons, so whenever there was a school vacation, he chose one of his kids to be his sidekick. They always fought about whose turn it was because they loved sampling food as much as their father did. Wide-eyed, they followed him from vendor to vendor, picking up treats at every stop. Who wouldn't love that?

I worked with an extraordinary group of people. I think it said a lot that so many of them came back every summer—the telephone started ringing in January as the kids checked in with me to secure their summer spots. The repeaters took on more and more responsibility each year. Some of them ended up going into the food business after college because they fell in love with it at Barefoot.

The new applicants were harder to manage, like herding cats. I told each one up front: This. Is. Not. An. Easy. Job. The hours are long, especially after a late night at the disco. Customers can be difficult: make eye contact and keep smiling. Gorgonzola is stinky, and, yes, you have to touch it. But the biggest problem was persuading them to stay through Labor Day. They always swore they wouldn't leave. Then their parents would say, "You know what? You worked really hard this summer. I think we should go to Europe in August." I couldn't compete with that. A late-summer vacation with the family was much more appealing than getting up early to slice bagels, scoop salad, or mop floors, so they'd be out the door on August 1. Sadly, the kids who actually honored their commitments and stayed for the whole summer had to pick up their work, which wasn't at all fair. I worked extra hard to make sure they knew how much I appreciated them.

We turned on the ovens in May and didn't turn them off until September. Even with three eight-hour shifts every single day, we couldn't satisfy Westhampton's insatiable appetite for baked goods. I loved supporting local businesses, so at one point, I started ordering from Kathleen King, a very young baker in Southampton. I think she was twenty-one at the time, but she'd been making cookies since she was eleven, and they were perfection—thin, crisp, with just the right balance of chocolate, butter, and salt. Eventually, she launched Kathleen's Cookies, which became Tate's, the company that defined the chocolate chip cookie.

I was as serious about business issues as I was about cooking. Pricing at Barefoot Contessa was never a whimsical decision. It was a mathematical formula based on the price of ingredients and the cost of labor. In the early days of computers, I had the idea of hiring a programmer at New York University to design a basic program for me, so I could input the cost of bulk ingredients and figure out the cost of an item. I started with the ingredients for my brownies—flour, sugar, butter, eggs, vanilla, chocolate, chocolate chips, walnuts—and when I was finished, the computer told me each one should sell for $2.50, at a time when the average brownie cost about $0.75. Oops! I adjusted a few ingredients and was able to get the price down to $2.25, which was still insane. *Absolutely no one is going to buy this,* I thought.

There was only one way to find out. I baked a tray of brownies and put them out to see what would happen. They were gone in five minutes. So, I baked more . . . and more. I think I made something like sixteen hundred brownies that weekend, and every single one sold. It was a good lesson. If you make something with the best ingredients, and it's as delicious as it looks, people don't care what it costs because it's worth it. A seventy-five-cent brownie tastes like a seventy-five-cent brownie. Our customers wanted the best brownie, and they were willing to pay for it, which gave me a lot of freedom to be creative.

Which brings me to the story about the duck. A woman came into the store to pick up a roast duck she'd ordered. The man standing next to her eyed that duck like it was his next wife, the only thing he'd ever wanted. He told the salesperson that he'd like a roast duck, too, and was not happy to hear it was a special order and he could come back in two hours and pick it up. It was the eighties: greed was good. This Master of the Universe turned to the woman and offered to buy *her* duck. She laughed at first, then saw that he was dead serious. "How much for the duck?" he pressed, clearly not taking no for an answer. The woman grabbed her duck and escaped to the cash register to pay for it. He followed her to the register and then out the door, down the alley, to the parking lot, the whole way, upping his offer. "This is my final offer," he shouted. "One hundred dollars for your duck!" we heard as she got into her car and drove away. He was a Wall Street trader type of guy; he didn't understand how she could have paid fifteen dollars for a roast duck and five minutes later would turn down a hundred—think of the return on her investment! (Of course, she saw that duck as dinner and couldn't have cared less for the ROI.)

Meanwhile, he was so intent on getting *her* duck that he didn't order his own. That would have been too easy.

The funny thing is that whenever I tell this story, half the people actually can't understand why she didn't take the money!

It wasn't unusual for the cooking staff to work late hours, and I always tried to keep everybody's spirits up during those grueling baking marathons. "Okay," I said conspiratorially very late one night, trying to make it a game. "Let's each tell the worst thing we've ever done." Well, that turned out to be a really bad idea. I expected the usual stories about a wild party or a dangerous prank, but when it was the cook's turn, she confided, "I used to steal." I was shocked! Steal what? Define "used to." Was this a confession or a heads-up?

Absolutely a heads-up. Not long after she alerted me, I caught her red-handed and had to fire her! Why was I surprised when she had just told me who she was? People don't stop doing things like that. Moving forward, I tried to be more careful with my hires—and I also thought twice about playing truth games.

I have often thought that everyone should work in retail at some point in their lives, kind of like mandatory military service.

They would understand two things—first, that serving customers all day can be a very difficult job, and second, that being kind is so much more effective than being nasty.

Every summer ended with a blowout party for the staff. They had worked so hard—and done an amazing job—and I wanted to show them how much I appreciated it. (Well, maybe also because it was so much fun!) The first year, the dress code was "creative black tie," with a menu of filet of beef and champagne—notably, the drinking age was eighteen then. I added a Groucho Marx mustache to my outfit, just to lighten things up. The next summer we went wild with a *M*A*S*H* theme and an operating tent in the middle of the store. Hunt dressed up as a helicopter, complete with a propeller on his head, and someone dressed up as a patient wrapped in "bloody" bandages. I borrowed my father's operating room scrubs and came as a surgeon.

But the party that stands out was the Barefoot Olympics. Sarah carried the torch—a flaming duck on a stick—while sitting on the hood of a car racing across a field at night (which seemed like a good idea at the time) for the Opening Ceremony, and each "game" had something to do with food, like the bagel toss, blindfolded "name that substance" (think pickled herring), and baguette javelin throwing. We worked hard, and we played hard, and there are a few stories I'm happy that I don't remember, one involving my employees dragging me out of someone's swimming pool at three a.m. (no, we didn't have their permission) when the police showed up.

I was so wrapped up in the store—some nights we had to push people out the door when we wanted to close—that I almost didn't hear opportunity knocking. During the summer of 1984, I got a call from a man who owned a building on Newtown Lane in East Hampton. Would I be interested in renting a space and opening a specialty food store there? The current tenant, he explained, was Dean & DeLuca, but they were leaving. I had always loved Dean & DeLuca. Whenever I had a day off, I went to East Hampton just to see my dream store. Barefoot Contessa was casual and accessible, which was the perfect vibe for its beachy location. But Dean & DeLuca was more sophisticated, and everything in the store was brilliantly sourced and beautifully displayed. It was the first specialty food store to use Metro racks for shelves, and they were stocked with encyclopedic offerings you'd find in an upscale European emporium. Fifty different vinegars! A hundred and fifty varieties of mustard! It was like a museum. No, it was heaven! *God, wouldn't it be wonderful to have a store like this,* I thought as I walked through the stunning assortment of food.

Given how I felt, I should have been thrilled by the offer. But I was already shaking my head. It was hard enough to run *one* store. A second store? No way. "Thank you very much, but I'm just not interested," I told him.

When I mentioned the conversation to Jeffrey, he had a different reaction. "Think of it this way," he suggested. "For the price of fifteen dollars a square foot, you could have your own Dean & DeLuca, your dream specialty food store, and all their customers, too." He pointed out that people were already used to coming to that space and buying good food. I wouldn't have to build the business; it was already there and successful. I would be taking over Dean & DeLuca—*FREE!*

Suddenly, I saw all the positives, but before I got too carried away, I wanted to make sure Joel Dean, one of the owners of Dean & DeLuca and a legend in the food business, knew about it. I knew him professionally, and I didn't want him to think that I would just rent his store out from under him. When we talked on the phone, he told me he actually wanted to stay in the space, but he wasn't paying $15 a square foot for the store. He had offered the landlord $14.50 a square foot, and he wasn't going to budge. *Really?* For fifty cents a square foot, he was willing to walk away from a successful business? That was crazy. I asked what he would do if someone else took over the space, and he said he'd move up the street and open Dean & DeLuca again. "Joel," I said, "please rent the store if you're happy there. It's not worth losing for fifty cents a square foot," but he'd made up his mind and I had warned him. I waited twenty-four hours to let Joel change his mind and then called the landlord. "Thank you very much. I'll take the space."

Fifty cents—that's crazy, I thought. First of all, it costs a fortune to relocate, and the new location would never be as good as the old one; second, there would now be another specialty food store in town competing with him; and third, it would take a year to move, so people would get out of the habit of going to Dean & DeLuca. I had tried to talk him out of it because it was the right thing to do, but in the end, it was a cautionary tale. I did open Barefoot Contessa in their old space; Dean & DeLuca moved to a terrible location up the street—at twenty-three dollars a square foot—and they never recovered. A few years later, they closed. It was sad, even for me, because I adored Joel Dean's store, but it was a reminder to never dig in your heels on a negotiation, especially if it's just about money.

There was another reason I was so excited about opening in East Hampton. As much as I loved Westhampton, it was strictly a summer place. Too much to do in the summer, nothing to do in the winter—that's the nature of a seasonal business, like a clam shack. But the stores in East Hampton never closed. I could have a place that was open all year, staffed by real food store professionals. Barefoot wouldn't feel so temporary, and I wouldn't need to hire and train a whole new staff every spring, which was exhausting.

I stopped in to see my friend Anna Pump at Loaves & Fishes so she'd hear it from me first, explaining that I wanted to expand,

and it was my dream to have a business that wasn't seasonal. And in case she was worried about proximity (the new place would be just five miles from her store), I had a bright idea. "Why don't we own the store together? We can be partners." Anna's answer was quick . . . and disappointing. No, she didn't want a second store, so that was that.

"But are you okay with me doing it?" I pressed, expecting her to react positively, the way I had when she opened Loaves & Fishes.

She really wasn't okay with it. I could see that she was anxious about having competition, especially since we had shared all our recipes and suppliers, and I found myself in a terrible situation, one I'd never faced before. If I pursued *my* dream, I might be hurting a friend, which is awful. Honestly, I didn't think having another specialty food store in the area would be a problem for either of us. Dean & DeLuca had been there for years, and new places popped up every summer. There were a lot of hungry people in the Hamptons.

I had to trust my own instincts, which can be really hard to do when someone you care about is telling you something is a bad idea. Anna's feelings and fears were real to her, and so were the consequences. When I moved ahead with my plan, she stopped speaking to me.

I think we both felt the loss of our friendship. I know I did.

Flash forward: Anna called me a year or so into our estrangement. "I know I was anxious about your being there, but it hasn't changed my business at all," she admitted. What I heard was an invitation to pick up our friendship where we'd left off. We did just that, a little older and a little wiser for the experience.

Everything was falling into place, even on the home front, because Jeffrey was negotiating to buy *The Southampton Press,* a local newspaper, and we were thinking about living together in the Hamptons full time. That lovely idea got derailed when the owner of the paper decided not to sell and the deal fell through. I felt terrible because Jeffrey was so disappointed, but I felt even *worse* about what happened next. Lehman Brothers asked Jeffrey to open a branch of the investment bank . . . in Tokyo. And he said yes!

"Whoa, wait a minute!" I said. "How's this going to happen? I just signed a lease for a store in East Hampton, so how are we going to live in Tokyo?" It would be inconvenient—no, *impossible*—and really expensive to travel between New York, the Hamptons, and Tokyo.

The reality of our situation and my cold-shower response made Jeffrey reconsider, and he immediately went back to Lehman, trying to get out of an offer that he had accepted without making it look like he'd changed his mind. He told his boss that in order for him to take a job like this, he and his wife would need unlimited first-class travel between New York City and Tokyo so we could see each other. Jeffrey figured that would put an end to that. "No problem!" his boss declared. Oh my God. What else could he demand that would get him out of the deal? Full housing and daily expenses paid? "No problem!" Furniture and art for the new apartment in Tokyo? "No problem!" his boss said. No matter what Jeffrey asked for, they said yes, so in the end, he felt obligated to accept the offer. (And I secretly think he was excited about the challenge of opening a bank in Tokyo.)

"Let me make this really simple," his boss suggested. "Whatever you need to make this work—unlimited first-class travel for both of you, an apartment in Tokyo, furniture, *anything*—we'll pay for it."

This is where Jeffrey is at his best. What he wanted to do and what I wanted to do were frankly incompatible. But Jeffrey likes to think we can make anything work. Instead of deciding that only one of us would get their dream job, he said, "Let's try both—I'll work in Tokyo and you'll work in East Hampton for a year, we'll each travel back and forth for one week a month, and if at any time it doesn't work, we'll make a change." I was totally game to try, and the best part was that he wasn't prioritizing his big-deal investment banking job over my small retail food store job.

I made a quick trip to Tokyo in December and found and furnished an apartment in one week, which was just insane. Jeffrey hates moving (as a kid, his family moved every year) and I wanted him to feel completely at home, so I re-created the apartment we'd just finished decorating in New York, right down to our Le Corbusier dining table as his desk and his favorite Alvar Aalto chair. I even loaded the CD player with the same music we listened to at home. When he was in the apartment, everything he loved would be within reach, except me. But we'd already decided to take turns going back and forth once a month.

It was only Tokyo, right? How bad could this be?

Outrageous Brownies

MAKES 20 LARGE BROWNIES

1 pound unsalted butter
1 pound plus 12 ounces semi-
    sweet chocolate chips
6 ounces unsweetened chocolate
6 extra-large eggs
3 tablespoons instant coffee
    granules

2 tablespoons pure vanilla extract
2¼ cups sugar
1¼ cups all-purpose flour
1 tablespoon baking powder
1 teaspoon kosher salt
3 cups chopped walnuts

Preheat the oven to 350 degrees.

Butter and flour a 12 × 18 × 1-inch baking sheet.

Melt together the butter, 1 pound of chocolate chips, and the unsweetened chocolate in a medium bowl over simmering water. Allow to cool slightly. In a large bowl, stir (do not beat) together the eggs, coffee granules, vanilla, and sugar. Stir the warm chocolate mixture into the egg mixture and allow to cool to room temperature.

In a medium bowl, sift together 1 cup of flour, the baking powder, and salt. Add to the cooled chocolate mixture. Toss the walnuts and 12 ounces of chocolate chips in a medium bowl with ¼ cup of flour, then add them to the chocolate batter. Pour into the baking sheet.

Bake for 20 minutes, then rap the baking sheet against the oven shelf to force the air to escape from between the pan and the brownie dough. Bake for about 15 minutes, until a toothpick comes out clean. Do not overbake! Allow to cool thoroughly, refrigerate, and cut into 20 large squares.

The Pinochle Club

I took over the new store on January 1, 1985, and immediately started renovating. We built a commercial kitchen in the back, then had the good idea of running the exhaust vents out the side of the building, so the scent of freshly baked bread perfumed the street—the best advertisement for what was inside. As a finishing touch, I added an old-fashioned screen door to the entrance—the sound of that door slamming shut was the essence of summer, of vacations and carefree times, a signal to relax, indulge, and eat!

By now, Sarah had graduated from Yale, so I convinced her to come to East Hampton to run the store with me, and I hired a wonderful group of people. As soon as the renovation was finished, I decided that we would all clean and stock the store together so we could get to know each other and start feeling like a team. With a lot of hard work, we were ready to open in May.

I was a little nervous about being accepted by the East Hamptonites, who viewed Dean & DeLuca as a very chic, high-end store, a place *New York* magazine described as "swellegant-elegant," like Soho at the beach. I knew they saw me as that woman with the "deli" in Westhampton. *Who is this person and why is she in my Dean & DeLuca?* The first few weeks it seemed I couldn't do anything right. The prices were too high, the food was too *"this"* or too *"that."* Then there was the rumor that Barefoot Contessa had pushed out Dean & DeLuca, which was untrue, and, if anyone bothered to think about it, extremely unrealistic, like a mouse clobbering an elephant.

I decided to test the market. I cut the price of the pasta salad in half to see if the customers were really responding to the cost, or if they were just annoyed by my replacing Dean & DeLuca. Then I cut it in half again. Guess what? They were just annoyed. No matter what I did, they didn't like it, even when I put samples out for them to taste, something Dean & DeLuca never did. I felt like saying, "It's a food store! Lighten up!" But they had strong ties to the past and needed time to adjust. I had to remind myself about the enthusiastic customers in Westhampton who couldn't get enough of our food, who lined up at the door before we opened and knocked on the window after we closed, desperate for just *one* more brownie.

Instead, I cranked up the music and smiled. This was my opportunity to make everyone feel that they were invited to my party. We added a dash of cinnamon to our brewed coffee, and the scent was an aphrodisiac. The coconut cupcakes (or frosting delivery systems, as we liked to call them) were like crack, everyone's favorite (legal) guilty pleasure. No one cared about the calories because they were so good! When customers barreled in on Fridays, still vibrating from the stress of the workweek and the tension of the infamous crawl on the Long Island "Expressway," we calmed them down. A houseful of very hungry weekend guests arriving any minute? Barefoot had something for every palate, from breakfast muffins and fried chicken to croissants and beef bourguignon. Eventually, we all adjusted, and it was fine. No, it was *wonderful.*

As I'd hoped, strangers became regulars, and when the screen door slammed, I'd look up to see a now-familiar face. Frank New-bold, a realtor who worked down the street, popped in every day for a lunchtime sandwich. The beautiful older woman who wore pristine white gloves? That was Estée Lauder, and when she ordered racks of barbecued ribs, we joked that those gloves would have to come off! Customers pretended *not* to notice when they spotted Steven Spielberg at the counter, but they spent twice as much time browsing and sipping coffee whenever he was in the store.

One day I was working at my desk, which was right by the cheese counter, when I heard a very imperious voice telling me, "I'd like a roast beef sandwich on a roll." I looked up, ready to explain that Barefoot didn't make sandwiches to order, when I realized that the voice belonged to the incomparable (and slightly terrifying) Lauren Bacall. What did I say? "Would you like mustard on that?" How could I—how could *anyone*—say no to Lauren Bacall!

I rented a house not far from the East Hampton store and treated it like a crash pad, flopping on the sofa when I had a free minute. This is when my memory gets blurry, because running two stores in separate locations *and* "commuting" to Tokyo turned out to be a lot harder than I imagined. I felt that I couldn't be away from the store on weekends, so I'd fly out on a Monday, secretly looking forward to the moment when I could collapse in first class (at Lehman Brothers's expense!), which was so much better than the living room in my rental house. The seven-thousand-mile flight was like a little vacation—the phone didn't ring, I didn't have to make any decisions or put out any fires, and I could relax with a drink and a good book and enjoy the quiet. That was the high point of the trip. I'd arrive in Tokyo on Tuesday, vaguely resemble a human being by Wednesday, then leave on Thursday to get home by Friday night. Jeffrey did the same zombie run two weeks later when it was his turn.

When I got home, it was time to race between East Hampton and Westhampton, no small feat in the summer, when heavy traffic meant that distance was calculated in hours instead of miles. I was such a regular for breakfast at Dave's Bun 'n' Burger that when the pay phone rang at six thirty a.m., I'd jump up from my booth to answer it, certain it was Jeffrey calling from Tokyo. He knew exactly where to find me at that hour. I ate my breakfast, he finished his dinner, and we caught up on the news until it was time for me to go to work.

No matter how often I showed up at the Westhampton store, though, it wasn't enough. "You're never here anymore," my old customers complained. Martine, who was managing the store, was doing a great job, but it wasn't the same as having the owner there 24/7. People were used to "Mom" being "home."

If I felt at all torn between the two places, I was definitely leaning toward East Hampton, partly because of the wonderful new friends I found there. Antonia Bellanca, an insanely talented florist, owned a small, jewel-box shop on Newtown Lane, right near Barefoot Contessa. I loved popping in, and on one visit she introduced me to Frank Newbold, the realtor who bought his lunch at Barefoot every day. "Only a handful of us live here full time in the winter," Antonia pointed out. "We all have to become good friends!" We sort of laughed, but then that's exactly what we did, calling ourselves the "Pinochle Club," even though we never once played pinochle.

Our little group expanded to four when Antonia met her future husband. We had such a good time together, going out for dinner just about every night, watching movies, planning parties at the drop of a hat. Suddenly I had an actual life outside of my work.

And Jeffrey loved his assignment in Tokyo. His job was to close a commercial bank for American Express and open an investment bank. When he wasn't working, he wrote for *The New York Times* and other publications. Our long-distance arrangement was going smoothly, so smoothly that after about a year, I had a terrible thought. I called Jeffrey and said, "I think you need to come home. It's not that I'm miserable. It's just the opposite. I'm perfectly fine. And I think that's really, really dangerous."

I was afraid that I was getting used to living without him, and I wasn't willing to let that happen. Jeffrey understood what was at stake and agreed to wrap up his business in Tokyo. He just had to make one quick stop in Hong Kong to visit an important client, then he'd come right home, he promised. "One quick stop" turned out to be the understatement of all time.

When Jeffrey arrived in Hong Kong, his client, one of the biggest shipping companies in the world, was in the middle of the largest and possibly most complicated bankruptcy in history. Jeffrey's specialty in investment banking was restructuring sovereign debt—when a country is in bankruptcy and owes billions in loans it can't pay—but no one had ever restructured a personal debt that size. His client was convinced that Jeffrey was the only person who could do it.

The client begged him to stay, booked him a suite at the Mandarin Oriental, and urged him to start that very day. It was a dramatic and exciting project for Jeffrey, one of the most interesting challenges he'd ever faced. I was disappointed because spending another year apart wasn't exactly what I had in mind, but this was his big moment, and I wanted him to be happy. That's the key to a successful relationship, isn't it? Wanting the person you love to be happy, no matter what the cost, and knowing they want the same for you?

I traded my seventeen-hour flight to Tokyo for a twenty-four-hour flight to Hong Kong. Stressful and exhausting? Yes. But we figured it out and got through another year.

It occurred to me that this might be a good time to eliminate another source of stress in my life: the store in Westhampton. I'd turned into *Where's Waldo*, bouncing between the two stores and feeling like I was losing control wherever I landed. I decided to close it and put all my energy into my year-round retail and catering business in East Hampton. It was a difficult decision because I loved my first store and felt sentimental about my customers there, but it was the right thing to do.

Even with one store, the summers were insane. A routine day often turned into an all-nighter, especially when I'd get the dreaded call at three in the morning with the news that the baker wasn't coming in and *I* had to race to the store to make the baguettes before opening. *Literally, a thousand baguettes.* The demands never stopped. I was used to having a break in the winter when the Westhampton store was closed, when I had a few months to leisurely test recipes, explore new vendors, and recharge before the new season started. But the East Hampton store was open all year.

Financially, that was a good thing. The winter was busy because people came to the Hamptons for holidays and long weekends. In fact, New Year's Eve was usually our biggest day of the year. We decorated the store with thousands of black, white, and silver balloons and cranked up the music. The staff, dressed like Bob Fosse dancers in white shirts and black pants, bow ties, and bowler hats, served champagne to our happy customers. It felt like a party. And the shopping was insane! People ordered extravagantly—"I'll take that *big* tin of caviar" or "that whole side of smoked salmon"—so they could continue the celebration at home.

I never had a chance to catch my breath. I was beyond exhausted and maybe a little lost personally. My friend Antonia suggested that I see her therapist, which I did, and it was one of the most important decisions I've ever made. Her name is Cecily Stranahan, and she changed the rest of my life. I can't imagine where I'd be without her extraordinary advice. "I'm just working all the time," I told her. "I'm not having any *fun*."

She asked me what I would consider fun. I'd never asked myself that question, but I thought for a moment. *How about a convertible, because who can be unhappy in a convertible? And a masseuse to get the kinks out?* The next day, I rented a bright-red 1964 Mustang convertible and booked an appointment for a massage. Thirty-nine years later, I'm still driving a convertible, and I'm still seeing the same masseuse.

Cecily wisely intuited that I was searching for more than ways to have fun. Our weekly conversations during the next three years covered territory that was harder to explore. I was pretty unhappy in 1985, but it wasn't just because I was working too hard or missing Jeffrey. With Cecily's help, I asked myself tough questions about the root of my unhappiness and why I had such low self-esteem. I could link my self-doubt to my childhood, when I felt unseen and unappreciated—there was a lot to unpack there. But Cecily made me realize that the highly critical voice in my head was actually my parents' voice, not mine. It's really hard to separate yourself from that voice, but I started telling myself, *That's what my mother would have said. Everything you've done has come out better than you could have imagined, so listen to your own voice.*

Cecily helped me to understand that the past wasn't my only problem. How I was dealing with it, or more accurately, *not* dealing with it, was making me unhappy.

There's a wonderful quote attributed to George Lucas: "We're all living in cages with the door wide open." That was me until I realized I had the power—and the responsibility—to set myself free. To step out of the cage of whatever I'd experienced in the past, to think for myself, and to believe in my choices.

There was one legacy that had real consequences. When I was in my twenties, I had no idea why people have children. Because I had such a horrible childhood with my parents, with emotional and sometimes physical abuse, I couldn't understand why anyone would want to re-create that family. *I* didn't. There's a saying, "What goes in early goes in deep." After my experience, my mind was closed to the possibility of having my own child.

My brother, Ken, felt the same way. The subject of parenting came up when we were having lunch sometime in the seventies. We each said that we didn't want to have children because we were afraid of doing to them what our parents did to us. It was a painful feeling to carry, and it affected our choices in life.

Eventually, after I worked on some of my issues in therapy and spent time with friends who had loving, nurturing relationships with their children, I understood that it didn't have to be that way. But Jeffrey and I were content with our choices and our life. When Dolly Parton opened up to Oprah Winfrey about why she didn't have children, she said, "If I hadn't had the freedom to work, I wouldn't have done all the things I've done." I feel the same way.

Ken changed his mind when he was forty-five years old. He fell in love with a child who, as Ken says, "was looking for a father to adopt." Ken and his wife, Gail, adopted Alexander and embraced parenthood.

To be clear, therapy wasn't a quick or easy process, but it was effective, because I was learning to trust myself.

While I was seeing Cecily, I decided to invite my parents to visit us in East Hampton. We had spent time together intermittently over the years, going out for dinner and playing tennis. Jeffrey was a wonderful buffer who kept things pleasant. The weekend of their visit was one of those brutal summer weekends at the store when I came home exhausted, inert, the worst hostess. I didn't—no, I couldn't!—lift a finger. I didn't cook for them, didn't take them on a tour of East Hampton. Nothing. After they left, Jeffrey—who is *never* critical of me—suggested that maybe I could have been more attentive. He was totally right. I felt terrible when he pointed out that I didn't even buy flowers for the house when they were there.

I actually felt so terrible that I invited them back a few weeks later. Flowers for the house?! I went crazy and bought huge bouquets for the living room, but that wasn't enough. I dragged enormous clay flowerpots home, placed them outside the front door, and filled them with huge purple agapanthus. But that *still* wasn't enough. Our rental house was in the middle of the woods, so I decided to clear out the brush underneath the trees and plant a flowering shade garden with white astilbe, white Solomon's seal, and purple hostas. And what about trees? *Yes, we need flowering trees near the house,* I decided. A call to the local nursery took care of that, and a few days later they were planting a grove of beautiful white dogwoods along the driveway. Do you think I overreacted? Maybe, but this was the beginning of my obsession with gardens. I had no idea that I had any interest in them at all, but after that I just didn't want to stop.

Wait. We were in a *rental*. I was spending all this time and money landscaping a property that wasn't even mine! I can't imagine what was going through the owner's head, but I hope he was really, really happy (although I'm not so sure the bamboo I planted near the house was such a good idea).

More important, I think my subconscious was sending me a message: after so many years of moving from rental to rental, I wanted roots. I loved East Hampton, my business and my friends were all there, and I was staying for good. Jeffrey nailed it when he said, "It's time to buy a house."

This was so much easier said than done. Back from Hong Kong, Jeffrey decided to leave Lehman Brothers and teach at Columbia University while he figured out what to do next. In the meantime, I had fallen in love with a classic shingle-style house in the Village of East Hampton that we simply couldn't afford. One day, the seller miraculously lowered the price by 25 percent, and we swooped in and bought it. Of course, it required a total renovation down to the studs—new kitchen, new bathrooms, new everything—and as with all renovations, the cost just kept going up and up until we were literally out of money (sound familiar?). "Stop, just stop," I told the contractor. "At some point, we'll start again," I promised him (and myself) optimistically, but I really wasn't sure how. We continued living in our rental while our house, basically a construction site, was on an indefinite pause.

Then, Jeffrey, who was in New York at the time, called to say he'd been offered a job at Blackstone—*a major big-deal boutique investment bank.* I speed-dialed the contractor, and by the time Jeffrey got off the train from New York that Friday night, the construction crew was hard at work at the house again, building our dream.

We settled into a comfortable routine, back and forth between East Hampton and New York. In 1993, Jeffrey joined the Clinton administration and was appointed undersecretary of commerce for international trade, so his "commute" now stretched from East Hampton to Washington and back each week. By this time, navigating unusual living situations was "normal," built into our

DNA. We focused on our work when we were apart and on each other when we were together.

After several years in our new house, one problem we couldn't seem to solve was the lack of space. It wasn't a big house, and by the time I'd renovated it, it had just two bedrooms. Jeffrey needed a home office, but the only place for him to work was the dining room table, right smack in the middle of the house. We couldn't add on because of the property lines. Frank Newbold, our real estate friend, pointed out that there was an empty lot for sale right down the street. "Why don't you build the exact same house on that property, and you can add an office to it?" he suggested.

Weirdly, the idea made perfect sense to me. We could buy the lot, sell our newly renovated house, and build the new one. I couldn't afford an architect, so I designed the house myself, a fabulous big fancy shingle-style house with wraparound porches and lots of bedrooms, including an office for Jeffrey.

But wait! I realized that I loved our little house *more* than the big fancy one I was planning to build. Our street in the Village of East Hampton was mostly built in the early 1900s, with materials that were available at the time—wood shingles—and many houses on the road have the same basic layout, kind of like an early "development." I loved it in some part *because of* the original architecture. Why not be respectful of the community and build to honor what came before us?

I tore up my fancy architectural plans and, with a few small additions and changes, built almost exactly the same house that we already owned. I could walk through the rooms blindfolded and know where everything was.

Once my living situation was resolved, I needed to figure out my work life. Here's one thing I've learned about myself: I'm an adrenaline junkie. When my work no longer scares me or even challenges me, I get bored. Alarms were going off in my head. Business at the store was terrific, but the truth is the job I had loved for almost twenty years no longer scared me, so I had used a construction project—building a new house—to get that rush. It worked every time.

I thought about how I could approach work differently. Managing the store all day and catering several parties at night was becoming mind-numbing, like running on an endless treadmill. I decided that my first move was to stop catering. I did the math— private parties were taking up 95 percent of my time but making up only 5 percent of my income. Well, that doesn't work!

The last party I booked was a friend's wedding, and it was a doozie. There is a British comedy called *Noises Off* where act 1 is a play within the play—perfectly calm and lovely. In act 2, they turn the stage around, and you see the bedlam and chaos going on backstage—people fighting and being pushed onstage. The final act of the play is the original play again (act 1), but now you know what's actually going on backstage and it's hilarious. Catering always seemed to me like *Noises Off*. My goal was always that the client never saw the chaos, only how beautiful their party was.

For my last catering job, my friend was marrying a man who owned one of the major English china companies. He asked if he could send all the china for the wedding dinner. "Sure, no problem! I just won't order rental plates," I said, not giving it much thought.

The day of the wedding started a little crazy, anyway. The party was supposed to be outside under the trees on the lawn of a friend's house. Not a good idea, I advised. No tent? What if it's too hot or too cold, or worse—what if it rains? My client insisted, so I didn't order a tent. Two days before, when the forecast predicted rain, I scrambled frantically to find a huge tent at the height of the wedding season in the Hamptons. Whew! I found one! Then on the day of the wedding, as people were arriving, it wasn't just raining—it was like someone was throwing buckets of water at the guests. Of course, even the tent couldn't withstand that amount of rain, and it flooded. Now we had to set up a wedding for a hundred and fifty people inside the house! (Isn't catering fun?!)

When I arrived, I saw all the English china piled high in the sunroom, *in wooden packing crates.* It was like walking into the last shot of *Raiders of the Lost Ark.* There were a hundred and fifty guests, and each place setting had five pieces of china—that's seven hundred and fifty plates and cups individually wrapped with various layers of packing materials, including straw and wood excelsior, sealed in wooden crates *with nails.* This wasn't catering. It was a construction job!

The china was the most gorgeous I'd ever seen—hand-painted with lots of gold details. I assumed it was at least $1,000 a plate. I couldn't let anyone else touch it, so I got to work with a hammer, opening crate after crate after crate, trying desperately not to break a single plate, because I actually needed every one. (Not to mention what it would cost to replace a broken plate!) I just kept saying to myself, like a mantra, *This is the last party I'm ever doing. This is the last party I'm ever doing,* as I pulled nails out with the hammer. Oh yes, did I mention that as people arrived inside the house, a pipe burst on the second floor, pouring water down through the ceiling in the foyer? *This is definitely the last party I'm ever doing!*

It was a relief to stop catering, but I still had to deal with the daily problems—and dramas—at the store. Who wants to spend a minute thinking about theft? But that's an unpleasant reality for all retail businesses. Barefoot had shoplifters in all shapes and sizes, from clueless teenagers to the crafty East Hampton matron who rigged her designer purse with a false bottom so she could hide the items she stole. Or worse, the woman, whom I'll call Jane, who simply refused to pay her huge, long-standing bill. One day, I decided it was time for a conversation. "Jane," I said politely, "you need to settle your account."

She looked me right in the eye and said, "Oh, you must be confusing me with someone else. I'm not Jane."

At that very moment, one of my salespeople walked by and chirped, "Hi, Jane!"

Outed!

Instead of being embarrassed, Jane turned on me and said it was *my* fault that her bill was so big because I kept letting her charge. Then she begrudgingly wrote me a check—a bad check.

Moving forward, we got a lot smarter. When customers asked if they could have a house charge, we'd say, "Of course! We have American Express house charges. Leave your credit card on file and just say 'charge it' at the register."

But the all-time prize for Outstanding Chutzpah went to a brazen thief I stumbled upon in the dark of night. I was on my way to meet Jeffrey in New York when I decided to make a quick stop at the store. It was after hours, so I unlocked the door and was reaching for the light switch when something caught my eye— two huge shopping bags filled with groceries on the counter by the register. Two pints of ice cream sat on top, so I knew the thief had a key to the store and he or she would be back soon.

Channeling my inner Columbo, I waited, quietly calling Suzanna Giuliano, my friend and accountant, to whisper that if someone walked in and killed me, at least I'd be able to tell her who it was! Eventually, the door leading to the offices upstairs (I owned the building and rented to tenants) opened, and in walked one of my tenants. He spotted me in the shadows and coolly admitted that he'd been stealing from Barefoot for years. "Why not? Stores overcharge," he said unapologetically. He felt he had a right to steal from them, from *me!*

Was he nuts?

It wasn't like he just walked in and swiped something. He had to work for his loot. He had gone into the walk-in refrigerator and taken out a cake, then walked all the way to the bakery, made a box, and found Scotch tape to seal it. When he took a bottle of olive oil, he moved all the other bottles on the shelf, so it didn't look like anything was missing. I mean, he had gone to an enormous amount of trouble to fill those bags, elevating shoplifting to a new level. And this wasn't his first rodeo. Not that I was giving him any credit. The resolution to this nasty episode was long and complicated and left me disheartened.

After eighteen years of being in the food business, what I didn't like about running Barefoot Contessa was overshadowing what I used to love. I felt that I wasn't doing anything new, and I certainly wasn't bringing any creativity to my work. I knew the business would suffer if I continued running it on autopilot, and I remember thinking to myself, *I can't tell the employees to close the bathroom door one more time.*

That's when Suzanna and I devised a plan to sell the store. Today, the COVID-19 pandemic has prompted people to question whether their jobs are satisfying and consider quitting and doing something new and exciting. In the nineties, it seemed insane to walk away from the success of Barefoot Contessa. But I was pretty miserable and couldn't see another way.

First, I had to figure out how to sell the specialty food store business, which was not an easy thing to do. Without me, Barefoot Contessa wasn't worth that much, especially if the buyer had to hire someone to manage the store, which is what I did. Suzanna came up with a brilliant idea. She suggested that I sell the business to Parker, my chef, and Amy, my store manager. I'd finance the sale, and they could pay me from their profits. It was a perfect solution because it presented an exciting path to ownership for them, and an effective way out for me.

What else could I do? I wondered. What would challenge me? Make me work twice as hard? Keep me up at night solving problems? Cecily had become my dear friend and trusted adviser. She saw that I was struggling for answers and tried to reassure me. She told me that "Type A" people (I guess she was talking about me!?) can't begin to think about what to do next until they stop what they're doing. They need space and time to allow "the universe" to reveal what is next. I frankly had no idea what she was talking about, but I trusted her so much that I decided that selling the store and doing nothing for a while was a good idea.

Easier said than done. That year turned out to be the hardest year of my life. One day, I was running a store with fifty employees and sometimes baking a thousand baguettes, and the next day, I literally had nothing to do. Not a happy place for an adrenaline junkie like me. I took over one of the offices above the store, right next to my old office, and forced myself to go there at nine a.m. every morning. At first, I was busy with the Barefoot transition, ready to help Parker and Amy any way I could. I still had a financial interest in the store, so I was very present. The internet was a big question mark at this point, but I thought it was important for Barefoot to have a website, so I designed one for them as a gift. Who knew that you needed a website? This was 1996, and looking back, I'm proud (and a little surprised) that I was an early adopter! After that, I had nothing to do. I mean *nothing*.

I copied over my address book. I read magazines, popped downstairs to Barefoot for a cup of coffee, studied how Warren

Buffett invested in the stock market (after a year of investing, I decided I definitely *wasn't* Warren Buffett and gave that up!!). I made a business plan for a luxury bus service between the Hamptons and New York City (with more amenities than the existing Jitney) and looked at real estate investing (my other love beside the food business). I even ran the numbers for buying the A&P and turning the building into a parking lot. (Really?) Nothing interested me. Nothing got my creative juices going. But instead of giving up and doing something fun like traveling, I kept my office schedule and sat there, day after day, bored out of my mind.

At this time, Jeffrey was commuting from Connecticut, where he was happily working in his new position as dean of the Yale School of Management. One Monday morning, nine months into my misery, as he was heading back to New Haven, he asked me what I'd be doing for the rest of the week. I flipped through my calendar. Nothing Monday, nothing Tuesday, but on Wednesday, I had a manicure! How sad was that? It was the only thing I had to do all week. A manicure isn't something to do, it's what you squeeze in between appointments, like going to the bank. I knew it was pathetic. What I didn't know was that that's the process. As Cecily suggested, I had to get good and bored. I'd been standing on the side of the pond, looking in, and deciding not to jump in the water. *Maybe it's too cold? Too deep? Who knows what's in that pond?* It was all too scary.

Jeffrey felt terrible watching me suffer and said to me, "You love the food business. Why not think of another way to do it?" I actually had begun to think that my career—the one I had loved—might be over. *Maybe this is the end of the line. Maybe I'll never find anything as exciting and as engaging as running Barefoot Contessa.*

In the meantime, though, I thought, *Why not just do something— anything!—while I figure out what's next.* My customers were always telling me I should write a cookbook. I was afraid writing would be a lonely occupation, but at least it was something to *do!* *Maybe instead of standing on the side of the pond speculating about it, I'll jump in the pond, splash around, and see how it feels.*

The Pinochle Club on our way to Nantucket

Coconut Cupcakes

MAKES 18 TO 20 LARGE CUPCAKES

¾ pound unsalted butter at room temperature

2 cups sugar

5 extra-large eggs at room temperature

1½ teaspoons pure vanilla extract

1½ teaspoons pure almond extract

3 cups all-purpose flour

1 teaspoon baking powder

½ teaspoon baking soda

½ teaspoon kosher salt

1 cup buttermilk

14 ounces sweetened, shredded coconut

Cream Cheese Icing (recipe follows)

Preheat the oven to 325 degrees.

In the bowl of an electric mixer fitted with a paddle attachment, cream the butter and sugar until light and fluffy, about 5 minutes. With the mixer running on low, add the eggs one at a time, scraping down the bowl after each addition. Add the vanilla and almond extracts and mix well.

In a separate bowl, sift together the flour, baking powder, baking soda, and salt. In three parts, alternately add the dry ingredients and the buttermilk to the batter, beginning and ending with the dry. Mix until *just* combined. Fold in 7 ounces of coconut.

Line a muffin pan with paper liners. Fill each cup to the top with batter. Bake for 25 to 35 minutes, until the tops are brown and a toothpick comes out clean. Allow to cool in the pan for 15 minutes. Remove to a baking rack and cool completely. Frost with the icing and sprinkle with the remaining coconut.

Cream Cheese Icing

1 pound cream cheese at room temperature

¾ pound unsalted butter at room temperature

1 teaspoon pure vanilla extract

½ teaspoon pure almond extract

1½ pounds confectioners' sugar, sifted

In the bowl of an electric mixer fitted with a paddle attachment, blend together the cream cheese, butter, and vanilla and almond extracts. Add the confectioners' sugar and mix until smooth.

"I Can Sell This Book in La Jolla"

The first thing I did was put together a book proposal, thinking no one would ever see it. But I threw myself into the project because that's what I do—it was fun and creative and much better than just sitting in my office. I decided to call it *The Barefoot Contessa Cookbook,* and it would be the story of the store, including many of the most popular recipes. I got some eight-by-twelve-inch whiteboards and cut out photographs from books and magazines that showed how I wanted the book to look. I tested a few recipes, like Perfect Roast Chicken, the Outrageous Brownies that sold so well, and those Coconut Cupcakes that no one could resist.

And because I didn't know anything about publishing, I asked my friend Lee Bailey, who had a bestselling cookbook, to recommend an editor. He suggested Roy Finamore at Clarkson Potter, the top editor at the top cookbook publisher in the country. *Well, this is never going to happen,* I told myself, but I always swing for the fences, so I told my agent to send the proposal to Roy, thinking that would be that. A week later, Roy came back and said, "We will publish your cookbook on the condition that of the ten thousand books we print, you will buy five thousand of them to sell in your store." Are you kidding? I would have bought all of them and stood on my head for a week if that's what they wanted!

And just like that, I had a book contract. Yikes! How was this going to happen?

I later found out that Roy sensed that there was a hole in the market and thought *The Barefoot Contessa Cookbook* had all the hallmarks of the food Lee Bailey had made so popular in the 1980s: simple but elegant, comforting without being boring, and beautifully styled. That was a tremendous compliment, because I loved Lee, a real Southern gentleman, and his amazing cookbooks.

Later, I also learned that Chip Gibson, the wonderful head of the Crown Publishing Group, Clarkson Potter's parent company, had his own reasons for believing in the project. When he was visiting Martha Stewart one summer weekend, she had taken him out for a drive. Suddenly, with a screech of brakes, she swung her giant black Suburban into a death-defying U-turn on Newtown Lane, announcing she *had* to stop at Barefoot Contessa to pick up lemon bars. Chip wondered why they were risking their lives for a dessert until he tasted them. The memory of that ride—and those delicious lemon bars—had stayed with him.

Chip was always looking for his next bestseller, and when Roy told him about *The Barefoot Contessa Cookbook,* he immediately saw its potential: a collection of uncomplicated but showstopping recipes that looked pretty easy to make *plus* gorgeous party platters built around prepared foods that required no cooking at all (the beginning of *store-bought is fine!*). And, like Roy, Chip sensed that the Hamptons wasn't just a place—it was becoming a state of mind, synonymous with celebrity, luxury, and high-end fun. Its cachet could extend far beyond an East Coast beach.

I can sell this book in La Jolla, Chip thought.

Roy suggested that we meet for lunch. Okay, I like lunch! He told me to meet him at Vong, one of Jean-Georges Vongerichten's first restaurants in New York City. This was 1997, I'd never been, and I thought, *How exciting and glamorous!* When we sat down—in the bar! *Very* New York publishing—I suggested to Roy that we needed to hire a writer. "I used to write nuclear energy policy papers at the White House," I told him. Not exactly a bestseller!

"Nope," he said, "you'll write it yourself." *Really?*

I couldn't even imagine how that was going to happen, but once I got started, I felt as though I'd always known how to write a cookbook. I have no idea where it came from, but I had a very clear idea about how to design the book, which recipes to include, and how they should be written, and, it turns out, I did know what I wanted to say in the text. I didn't want to write about broccoli and string beans—that would put me to sleep! I wanted to tell the story about building the store, cooking for customers, and, most of all, what I had learned about entertaining over the past thirty years of giving my own parties. Like the time I invited six friends to lunch and they each brought houseguests with them, so twelve hungry people showed up, and what I did about it. (I made the lobster salad sandwiches I'd planned into open-faced sandwiches and told Jeffrey, "If anyone asks, you're allergic to lobster," because he and I had sandwiches made from leftover chicken salad I had in the fridge!) For me, cooking wasn't the goal of entertaining; being with friends was the goal, so I wanted to make easy recipes that anyone could prepare and know their guests would be delighted.

Gradually, I developed my own writing process, and it's always the same. I'm sure I have absolutely nothing to say, so I wait until the last second, then clean out my closet, then finally I force myself to sit at the computer, searching for the elusive opening sentence. When I have that, the rest just seems to fall into place.

Obviously, I was much more secure about cooking. Me, in my

small kitchen, pulling out my recipes and remembering why I loved making them for customers in the store. Sun-Dried Tomato Dip, which was insanely popular; Perfect Roast Chicken (now famously called "Engagement Chicken," because Emily Blunt, Meghan Markle, and other happily married women swear that this dish, fresh from the oven, prompted their boyfriends to propose); and Banana Crunch Muffins, which made *anyone* want to get out of bed in the morning. In fact, I had a secret test for myself to see if I should sell something in the store: would a customer get out of bed, put on their clothes, get into the car, drive to town, find a parking space, and walk to the store to buy this dish? That was a hard test to pass, and I wanted only those recipes in the store and in the book.

Even though I'd been making these dishes for more than twenty years, I had to test each one repeatedly before I considered including it in the book. Publishers never actually tasted—or tested—the recipes in their cookbooks; they relied on authors to do that. And most authors wrote recipes very casually, without understanding how somebody was using them. I care deeply about the user experience because I want anyone who makes a recipe to end up with a perfect dish every time. As a friend of mine who worked in advertising used to say, "It's not what you say that counts, it's what they *hear*."

I approached testing like a mad scientist: obsessively, and with no limits. First, I had to deal with scale. The store's master recipes were designed to make huge quantities. I had a chocolate cake recipe for forty cakes, but now I needed to make *one,* and it was never as simple as dividing the ingredients. If I decided to change one tiny component, I'd make the whole thing again, and again, and probably again, until it was perfect.

I could have stayed in my testing bubble forever, but a cookbook is so much more than just recipes. The cover, the layout, the photographs. Ignoring my nagging inner voice that kept asking, *"What makes you think you can do this?"* and *"Why would you be good at it?,"* I pushed past my insecurities. I was the first to admit I wasn't a professional, but I had a clear vision of what the book should be. I wanted you to open it, look at a photograph (because I think most people are visual), and say, "Oh my God, that looks delicious!" Then, I wanted you to read the recipe and think, *It's easy enough that I can make it myself.* And third, I wanted you to go through the list of ingredients and say, "I can actually get all of them in a grocery store." No black garlic. No trip to India for some spice. Funny, thirteen books later, I still feel exactly the same way.

To make this happen, I had to find the right photographer. I was writing a column for *Martha Stewart Living,* so I called Susan Spungen, then the head food stylist, for recommendations. I wanted someone who would photograph real food, including food that's a little messy, as real food looks. Like a filet of beef that's not on a beautiful platter decorated with herbs, but rather one that's juicy on a cutting board with a slicing knife. She said, "I'll give you four names, but you're going to hire Melanie Acevedo." She was so right—I looked at Melanie's photographs, and she was the one. Then, because I knew Melanie would want gorgeous food to photograph, I asked her who she'd like as a food stylist. She suggested Rori Spinelli Trovato. I hired Rori, then asked *her* who she would hire as a prop stylist, thinking she would like her food on a gorgeous plate. She said Denise Canter. The whole add-a-pearl process was easy and organic, and suddenly I was an art director with the best team.

The first day of the shoot, I was terrified. I thought, *How am I ever going to give them direction? I have no idea what I'm doing!*

And how am I going to make all that food? We had seventy-five recipes. I mean, I'm an okay cook, but I'm not a professional chef or food stylist. The first day, I was a wreck. I said to Rori, "Okay, what do you want me to make first?" I assumed she would be taking what I was cooking, putting it on a beautiful plate, maybe brushing it with motor oil to make it shine, and giving it to the photographer.

She looked at me like I was crazy and said, "That's what I do. *I* make the food for the shoot."

Oh my God, I was so relieved! This was actually going to be fun!

It turns out that I did know what I wanted. I just needed someone to ask the right questions and make my ideas come to life. I found that I was drawn to strong, natural light, bright colors, and photographs that were in focus instead of the soft, diffused look that was popular at the time. I knew from the store that people wanted to buy a dish because of how it looked. They'd respond to a photograph accompanying a recipe in that same intuitive way. Rori took the gorgeous wooden bowl of chunky guacamole outside in the sun, and it looks amazing and delicious, and not styled. The Roasted Carrots are photographed right on the sheet pan—messy with olive oil, salt, and pepper. Those Coconut Cupcakes are on a pretty blue plate, and the image just jumps off the page. On the other hand, there's no picture of Indonesian Ginger Chicken in *Barefoot,* delicious as it was (and is). After we photographed it, I realized that brown chicken in a brown sauce looks, well . . . *brown* . . . so the recipe is there but not the photograph.

I also decided that the quality of the ingredients mattered. I wanted the food in the photographs to be good enough to eat, not prop food faked for the camera. If we showed a glass of wine, it had to be good wine, the kind I'd serve to guests. I loved when we made the Kitchen Clambake and photographed it with some beer in the background, and, when we were done, everyone just quietly pulled up a chair to the table it was photographed on and dug in! I knew then that we had something special.

At the end of that first day, I put all the Polaroids we had on a big whiteboard and studied them. I thought, *Oh my God, we did it! This is exactly what I imagined.* That was one of the best days I ever had writing cookbooks—I had a fun, creative team who were all stunningly good at their jobs, and I realized I got to publish all of these recipes and photographs. Was it possible that I actually knew how to do this?

Next, I sent the book to my editor, who really taught me how to write a recipe. I'd write, "Put the butter in the bottom of the pan," and he would write, "Where else could you put it?" and delete "the bottom of." I loved that part of the process! He taught me to put ingredients in descending order, with the salt and pepper last. I developed a sense of how to write a recipe as concisely as possible without missing a word of instruction. I was learning how to write a cookbook!

The design process was harder for me. I sent the materials to my editor and told him I was eager to speak to the book designer to explain the story I wanted the book to tell. It was an important conversation, and I thought we'd have it immediately. But we didn't speak, so I asked again and kept asking. My editor said okay, but then ignored every one of my requests. Eventually, I was told that the book was almost done, so why not wait until I saw it? That's when I realized that the absence of communication was deliberate. I'd been shut out of the design process because, for some crazy reason, my vision for the book wasn't considered important.

Big mistake. When I finally saw the layout, I hated it. I knew instantly it was wrong, just wrong. *Barefoot* was a story about my specialty food store. It was about me. And it was about the food I prepared. The three most important elements of the story. When I flipped through the first forty pages, I saw beautiful photographs of ripe raspberries, the Hamptons countryside, and juicy tomatoes being cut, but not *one* (and I'm not exaggerating) photograph of the store, me, or any of my food. This was somebody's book, but it wasn't mine! Up until this moment, I was so committed to making the book a success that I said yes to everything. When it was suggested that it would be a great idea to serve a *Barefoot* breakfast to the publisher's sales team at a nine a.m. meeting, I was there at eight a.m., with platters in hand. Goody bags for a convention? Sure, I'll pack them up and send them out.

This time, I wasn't saying yes, not a chance. The book had to be changed. I knew what I wanted and wouldn't back down. Usually, I think I'm wrong about everything, but for some reason, this time, I was confident that I was right. I thought to myself, *I don't really care what anyone thinks of me. If I'm right, they'll think I'm a genius. If I'm wrong, and the book fails, they'll never have to see me again anyway.*

I fought like hell, and I was lucky to have Chip Gibson in my corner. Chip believed in me and in my vision for the book. He intervened and told my editor to let me have what I wanted. Eventually, I did change the book design, but it would have been so much easier on everyone involved if I could have talked to the book designer first rather than have him do a design and then go through the pain of having him change it. It's possible, too, that most authors don't get so involved in the design process, but not only did I think it was fun and interesting, I thought the design was as important as the recipes. By the time *Barefoot* went to the printer, it was everything I'd hoped it would be.

Even though I had Chip's support, there were other obstacles ahead. Someone told me that when the newly printed copies of *Barefoot* arrived from the printer, one executive at the company picked up a copy, slammed it down on her desk, and said, "Who let this happen? This book will never sell!" Why? Because *Barefoot* was an outlier. At the time, bestselling cookbooks were "bibles" that had hundreds of recipes—how to cook *everything*—and zero photographs. Instead, *Barefoot* had seventy-five recipes and full-page photographs. How many recipes does anyone need, anyway? That executive was only interested in selling what had worked in the past. I had written the book I wanted to buy, and it's hard to get support for a vision that's seen as risky.

I had heard plenty of grumbling from friends that publishers don't do enough publicity for new authors, so instead of complaining, I decided to hire the Susan Magrino Agency and worked with Amelia Durand, who turned out to be stunningly good. She was the perfect advocate for *Barefoot*, landing stories about the book and me in newspapers across the country. Now I just had to wait—nervously—for April 6, 1999: publication day. The first printing was supposed to be ten thousand copies, but my publisher optimistically upped it to twenty-five thousand because of all the publicity that Amelia had arranged.

Around that time, I got a call from Clarkson Potter asking where I wanted them to send my books. Books? Oops! I'd totally forgotten that, as part of my original contract, I had agreed to buy five thousand books. It didn't seem like a big deal at the time. I knew it made sense to sell *The Barefoot Contessa Cookbook* at the Barefoot Contessa store, but I never thought about the logistics and had no idea what five thousand books looked like. Could they fit in a car, or would they come in a eighteen-wheeler? And where was I going to put them?

Worse still, they said they needed a check for $85,000! I hadn't done the math when I signed the contract—where was I going to get $85,000?! It turns out five thousand books is a huge number of books, so I called a moving and storage company to store them there. Oh great, another expense!

But then, three days after the book was published, I got a call from the same executive who'd announced that the book would *never* sell.

"You know those five thousand books? We need them back *now*."

They had already sold all the books they had and needed the five thousand I had in storage. Whew! Now I didn't have to send that check! (By the way, that executive was dead wrong; we've sold 1.4 million copies of *The Barefoot Contessa Cookbook*, and it's still selling twenty-five years later.)

My first book tour was a series of appearances at small venues— garden clubs and women's groups—in Southern California. My biggest fear was that nobody in California would have heard of me, and I would end up talking to myself in an empty room, which would be *really* embarrassing. Jeffrey knew I was nervous and took time off from work to go with me. As we drove through Newport Beach, I spotted a Barnes & Noble. Martha Stewart had told me that whenever I saw a bookstore, I should stop and offer to sign books because that's a great way to boost sales. I walked in, stealthily looked around, and finally spotted one lone copy of *The Barefoot Contessa Cookbook* on a high shelf. Then I asked to see the manager and told him I'd written a book. Would he like me to sign it?

What if he said no? None of this came naturally to me!

"What's your book?" he asked offhandedly. When I answered *The Barefoot Contessa Cookbook*, he perked up and said, "Oh!

We have fifty copies on a table in the middle of the store!" as he walked me over to the table. *Fifty copies?!* But when we got to the table, there wasn't one book left—not one. The manager said he'd been off the day before so they must have sold them all. I signed the one remaining book (which did not go back on the high shelf) and went to Jeffrey in shock, saying, "Holy crap! They sold fifty copies yesterday!," which we kept saying to each other the whole way down Highway 1. That was when I thought, *Oh my God, this could actually work out!*

Everybody was happy, most of all *me,* and my publisher wanted another cookbook immediately. I came out of this experience learning two important lessons: Stand up for yourself, even when it's hard, even when it means taking a risk. And in any endeavor, find just one person who really believes in you. That person at Crown was Chip Gibson.

With one book behind me, I was more experienced, but I'm always looking for ways to make something better. Then, one night, our friend Richard Avedon dropped by for dinner.

Avedon was one of the world's greatest photographers, famous for his iconic portraits of John F. Kennedy, Audrey Hepburn, Marilyn Monroe, and every other celebrity on the planet, plus his extraordinary fashion shots of incredibly glamorous women swanning through the boulevards of Paris, which I adore. But whenever he came to our house, he was just Dick, a gorgeous man who loved good food and lively conversation. He had an extraordinary house all the way out in Montauk—the last house on the coast, in fact, high up on the cliffs, with long stairs leading down to the ocean—and he was often there on weekends. From time to time, he'd call and say, "What are you up to?" which I took as code for "I'd love to come for dinner," and I'd invite him over. He was the best company, because he really liked to dig under the surface and get to know you, which he usually accomplished by asking a lot of questions.

That night, we were sitting in the living room with our friend Marla, who had introduced us, when the conversation turned to our books. Dick's latest book, *The Sixties*, a collection of his most provocative photographs from the era, had come out the previous winter, just before *Barefoot Contessa*. "How's your book doing?" he asked. I was excited to discuss it with him, so I answered honestly, "It's just unbelievable. It's doing incredibly well, and I can't figure out why." Of course, I was thrilled that the book was a success, but I was thinking aloud because I was looking ahead to my next book, and I wanted to understand *why* readers found it appealing, so I could make it even better the second time around. Dick listened—he was a really good listener—then asked me, "What do *you* think?"

I rambled a little, suggesting it was the recipes, or the photographs, or maybe even the book design, because I loved the way *Barefoot* looked. When I mentioned design, Dick turned to me and said, "It's the worst I've ever seen."

Wait . . . what? Did I hear him correctly? *The worst he'd ever seen?*

In that split second, I should have been offended, angry, or crushed! Or all three. Dick, the charming man sitting next to me on my sofa, was Richard Avedon, a master of the visual arts, and he hated the design! Devastating, right? But weirdly, that's not how I felt. Instead, I slid right over to him and said, "I need to see what you see."

Dick was full of opinions, advice, and, yes, criticisms as we turned the pages together, yet there was something about the way he delivered his comments that was loving and supportive. He wasn't trying to tear me down: he meant it to be a teachable moment, and I was so hungry to learn that I listened. Try a new art director, he urged, offering to set me up with his art director, Mary Shanahan, who was the art director at *Town & Country* magazine.

That was funny because I didn't even know I needed an art director; *I'd* essentially been the art director on *Barefoot,* and I was doing the same for my new book without realizing that it was actually an important job. As much as I was looking forward to working with my fabulous team on my second book, I was tempted to follow Dick's advice and consider a new approach. Who wouldn't listen to him, genius that he was?

I spoke to Mary Shanahan, who was wonderful. But, over the next couple of weeks, I realized that something was off. I remember thinking to myself, *Dick does art. And it's gorgeous, but I don't want my books to feel like art.* What did I want? Books that were accessible—warm and friendly. Not impressive and formal, like a work by Avedon, but inviting. A happy and familiar place to be. The fact that *Barefoot* sold beyond anyone's expectations meant that I was obviously onto something. That's when I decided to stick to what I believed my books are about and how they should be experienced, and I have been the art director ever since.

So, what did I learn from Avedon? First, that he was incredibly generous. He didn't do the easy thing, which would have been to say, "Oh, it's gorgeous," even though he didn't think so. I admired him for telling the truth because it made me feel trusted and respected. But I realized that it was *his* truth—a different vision for a different kind of book. I also learned that it's important to listen to advice and then decide if it's true to who *you* are and what you're trying to accomplish. Here was a world-class creative genius sharing his knowledge and experience, but I had to have the confidence to understand—and to believe—that what may have been a good idea for Avedon was not necessarily a good idea for me.

Happily, Dick didn't mind that I stuck to my own way of doing things. I saw him a few months after our dinner, and my book came up again. "Well," he told our mutual friend Marla, "Ina's book sold better than mine, so how was my advice?" That was pure Dick, so funny, so charming—and always able to laugh at himself! That takes confidence, too.

Lunch on the dock with Avedon

407 EAST SEVENTY FIFTH STREET
NEW YORK, N. Y. 10021

Dear Cna + Jeffrey

Wow !
SLURP!

Dirk

And a charming thank-you note from him

Working with Barbara Libath

"Lose My Number"

Who doesn't love a great party? I've always felt that way, whether I was hosting a small dinner at my first house in Washington or a garden party for three hundred and fifty people in East Hampton. The *idea* of having a party is so exciting . . . until reality sets in and the to-do list overwhelms the panicking host: decisions about the menu, shopping, cooking, then pulling it all together on the big day. Why is it so stressful when we just want to have fun with friends? The question led me to the subject of my second book, *Barefoot Contessa Parties!*

I knew I'd have fun writing it, and I couldn't wait to get back into the kitchen to work on the recipes, but with the first book's success, I found myself with way too much to do. Suddenly there were book signings, interview requests, columns to write for *Martha Stewart Living,* and expenses to track on top of the day-to-day shopping and cooking. Despite all this activity, I never imagined that anyone knew who I was. Then I was standing at the elevator in Takashimaya, one of my favorite department stores in New York (sadly, it closed in 2010), when I noticed a mother and daughter behind me whispering, and I sensed they were talking about me. I thought my hem had come down, or my shoes were on the wrong feet, until I heard them say, "That's really *her.*" I was shocked!

Jeffrey suggested that I hire someone to help me, but I didn't really think of myself as someone who needed an assistant. A day later, I knew he was right—I desperately needed help! I reached out to the person who could do every job, Barbara Libath. She was married to Tedd Libath, who had driven to New York all those years to pick up food for the store, and all their children had worked at the store at one point or another. Barbara was smart and capable; she had helped me with the first book's photo shoot, and I loved working with her so much that I wanted her back.

She already had a job working for an accountant, but I wasn't going to let *that* stand in my way. I called her and said, "I'd love you to come work with me. This is the deal—you can work as much as you like or as little as you like, you can pick your days, and you can name your salary." I didn't even pretend to negotiate. Who would turn that offer down? The next day she called and said, "I can start tomorrow!" Barbara had figured out a way to work part time for both of us. From that day on, I'd hear her cheery "Good morning!" when she walked into the house, and we'd sail through the day together. I was so happy to have her positive energy and her extraordinary counsel. We were working in the kitchen at my house—which is surprisingly small, but we worked so well together that it was never a problem.

Barbara did all the shopping, and as she discovered, finding exactly what I wanted wasn't always easy. It usually involved going to multiple stores, sometimes several times in one day, to find the best cut of meat or the brand of white beans I liked. If I was testing a peach tart out of season, she would order peaches from California, where they were in season. Shopping was just one of Barbara's many jobs. On her own, she organized my photo shoots, answered the thousands of customer emails, started a mailing list, and collected addresses whenever I did a book signing. She was smart and proactive, and she had a great sense of humor—the kind of person who was fun to spend the day with. Eventually, I had so much for her to do that I convinced her to leave the accountant and work for me full time. Not only was I now someone who had an assistant, but after a month with Barbara, I had no idea how I'd ever gotten through a day without her!

One day when I was in the kitchen testing a recipe, I looked at Barbara, who was busy doing something else, and said, "You know what? *You* make it." She thought I was kidding—she could cook for her family, but that was it. Which was precisely why I wanted to watch *her* make the dish. When I'm working on a recipe, I make it at least a dozen times, sometimes twenty-five. I've had twenty years of experience cooking in a specialty food store. I know the ingredients, quantities, and steps by heart. But how does a recipe look to someone reading it for the first time, who doesn't have my experience? Are the ingredients straightforward? Are the directions clear and logical? Are there any surprises, like something bubbling up violently, that I want to warn you about? Is there potential for a mistake? Barbara was the perfect stand-in for my reader. If she found the recipe confusing at any stage, a thousand other people were bound to feel the same way, and I wanted to eliminate any mystery so the recipe would come out perfectly every time, no matter how experienced a cook you are.

Barbara and I settled into a comfortable rhythm, working happily on *Barefoot Contessa Parties!* At this time, Martha Stewart and I had been friends for several years, and I was writing a column for her magazine. Her TV production company was interested in producing new cooking shows in addition to her wildly popular show, *Martha Stewart Living,* and they proposed doing a show with me as the host. What? Really?

The concept seemed warm and accessible—me cooking in my

kitchen, sometimes with friends or other cooks. Of course, I had my doubts. Why would I want to cook in front of a camera, and, even more important, why would *anyone* want to watch me do it? I pushed my second and third thoughts to the back of my mind and tried to be enthusiastic about the project. *If they hate it, no one will ever see it,* I told myself. *What have I got to lose? This is Martha Stewart; of course,* I thought, *her team will produce a great show!*

On the first day of shooting, two giant trucks loaded with equipment pulled up in the driveway. Then the crew of fifty people swarmed through the house and grounds, setting up their various stations. There was one huge tent in the side yard that was just for *props.* Another big tent was set up that was the prep kitchen (remember, my house kitchen was now the TV set, not an actual working kitchen!). There was a third tent in the side yard that was *just* for lunch for the crew—feeding fifty people every day was a whole other project! Inside my house, the edit board took up most of my dining room. The research people and "back office" took over what used to be my library. My little kitchen was filled with cameras, lighting, and sound equipment stuffed into every available corner. There was barely room for me, let alone the people I'd invited to be on the show.

All this was happening while Jeffrey and I were living in the house—or *trying* to live in the house—so we had to live in the two bedrooms upstairs for the entire eight weeks I was filming. It was a nightmare. We filmed from eight in the morning until sometimes ten at night, and every morning, I would drag my exhausted self downstairs to make breakfast, and I'd realize, *This is a TV set. Where the fuck are my coffeepot and the toaster?!* It was like a scavenger hunt every morning, and I was getting cranky. If I wanted a moment alone, I had to run up to the bedroom and shut the door. Jeffrey was such a good sport, but it must have been awful for him—two months without a house. Any reasonable man would have been considering divorce.

Each filming day started with the same drill. At eight a.m., I would have my hair and makeup done upstairs, then I'd get myself dressed and downstairs by nine a.m., when the director was ready to start filming. As I walked to the kitchen the first day, a lovely young woman handed me the "script," or what I was supposed to say for the entire day. *What!?* I'd never even spoken to her, so she could have no way of knowing what I wanted to say. And did she think I would memorize the words? The script was totally useless to me. This should have been the first alarm bell that something was wrong, but what did I know? I'd never filmed a TV show before. As nicely as I could, I handed that script back to that lovely young woman and said, "I'm so sorry, I know you worked hard on this, but I really can't use it." Every single day for the next eight weeks, she would write a script, as her bosses directed her; every day she would hand it to me at nine a.m.; and every day I would—as compassionately as possible—say thank you and hand it back to her. It was slightly insane.

And then we would start filming. The director would tell me what we were doing that day, and I would just talk as though I was teaching someone how to make Indonesian Ginger Chicken or Roasted Carrots. The food stylists would prep everything in little bowls, and I would say to them, "No, that's how Martha does it; I want the carrots on the board so I can show people how to cut them." Flour and sugar were also premeasured into little bowls, and I'd say, "No, I want the flour in my glass canisters, and I'll show people the best way to measure it." It was a constant struggle, but I held my ground.

Their way of doing things sometimes mystified me; they'd

shoot every step of a recipe but then forget to film the "beauty shot," the mouthwatering image of the finished dish so people could see how delicious it was. In one episode, I made a soup, ladled it into a bowl, and dipped a spoon to taste it. The camera showed the spoon going up and down, but not my face. It made no sense to me. All day long, I would say to the director, "No, that's the way Martha does it! You already have Martha. You want me to do it the way I do it, which is simpler and more casual." I have no idea how I knew that or how I had the temerity to tell the director, but I knew anything else would feel wrong.

The atmosphere was tense, with no end in sight. Those eight weeks were the most difficult and exhausting work I've ever done. I couldn't imagine anyone being interested in this show, least of all Eileen Opatut, the head of development at Food Network. Eileen had bought the show and planned a visit to the set to see how it was going.

The day she arrived, I was making gorgeous little cheddar and chutney tea sandwiches on brioche. While the cameras were rolling, I picked one up, took a bite, and *actually chewed it.* "Delicious!" I said, with my mouth full, prompting the outraged director to yell, "Cut! You can't talk with your mouth full." Martha would *never* do that. *But I'm not Martha*, I wanted to say. My frustration was building by the minute and about to boil over. Then all hell broke loose outside the house.

The entire crew was on set, meaning fifty people were using the bathroom in my little two-bedroom house, so the septic system was totally overloaded. At some point, it decided, *ENOUGH,* and sewage started bubbling up in the middle of my lawn. A cesspool truck rushed over to take care of the problem, but the grass was muddy with—never mind!—and the truck's wheels got stuck in the muck. While Eileen was there watching me film, the crew had to go outside and push the truck out of the mud, leaving big muddy tire tracks in my nice green lawn. The director was so distressed that she wrapped herself in a pashmina shawl, went out in the back garden, and threw up. It was total chaos. I'd officially had enough. The next morning, I called them all together and said, "I'm done. I'd like everybody to leave, please." And I sent the crew packing. I decided I would never film a television show again. But apparently the universe had other plans for me.

A few weeks later, Eileen Opatut called me to say she would like me to do a show on my own—without the Martha Stewart film crew. "What in the world did you see that day that would make you want to film a show that was such a fiasco?" I asked incredulously. She told me she loved that I'd taken a bite of that tea sandwich and praised it, full mouth and all. She knew that if I had to taste it because it was *so* delicious, the people watching the show would want to taste it, too. And when she showed the tape to her team at Food Network, they were equally enthusiastic about my potential as a host.

Her response was flattering, but there was no way I would subject myself to the ordeal of shooting another minute of television. Eileen was so determined to change my mind that she kept calling, promising she'd do the show differently, with a smaller crew, less equipment, more spontaneity, and a better sense of who I was. I listened because Eileen is charming, but what I really wanted to say was *"Lose my number!"*

The funny part is that I think Eileen thought I was playing hard to get. Everyone wants to be on television, right? She later told me that people send gifts of hams to get a show on Food Network! Not me. I was perfectly happy in my cookbook world and never wanted to see a camera and crew in my kitchen again. "I'm not *negotiating,*" I explained patiently. "I just really don't want to do it."

The television show receded in the rearview mirror as I focused on what I enjoyed doing most—writing a new cookbook—and then Jeffrey had the craziest, most improbable and wonderful idea for a project for me. When *The Barefoot Contessa Cookbook* sold beyond anything I'd imagined, I had some money I didn't expect. "How should I invest it?" I asked Jeffrey, thinking he would suggest something like stocks or bonds.

"Why don't you do what you've always wanted to do?" he said.

And I asked, "What? What's that?"

"Buy an apartment in Paris," he answered matter-of-factly—as if it were the most obvious idea in the world.

Buy an apartment in Paris? Are you kidding? The thought had never occurred to me because it seemed entirely out of my realm. "Would *you* like an apartment in Paris?" I asked. I'd barely finished the sentence when he said he'd *love* it. I remembered the words Jeffrey had written to me right before we got married. We'd go to Paris and live in "some small apartment . . . maybe we'll have some money, and then we'll want to do only the things we did when we didn't have any. I'm so excited about this idea. You're going to make my whole life so exciting."

Exciting was an understatement! Before he could change his mind, I booked a seat on the next Air France flight to Paris and called friends for real estate advice. I learned that brokers in Paris don't share listings, so if you want to see apartments, you have to work with multiple agents. Our friend Ted Wolter, an antiques dealer in East Hampton, introduced me to Richard "Steeve" Giraud, a great Paris broker. I met with other brokers, but I remember thinking they'd all forget about me the minute I left Paris, except Steeve. I had a feeling he was going to find me my perfect Paris apartment. And that's exactly what happened.

For the next year, I spent one week a month in Paris, dragging my sorry jet-lagged self around the city, looking at some of the worst apartments I'd ever seen. Inexpensive Paris apartments can be very higgledy-piggledy, with one nice room, then two stairs leading to a hall and the bedrooms, which might even be in another building. I wanted light, air, and charm, maybe with a Paris view, but with my budget, I didn't see anything even close. Then, when my friend Frank Newbold and I were visiting our friends Eli Zabar and Devon Fredericks in the South of France (poor Jeffrey was home working), Steeve called to say he'd found the perfect apartment and told me to come right away.

Eli is a pilot, so we jumped on his plane and flew to Paris. (How cool is that? We landed at Le Bourget Airport, where Charles Lindbergh landed after that first transatlantic flight.) It was a very windy day, the plane was bouncing around like a feather, and I was terrified. *Is this apartment worth dying for?* On the flight with Frank and me was Devon and Eli's architect Lia Kiladis, who had come along for the ride. I had never met her before, but the two of us were so terrified that we held hands for the entire flight. It was a good way to get to know someone! (Fast-forward—Lia became my architect too!)

We all arrived at the apartment—number 1 rue du Bac on the Left Bank—and, as promised, it was absolutely gorgeous. A plaque proclaimed that the site had been the home of the real-life d'Artagnan, one of the Three Musketeers. The apartment was on the fifth floor, with a wraparound terrace overlooking the Seine and the most beautiful panoramic view of Paris I'd ever seen. I walked in and burst into tears. Frank whisked me outside and asked, "Why are you crying?" I managed to say between sobs, "Because I can't believe a girl from Brooklyn can buy an apartment like this in Paris."

I called Jeffrey and got right to the point. "If you love me, we'll buy this apartment." He countered with his usual practical question. "Can you sell it for what you bought it for?" That's his litmus test. It's the simplest question to ask about real estate, and all he needed to know: Can you get out without losing your shirt? I tend to buy things with my heart, and Jeffrey is so much more practical. Happily, we can always agree in the end.

I'm a little more (maybe a lot more) impulsive, but I was certain the price was too low, so I made an offer. Long story short, I was right. The apartment was listed at well under its value and there was a bidding war—the apartment sold for more than twice the asking price!—so it did not go to the weepy girl from Brooklyn. But it turned out to be another one of those "You never know your good breaks from your bad" moments. Whenever I lose a deal, I think, *When the next comes along, I'll be so grateful that the first one fell through.*

The next time Steeve called, I was back in East Hampton. "I have your apartment," he said. I asked Jeffrey what I should do, and he said, *"Go now!,"* so I grabbed my purse and my passport (not even a suitcase!) and hopped on the next flight to Paris. I took a taxi directly to the apartment. The price was right, and the apartment was exactly where I wanted to be on the Left Bank—within walking distance of all my favorite food stores—but it was *dreadful!* It was a rabbit warren of rooms; the dark kitchen all the way in the back had only one window, and it was on the airshaft—and it had pink and gray Formica! Wait! I thought Parisians had style; what was gray Formica doing in a Paris apartment? Seeing the look on my face, Steeve suggested we take a break and go have lunch. After a fabulous meal and a glass (maybe a bottle?!) of wine, we went back to the apartment. I thought maybe it would look better after a bottle of wine. But sadly, it actually looked worse. *I could never live here,* I thought.

Then Steeve said the magic words: "Flip it." Move the living room and kitchen to the front of the apartment, where the light is, and put the bedroom, bathroom, and closet in the back, where it's quieter. Well, that sounds great, but now we're talking about doing a major apartment renovation in another country. Could I actually do that? It was too scary to even contemplate. Later that day, when I was flying back to New York, I fell into an exhausted sleep and dreamed about the apartment.

I saw what it could be. In fact, this apartment had all the qualities I was looking for. The location, in the heart of my favorite neighborhood on the Left Bank, was perfect. The apartment was on the top floor, facing south, filled with sunlight, and overlooking a park. It was surrounded by a foot terrace, one we could actually walk out on, shaded by awnings. The rooms were lined up in an orderly way, with windows (aka French doors) everywhere, an unusual feature in Paris. It had a working fireplace. Oh, and last but not least, it was the right price, meaning we could afford it. I asked my friend Frank what he thought, and he gave me the best advice: "You can change the apartment but not the location." I called the realtor the next day and told him to make the deal. *Wow. I'm going to have an apartment in Paris?!*

Now what? It was time to jump off another cliff and figure out how to fly.

On closer inspection, the apartment was full of surprises. It came with—so French—two designated wine cellars, or *caves*. Knowing we wouldn't keep that much wine on hand (we'd never be *that* French), my first thought was to sell the space to someone in the building who maintained a real collection. When I mentioned this idea to Steeve, his horrified response was *"Non!"* If we ever wanted to sell the apartment, surrendering the wine cellar would reduce the price because in France it's considered a necessity, like having bathrooms. We still own them, but we've never even ventured down into the dark caverns of the building to see them.

There were other quirks. The elevator barely accommodated two people, and only if they stood very straight and hadn't eaten a large lunch or dinner. Inexplicably, it stopped *between* floors, so you always had to walk up or down steps to use it.

My favorite *La Bohème* touch was the *chambre de bonne,* or maid's room. Like the wine cellar, every apartment comes with one. The *chambre de bonne* was the legacy of Baron Haussmann, the visionary architect who modernized Paris in the mid-nineteenth century and whose name defines a style of building from the period. Haussmannian apartment buildings like ours have five floors, a cream-colored stone exterior, iron balconies, and a warren of tiny rooms on the sixth floor tucked under the mansard roof to house the maids of the families who lived there. Given that the roof was made of zinc, these bedrooms (accessed by a separate back staircase, not the elevator) were hot in the summer and cold in the winter, and everyone had to share one bathroom in the hall. But from a nineteenth-century maid's point of view, it was a far better arrangement than what they used to do—sleep on the kitchen floor.

Today, these small spaces are used for anything *but* domestic help. They're sometimes used for storage but more likely to be rented as *studettes,* or small studios. Because we were on a high floor, our *chambre de bonne* was right above our apartment, so Jeffrey could use it as an office. I fantasized about buying the adjacent *chambre* (because it had a gorgeous cupola) and expanding the space into a proper second floor, but the French are SO discreet about real estate that I wasn't permitted to even know who owned it, let alone how to get in touch with them.

I love building things—apartments, houses, gardens, any-where we're going to live—while Jeffrey is happiest coming in for the finish. I would buy something, renovate it, furnish it, and one day move all his belongings and clothes into the closet of the new place, and then he would arrive—voilà! He's home. For me, it was great because I never had to negotiate with someone who wanted a red leather sofa in the living room, and he never had to experi-ence the logistical discomfort of moving.

It had worked beautifully for the past thirty years, so I decided to do the same thing with the Paris apartment—Jeffrey wouldn't see it or be involved in any of the renovation decisions until it was completely done. It would be a gorgeous present.

My dream was that he would arrive to find all the furniture in place, the pictures on the walls, French music playing, and the smell of warm croissants and coffee wafting through the apart-ment. Even when he accompanied me on one of my frequent trips to Paris, the apartment was off-limits. I'd handle every detail of the total renovation myself. It wasn't unusual—I'd overseen our other projects, building and renovating our houses in East Hamp-ton and apartments in New York, and furnishing his apartment in Tokyo—but I'd never actually *renovated* and furnished anything in a foreign country. How hard could this be?

It was really hard! The first thing I needed to do was open a checking account so I could pay the bills. I gathered my papers (and my French vocabulary) and went to the Banque de France, an impressive stone building across the street from the apart-ment. It looked more like a museum than a bank, but that was true of many buildings in Paris, where everything is so grand and elegant.

I walked in and said in my best French, "Please, I'd like to open a checking account." The bank officer looked at me strangely and didn't respond, so I figured there must be something wrong with my French. I found somebody else, hoping they would understand me, but I got the same puzzled reaction. Frustrated, I walked outside and called Jeffrey on my cell phone. "I'm doing something wrong, but I'm not sure what it is. I'm at the bank, trying to open a checking account, and no one understands me."

"Which bank?" he asked.

"The Banque de France."

Jeffrey thought this was hilarious. "Well, that's a little like walking into the Federal Reserve and saying you want to open a checking account," he told me, which explains why the people who worked there were so mystified (and probably annoyed) by my request. The Banque de France, the central bank of France, was founded by Napoleon to manage the treasury and set monetary policy for the entire country and beyond. No, I would not be getting a checkbook at that "bank."

I found a bank for humans across the street and wrote more checks than I care to remember as I assembled a fleet of professionals to transform the apartment. I started with architect Lia Kiladis (the woman whose hand I had clutched on the plane when I thought I was going to die), who knew exactly what to do. We ripped out the walls, tore up the floors, and started from scratch. My French vocabulary didn't include critical words (how do you say *air conditioner*?), so my learning curve was steep. In addition to making decisions about structural changes (how do you say *gut job en français*?), I had to think about style and how to furnish the apartment—in this, I was pretty much on my own.

I kept saying to myself, *I don't want an apartment in Paris—I want a Paris apartment,* meaning not a New York City transplant with all the American trimmings. Our home away from home had to have a real sense of place and history. I wanted to mix modern and antique—both in the architecture and in the furniture. If you have just antiques, it's too busy and feels old-fashioned, like a mishmash of your grandmother's furniture. And if you're strictly modern, it can be too austere and cold. But if you start with modern and bring in antiques, everything can fit together cohesively and the room has personality.

I thought I would buy some beautiful modern furniture from Christian Liaigre, a great Paris interior designer who had a furniture store nearby. But I wanted to mix in antiques, so I went to the famous Paris flea market called Les Puces de Saint-Ouen. Sounds simple, right? It wasn't! All the furniture I found in the market was either mid-century modern (not right for me at the time) or nineteenth century, which just didn't look right with my modern furniture. I was in a panic!

I called my friend Ted Wolter again (the man who had introduced me to the real estate agent Steeve). No one has more style than Ted. "Help! Do you ever come to Paris, and will you help me do the apartment?" Fortunately, Ted said he was planning to be there the next time I'd be in Paris, and he saved the day. The first thing he did was teach me that nineteenth-century furniture is too ornate to go with modern pieces; only seventeenth- and eighteenth-century furniture was simple enough to work with the modern Liaigre furniture I'd already bought. Once I saw what he was talking about, I knew, of course, he was right.

Ted was the first person to take me to visit a visionary designer and antique dealer in Belgium named Axel Vervoordt. As Axel tells his story, he fell in love with an antique trunk when he was a teenager and turned that early passion into a lifelong appreciation of all things old and beautiful. Ted took me to Vervoordt's castle outside Antwerp, where every room displayed incredibly beautiful furniture and objects from previous centuries—preserved but never restored, because Vervoordt believed age was a virtue, that it was actually a form of storytelling. The pieces he collected and sold—wood, leather, canvas, stone—were simple but with the kind of extraordinary patina that takes centuries to develop.

The interesting thing about Vervoordt's castle is that it is also his home. All the furnishings—the lamp on his night table, the medicine chest in his bathroom, the round tables where the staff have lunch every day—are for sale. I walked from room to room, loving his unerring eye for timeless style, and I found an English wood table that could serve as the table for lamps behind the sofa, a desk, and, when we pulled it out, a dining table for dinner parties. I've never liked things that are purely decorative, and Vervoordt's approach to design confirmed my feeling that if a room is filled with objects you love and actually use, it's warm and inviting instead of feeling "decorated."

Many milestones passed while the apartment slowly took shape. *Barefoot Contessa Parties!* came out in March 2001. When I finished my first book, I thought, *Okay, that's it—I've used all my recipes!* After *Parties!*, I again thought I'd be totally out of ideas. I admitted to Jeffrey that I was scraping the bottom of the barrel—not a good creative place to be! But then something happened; I imagine it's like exercise—the more you do something, the better you get at it. Eventually, I found that I could sit down and write a list of fifty recipes that I wanted to work on, so I made a list and began writing *Barefoot Contessa Family Style*.

Ideas came from everywhere—a recipe I'd seen in a magazine, a dinner we'd had at a restaurant, a new ingredient I'd just discovered, like sriracha. I love to base recipes on remembered flavors. One of my favorite recipes in *Family Style*—Parmesan Chicken—came from a dish my mother used to make, one of the few delicious things she made. But I put a green salad on top with a fresh lemon vinaigrette, the way Italians do with a veal Milanese, to give it more texture and flavor. The Potato Basil Frittata in the book came from my memory of the frittata that Anna Pump made for me the day I interviewed her for the position of chef.

Traveling was always good for inspiration, because I would see dishes I'd never seen before. Tiramisu came from a wonderful trip to Milan. Summer Pudding—an old-fashioned English dessert with layers of bread and fruit all melded together—came from a fun week in London. Wait, this is work and it's tax-deductible too? For each recipe, I might start with the common ingredients but then think, *What if I added this, or changed that?*

Paris alone was a food writer's dream. Our apartment was within walking distance of some of the great bakeries (Poilâne), butchers (Boucherie du Bac), fish markets (Poissonnerie du Bac), cheesemongers (Barthélémy), and produce stores (Roseraie de Grenelle), not to mention the enormous Grande Épicerie at Le Bon Marché department store, which is the most extensive international specialty food store I've ever seen. Shopping in East Hampton is just about getting into the car and collecting ingredients. Shopping in Paris is a totally sensual experience—all the stinky cheeses, fragrant breads, and sweet ripe fruit you can gather, plus a walk around the neighborhood. Old buildings, bright-blue skies, familiar shopkeepers greeting you (in French!). It's such a happy experience.

The Boulevard Raspail Market, or Marché Raspail, was another irresistible destination, and I've always remembered going there on our camping trip. It's a traditional market every Tuesday and Friday but completely organic every Sunday, including on Christmas Day and New Year's. The market has dozens of stalls that go on for blocks, selling perfectly ripe seasonal produce (asparagus sold by the stalk in spring, several types of strawberries in summer, and big chunks of enormous potiron squashes in autumn) alongside meat, fish, cheese, baked goods, flowers, and other temptations. Our apartment was a block from the market, and when I walked from vendor to vendor, I was transported back in time to our camping trip, when my passion for everyday French food began. The hardest part was passing the stall that sold freshly made, hot potato pancakes. They were so fragrant and crispy that it was totally impossible to walk by without stopping!

I also roamed the amazing aisles at Dehillerin, the historic cookware emporium patronized by the world's greatest cooks for over two hundred years. In fact, a Dehillerin bain-marie, a pan used to heat food in a bath of water, was salvaged from the wreckage of the *Titanic*. The store was beloved by Julia Child, who swore by their copper pots. I went there, too, on our camping trip, and if someone had told me then that my photograph would be on their wall next to Julia Child's, I would have thought they were completely insane! Sometimes I didn't know how to use a particular utensil or pan, but I had to have it. I'd buy it and then figure it out later, which was also a form of inspiration. I was like a kid in a candy store; I couldn't stop myself from buying all kinds of gorgeous professional cookware—pots, food mills, tart pans—for the Paris apartment and to take home to East Hampton, too. I do remember Jeffrey on the plane with me with a very large copper paella pan in his lap. (He's a *very* good sport!)

My adventures led to the theme of my next book, *Barefoot in Paris*. I wanted to share recipes for easy French food you could make at home, with all the style and WOW but none of the intimidating complications. I loved Julia Child's *Mastering the Art of French Cooking*, but many of the recipes were too complicated to make now; could I simplify them so that they would still have the same deep, satisfying flavors? Everywhere I went there were inspirations—the warm goat cheese salad from Café Varenne and the blue cheese soufflé I loved at Le Récamier. My goal was to make these dishes accessible for Americans at home with American ingredients. We don't have the classic French potiron squash, but I found the combination of canned pumpkin and fresh butternut squash made the perfect classic soupe au potiron—without the potiron! I loved writing this cookbook because I was living it!

My happy tour of Paris took a sad turn on 9/11, a terrifying day and a difficult time to be in a foreign city, so far away from New York. Friends invited me to their home for dinner. I remember sitting at the table, the whole group mesmerized by the unimaginable events unfolding on the television. The room was silent because we were too shocked and distressed to speak. All I wanted to do was go home, but it was impossible to even get a flight. The one time I ventured to the airport to see if I could get any flight, it was closed because there had been a bomb scare! I went for a walk, and when I reached the Luxembourg Gardens, I heard familiar music. Right in the middle of the park, a band was playing our national anthem, expressing France's solidarity with a grieving America. It was heart-wrenching to hear the song in this context. Stores throughout Paris displayed signs with the message "nous sommes américains," or "We are American," showing support for us. It was quite extraordinary and very emotional. I managed to get home several days later, still deeply impressed by how the French embraced Americans during that terrible time.

I continued to make monthly trips to Paris to check on the renovation, and I just happened to be there the day my stove was delivered. I'd always wanted a French La Cornue stove because they're so beautiful, but for testing recipes at home, I need an American range that's more like everyone else's stove. However, here in Paris, I could totally justify ordering the best French stove, right? I had imagined how beautiful a massive black La Cornue would look in my new kitchen, but my fantasy didn't include the logistics of getting that three-hundred-and-fifty-pound *monster* up to the fifth floor. There was no chance it was going into that tiny elevator, so it would need to be brought up the long, narrow flight of twisting stairs. Yikes!

The truckers arrived, deposited the stove on the sidewalk, and drove away. *What?* How was this going to happen? I called the kitchen designer, a gorgeous French Iranian woman named Shoré, and asked her what to do. She said, "Don't worry! Four really handsome men are going to come, pick up the stove, and walk it up the five flights of stairs. And you're going to want to be at the top of the stairs when they arrive because they're going to be *really* sweaty."

How French is that? I have to confess, I was there at the top of the stairs—and Shoré was there with me, too!

As much as I enjoyed Paris, I had a lonely husband at home who missed me when I was away and a new book to plan, and Food Network was still calling. Eileen Opatut refused to "lose my number." She wanted to speak to me, and I steeled myself to give her another hard no.

"Put My Jugs on the What?"

I started filming *Barefoot Contessa* in August 2002 . . . wait, didn't I say I'd *never* do another television show? Whatever possessed me to change my mind?

A friend had just returned from a trip to Australia, where he'd seen an episode of the British cooking show *Nigella Bites,* hosted by Nigella Lawson. He raved about it, saying she was spontaneous and personable (and gorgeous). She was clearly a great cook—the food looked amazing—but better still, she didn't stand behind a counter doing a tutorial. She even dipped her finger in the frosting and tasted it. The show wasn't broadcast in the United States then, so I asked Eileen if she could get me a tape of Nigella's show.

I certainly wasn't thinking of ever doing a cooking show again, but I have to admit, I was curious.

Of course Eileen could get me a tape—she knew all the British shows and had been responsible for bringing Jamie Oliver to the United States. She had high praise for Nigella and Pacific, the production company that worked with her, and was happy to get me a tape—anything to keep our conversation going in the right direction.

I watched the show and saw that Nigella lived up to her reputation. She was fantastic—warm, charismatic, and completely at ease in front of the camera. Still, my one thought was *Well, she's great, but that's not me.* Which is exactly what I told Eileen. "Thank you very much," I said, "but I'm not Nigella and I'm still really not interested."

Refusing to throw in the towel, Eileen tried to reassure me. "The most important thing is to match the personality to the program. I promise you we will be thinking of who *you* are." And lastly, she made a request. She asked if I would just have a conversation with Rachel Purnell at Pacific Productions in London. *One conversation won't kill me,* I thought, especially since I clearly admired Rachel's work. We'd speak, I'd be friendly but noncommittal, and that would be that.

But then I had a really interesting talk with Rachel. I was very impressed. She was smart, knew my cookbooks, appreciated my style of food, and clearly understood who I was and how to tell my story. She didn't want to turn me into Martha, Nigella, or anyone else; she wanted me to be myself. On the technical side, Rachel explained that she and her co-producer, Olivia Grove, used a small crew, just a handful of people who wouldn't take over the whole house, set up tents on the lawn, or destroy my septic system.

I was tempted but not convinced, until Eileen said the magic words: "Let's just do thirteen episodes; if you don't like it, we'll call it a day." By this point, I was as tired of saying no to Eileen as she was of hearing it. Okay, I would try it—film one season, and still have an escape hatch if the show was awful.

I found the challenge of bringing *Barefoot Contessa* to life terrifying but totally engaging. The show's primary focus was food and cooking, but we wanted to make it more than that. Cooking for me isn't an end; it's a means to an end. I cook for people I love, and when you cook, everyone shows up. How many times has someone called you and said, "Come for dinner!" and you said,

"Nah, I don't really want a home-cooked dinner and an evening around the table with friends"? Never! I wanted the show to be true to my life and about the world I'd created with great friends and good food in East Hampton. I would invite people who were genuinely a part of my life—Jeffrey and our friends. No endorsements, no product placements: just me cooking delicious dinners and sharing them with the people who meant something to me in the places I loved.

I wanted viewers to feel that they were *right there* with me throughout the whole day, as though they were sitting on a stool on the other side of the counter in my kitchen, watching me cook, or by my side when I went grocery shopping. "Where she goes, we go" was the crew's modus operandi—they'd jump in the car with their cameras and follow me everywhere, capturing the natural beauty and charm of the Hamptons along the way.

It wasn't easy, but this time the process was far more bearable—even enjoyable—thanks to Pacific. They rented houses in the Hamptons (depending on what was available, it might be an empty mansion or a no-frills place that was more "keep calm and carry on"), and we settled in for the long ten-week shoot.

In the early days, everyone on the crew was British, which meant they all sounded bright, charming, and exceedingly polite. "Darling, would you mind moving the camera?" one crew member would say to another. When my director checked the monitor each morning, he'd walk around to me behind the counter and tell me, "You have no idea how gorgeous you look." (And I believed him every time!)

It was all so civilized! They behaved like a family; in fact, in the years to come, my producer Olivia and one of her assistant producers each married one of the cameramen, so then it really was like a family!

In the beginning, as I had felt when I started writing cookbooks,

I was lost. I couldn't imagine that I could do this well, and I didn't know how it worked. Frankly, I didn't even know what a producer did! In feature films, was the producer the person who financed the project, or did they actually work on the set? And how was making a film different from television? (I now know that in film, the director runs the show, and in television, the producer runs the show. And yes, they are on the set all day every day.) But Rachel and Olivia put me at ease. They wanted the shows to come from my life—what did I *actually* make for Jeffrey when he came home from Yale every Friday night? Who were my friends, and could I invite them for dinner, as I did all the time? Did we ever go to the beach and have a picnic with friends? What do I like to do for table settings for a big party?

There was, unfortunately, one moment when Rachel asked me if I ever took a bath before a dinner party, and I found myself—with an entire camera crew!—in my bathroom in a big bubble bath (with a bathing suit on!!) while they filmed me reading a book. I think it aired once and never again. After long days of filming, I would question whether I could learn how to do this, but I remember that Rachel and Olivia would tell me the one thing I needed to know: "We won't say 'cut' until it's really good." And I trusted them.

Sometimes there was a little confusion because they didn't speak "American English." I was shocked when the director asked me to put my jugs on the hob. "I'm not doing *that*," I said, imagining the worst. What does that even mean? Turns out he wanted me to put my measuring cups on top of the stove. And there was one cultural difference we couldn't bridge. One day, between takes, we were talking about what we used to eat as children. They thought our PB&J sandwiches were disgusting, so they insisted on making me their ultimate comfort food—cold beans (yes, right out of the Heinz 57 can!) on white toast with a Kraft single on top. I politely said, "Thanks, I'll take this to my room," and promptly filed it in the trash. I think that was the last time they offered to "cook" for me!

The first day was grueling; we worked from eight o'clock in the morning until ten o'clock at night. Remember, this isn't like a movie where I'm in every other scene. If I'm not being filmed, the crew has nothing to do, so I worked straight through with just an hour off for lunch.

We filmed each take three times to get the best one, which is harder than you think on a cooking show. The first take is natural—talking about cooking, picking up a wooden spoon, and telling a story. But then for the second and third, I had to remember exactly what I'd said, in what order; how I'd told the story; and which hand I'd used to pick up the wooden spoon at what point in the story, or they wouldn't be able to edit the shots together. It was nerve-racking—the hardest thing I'd ever had to do. That's actually the way we filmed for a year, until I threatened to quit and Rachel admitted that my first take—the natural one—was so much better than the next two, and we started doing only one take.

When the first day of filming was over, I was about to drag myself to bed at midnight when the phone rang. As if there wasn't enough going on in my life, it was Maria, the *gardienne,* or caretaker, of our apartment building in Paris, calling about an emergency. "Madame, madame!" she screamed into the phone, followed by a rapid burst of incomprehensible French. The only word I understood was *pompiers,* which means the fire department. *FIREMEN?!* In my brand-new, just-finished apartment? "Oh my God," I said. "What happened? Is there a fire?"

She slowed down and told me no, not fire: water—the pompiers also show up if there is a flood. It seems that someone in a *chambre de bonne* above our living room had turned on the water in the bathtub, forgotten about it, and left the building. I should have been distraught about the damage; that would have been the normal reaction. But, no, all I could think about was real estate. This was the *chambre de bonne* above our living room that I had wanted to buy. *Now I'll be able to find out who the owner is because we'll have to talk about the insurance!*

This time I did know "my good breaks from my bad," and this was very good! When I eventually spoke to the owner, I said, "How about this? You don't have to pay for the damage if you will let us buy your *chambre de bonne.*" Happily, he agreed, and suddenly I had my cupola and a bigger second floor.

Back on set, we continued filming the first episode, "A Mediterranean Feast." I prepared lamb and couscous. My friend and stylist Miguel Flores-Vianna decorated a table in the garden, and I welcomed friends who often came to our house for the exact same meal. It felt natural to me because it was an evening I would have hosted in real life, without a crew and cameras. Still, I was nervous about how it would look on film. *I'm just bad at this and it's going to be crap,* whispered the nasty little voice in my head.

Pacific FedExed the raw footage to London for a quick edit. I'm my own worst critic, so I dreaded watching it and expected the worst. But I remember thinking, when I saw the rough edit, *Well, it's not as bad as I thought!* Not that I thought it was good, but it wasn't terrible, considering that I had just started filming. Feeling a bit more confident, I said to Olivia, "If that's what I could do on day one, just imagine how much better it's going to be when I get good at it."

Her reaction surprised me. "Not necessarily," she said, explaining that my nervous energy played well on the screen; it made me really show up. *Amazing!* To hear Olivia put a positive spin on it was liberating. I could be myself, nerves and all, working scared, and know it would make the show better, not worse. The funny thing is that twenty years later, I'm still nervous while I'm filming, but I suppose that it's still working for me!

Looking back at the shows we made during the first season, I'm surprised to see that my approach to food and entertaining hasn't changed all that much in the past twenty years. I made roast chicken for Jeffrey, I suggested that the best way to entertain someone "important" was to surprise them with casual comfort food like meatloaf and mashed potatoes, and I showed how to transform boring leftovers, the ones that usually end up in the back of the refrigerator, into a completely new meal.

I don't think people need new and exciting ways to entertain; they just need the experience to make dishes they feel confident preparing and a few tips for showing their guests a wonderful, relaxed evening. Gone are the days of a tricked-out piñata party with South American–themed food; instead, I've always preferred a dinner of Slow-Roasted Pork Shoulder with Maple Baked Beans, both of which cook slowly in the oven for six or seven hours and are ready to serve whenever we sit down for dinner. That was the idea of the show, and I think it still holds true today. By the time we finished shooting the first season, amazingly, I agreed to do it again. I loved my British family and saw that while filming a television show was really hard, doing it *and* working on cookbooks at the same time would present new challenges, engage different yet complementary muscles, and make me feel doubly creative. But first, a vacation—and I knew exactly where to go!

The Paris apartment was finally finished, and it was time for the big reveal. I planned Jeffrey's long-anticipated first look with military precision. I flew to Paris on a Tuesday and scheduled Jeffrey to arrive from his business trip the following morning. I was so determined to get every detail right that I even booked a class with the famous Parisian floral designer Christian Tortu that afternoon. His beautiful compositions, inspired by nature, upended decades of traditional flower shop arrangements. A signature Tortu bouquet was perfectly imperfect, not too symmetrical, with mixed blooms of varying heights and grasses and branches, as they would grow in a garden. I loved how he used one color, often just subtle shades of green and white, to create an elegant but completely natural display.

Following Tortu's style, I arranged flowers all over the apartment; it made me feel very Parisian. When Jeffrey arrived the next morning, the room was filled with the scent of warm croissants and hot coffee, with French music playing softly in the background, just as I'd dreamed it two years before.

I'd learned so much in the past two years; I'd presented myself with a challenge I wasn't sure I could meet and spent a ridiculous amount of money to do something a little crazy. Would we even *want* to go to Paris for every vacation? Construction in another country? That's not crazy—it's certifiably insane. And exhausting. And *terrifying*. I worried I might fail. I took a big risk—but when it was done, I felt like I'd nailed it. The apartment was so much better than I'd imagined at the beginning of this adventure. But would Jeffrey feel the same way?

He loved it!! PHEW! He couldn't believe that I had done it and that he now owned an apartment in Paris, complete with his clothes in the closet and his toothbrush on the sink. The first night he was jet-lagged and couldn't sleep—or was it the excitement?—and he walked around the apartment looking at all the details and the Paris city views, the park with a carousel outside our window. The next morning he told me how incredibly happy he was. It had been a long-forgotten dream and now he actually had an apartment in Paris.

The funny thing is that I didn't realize the full extent of how much he loved it until several years later. In 2009, our friend Susan Stroman, the extraordinary director and choreographer, premiered a new musical called *Happiness* at Lincoln Center. The premise was that each character had to look back on their life and pinpoint their happiest memory. We were there for the opening, and when the show was over, Jeffrey and I turned to each other to ask the question—"What was *your* happiest memory?"—and amazingly, we both had exactly the same answer. The best day of our lives was the day that Jeffrey came home to our new Paris apartment.

Living the dream did, however, come with certain realities. Cooking is hard for me anyway, but cooking in Paris is a whole new level of difficulty. Don't even think about celebrating Thanksgiving in Paris if you're a traditionalist, because the turkey (la dinde) is a completely different bird in France. There's no such thing as a cranberry, and celery is practically impossible to find. One Thanksgiving, Jeffrey managed to find a lone stalk in a little convenience store, but he had to beg the shopkeeper to sell it to him because the shopkeeper's wife had asked him to bring it home to her. Heavy cream isn't called heavy cream. Gelatin comes in sheets, not little packages of powder. If you want chicken stock, you have to make it yourself. And the metric system is a constant challenge for American cooks.

The first holiday we spent in Paris was New Year's Eve, and we invited our friends Walter and Patricia Wells for dinner. This was going to be an amazing night with great friends in the most beautiful city in the world. It just doesn't get any better than that!

The first thing I did was make a shopping list—Poilâne for bread, La Grande Épicerie for champagne and meat, Barthélémy for cheese (real French cheese!), La Roseraie de Grenelle for perfect produce, Berthillon for ice cream, and Marianne Robic for flowers. Other than Berthillon, everything was no more than four blocks from my apartment! Jeffrey and I made a trip to the Conran Shop, the British home goods store, also a block away, and bought all the tableware and linens we needed to set a beautiful table for four. Check!

On the plus side, I met the most accommodating butcher at La Grande Épicerie. I was shopping for the rôti de porc (roast pork), and just to test my French, while the butcher prepared my roast, I asked him how he would cook it. I expected a conventional response. But he told me something that sounded so crazy that I asked him to repeat it, thinking I must have misunderstood his French. Did he really just tell me to start the roast in a *cold* oven? I asked, "Could you write that down for me, please?" He wrote the instructions on a slip of paper—with his home phone number! "If you forget, you can call me at home," he promised. On New Year's Eve! How lovely is that?

Starting the pork in a cold oven was transformative. Ever the scientist, I cut the roast in half and put one half in a cold oven and the other half in a preheated oven, as I always had. The pork that started in the cold oven was the tenderest roast pork I had ever made. I was so excited and thought I was going to transform how people cook meat in the United States, but sadly, when I tried it back home, it didn't work with the leaner pork that we have here. Too bad!

Then, of course, I had to get my hair done for New Year's Eve!

I found a hairdresser across the street from our apartment, and since it was New Year's Eve, she asked, "Would you like your hair straight or curly?" I thought, *Oh well, it's New Year's Eve in Paris, maybe I'll do something different and surprise Jeffrey.* "Curly," I told her. After she did my "coiffure," I looked in the mirror and said, "*Mon mari dira 'Baise-moi vite avant que ma femme n'arrive,'*" which I thought meant "My husband will say 'Kiss me quick before my wife gets here.'" She looked at me in total horror. Occasionally, I experienced a "lost in translation" problem when my French collided with an idiom. One small word, if it's the wrong word, can make a really BIG difference. I thought, *Oh my God, what did I just say?*

Later, when we were having dinner with Patricia and Walter, who had lived in France for a long time, I told Walter the story. When he finally stopped laughing, he explained what had gone wrong—so very wrong. "*Un baiser*" is a kiss—but if the word is used as a *verb*, which is the way I had used it, it means something completely different and apparently very X-rated. "What you told her," Walter clarified, "was that your husband will say, 'Fuck me quick before my wife gets here.'" Oops!

No wonder the hairdresser was shocked! I never, ever made that mistake again.

Cooking with Elmo

It's a good thing the Paris renovation had a happy ending, because there was another big construction project on the horizon, literally in my backyard. Filming the television show in our house was not sustainable. For several years—for eight weeks, twice a year—we lived upstairs in two rooms while the crew took over the rest of the house (didn't they promise they wouldn't take over the house?!), and we didn't have any privacy. Ever. Jeffrey was a saint and never complained, but I knew we had reached the outer limit of our tolerance for camping out in our own house.

I literally could *see* the solution—an open field adjacent to our property, where it would be possible to build something that could serve as a test kitchen, a film set, and a party space right next to our house. The only problem was that we didn't own the land that could solve all our problems.

When we had originally bought the property to build our house, I had negotiated a right of first refusal to buy the property the sellers also owned next door. This meant that if they ever decided to sell, they would have to offer it to us first, or if they had an offer, we would have a chance to match it. In other words, the owner couldn't sell it without our knowledge. Over the ten years that we'd been living there, I had written every summer, politely asking if they'd consider selling. The answer was always a disappointing no. Now, after ten years, it was time to either buy the land and build a kitchen or, sadly, start looking for another place.

The owner was Reverend David Mulford, a deeply charming man whose family had owned the property since 1640, before East Hampton was founded. Mulford Farm, which is the historic property in the middle of the village, was part of their original farm. They also lived next door to us, and we had gotten to know and adore his whole family over the years.

The tenth summer that I wrote to Reverend Mulford, oddly, I didn't hear back, and I was wondering if something was wrong. Just before Christmas that year, he emailed and said, "Let's talk after the holidays." I was ecstatic because I thought it meant he was finally interested.

On January 2, as soon as it was polite for me to call, I phoned Reverend Mulford, and he told me that he wasn't ready now but he would like to sell the property in five years. Oh no! Five years? I simply couldn't wait that long. Jeffrey was in the next room and heard my disappointment. But I just couldn't let it go. I kept him on the phone while I reorganized my thoughts. I remembered those two things my father taught me about negotiations: First, you need to figure out what the other guy wants. Then you can structure a deal that gives him what he wants within parameters that you can live with, so everyone feels good about it. The second principle is, oddly, leave something on the table. Most people approach negotiations as a zero-sum game—you lose, I win. If you leave something on the table—meaning you don't negotiate every last dollar or last detail—everyone walks away feeling as though they won. Each person feels good about the deal, and isn't that the way we want everyone to feel when they do business with us?

I took a chance that Reverend Mulford might like the security of knowing that he had sold the property for his price in five years. I decided that rather than make him an offer, which might feel like an ultimatum, I would give him three choices so the decision to sell would be *his*. First, I offered to rent the property from him for five years and then—in five years—buy it at the market value. Second, I offered to rent it and set the price now for the sale in five years. And third—this was my swing-for-the-fences offer—buy it now for 10 percent more than the current market value. As I said, the best deals are the ones where everyone walks away feeling as though they got exactly what they wanted. Reverend Mulford answered, "Let me talk to my accountant and I'll call you back." The next day, he called and said, "Thank you very much; I'll take your third offer!" Door number three was the winning ticket and my favorite option! Yay!

Jeffrey and I bought the land, and then I tried to figure out what I wanted to do with it. A blank canvas is the hardest thing for me to deal with; when the possibilities are endless, I struggle to choose one style and stick with it. Finally, I decided there were two kinds of buildings that had always inspired me, and they were totally compatible both with each other and with East Hampton architecture. The first was the Belgian country farm buildings that I had seen on my trips to Axel Vervoordt in Antwerp, and the other was the main dining room of Dan Barber's wonderful restaurant Blue Hill at Stone Barns in Tarrytown, New York. They are both large open spaces, warm and textured with stucco, old wood, and stone, a little rustic yet modern and luxurious.

Next, I needed an architect to draw my vision. I always believe that the best way to work with an architect is to give them clear direction and see where they go with it. I called Frank Greenwald, an architect I adore who lives in Sag Harbor but does projects all over the world. Unfortunately, he explained that he didn't do small projects like this one. But just like when I was negotiating for the property, I couldn't let it go. "Are you sure? I've always wanted to work with you!" I said. After a moment of silence, he said, "Okay, I'll do it because this will be really fun!"

I outlined my ideas for the barn with Frank. I told him I admired the design of Blue Hill and also gave him all my books on Belgian farm buildings, putting Post-it notes on the details that I loved: French doors, clerestory windows, old wood beams, black Belgian stone floors, and English Crittall black metal French doors. Of course, I know that East Hampton isn't Antwerp, but the building materials are similar—shingled roofs, wood siding, stucco, and stone. I thought it would fit in well in East Hampton and still feel new. A few weeks later, Frank called to say he had the first draft of the plans. Could we get together?

I was so excited and nervous when Frank rolled out the plans on my kitchen table. How would it look? Would it be both beautiful and functional? It was the first time I was building something totally from scratch. As we looked at his drawings, Frank said, "This is just a first draft. Change anything you want to." I reviewed the plans with him and said something I had honestly never said to an architect before: "It's perfect exactly the way you drew it!" He absolutely nailed it. The look, the volume of the space (two thousand square feet with a gorgeous kitchen at its center), the huge French doors and clerestory windows that let light in everywhere. The generous rooms could accommodate the oversize antique furniture I loved, especially an eighteenth-century Swedish trestle table where I could work and Jeffrey and I could entertain.

As for the "commute"? Door-to-door was under sixty seconds unless, as I joked with Jeffrey, the rabbit traffic was heavy that day.

The designers and builders were just incredible, and I celebrated them by hosting a "barn warming" on my cooking show. It was so much fun to see them in the space they built, showing off their work to their spouses and trading stories while they sipped champagne and ate the meal I'd prepared in my kitchen.

There was a moment, though, when the landscape contractor offered to light a fire in the fire bowl on the terrace in front of the barn. He piled a massive number of logs in the bowl and lit them. I thought it was a nice touch, until a wall of flames shot up in the air as high as the top of the roof. NOOOO! I panicked. It was a barn *warming*, not a barn *burning*. I didn't start breathing again until the flames subsided. Then we went back to the party and had a wonderful time.

Amazingly, every day that I've walked into the barn over the past fifteen years, I still feel the same thrill I felt the first time. *I can't believe I get to work here every day.* Good architecture makes me want to do a better job, to live up to the promise of the space.

Whether I was writing a cookbook or filming *Barefoot Contessa,* my fabulous new space made everything better. There was always a lot to do and just enough stress to keep me at the top of my game. People are always surprised when I say that cooking is hard for me, but I'm not a trained professional. I've just done more cooking than most home cooks, and I've learned by doing. I'm always making something different, and each recipe has its own set of variables, including the ingredients. One day the carrots are sweet, the next they're bland. The first chicken is two and a half pounds; the second is four pounds. I have to think about every ingredient every time. And I'm a perfectionist with high expectations, so if the result is anything less than perfect it's a total disaster to me. Cooking is like shooting at a moving target. Of course it's hard!

But with experience, I learned to trust my instincts and the process. When I finished one cookbook, I'd instantly come up with seventy-five recipes I wanted to work on for the *next* book. When I was writing *Back to Basics,* I was thinking, *What is it that makes a dish something I would want to eat?* The answer is flavor and texture.

I use the words *flavor* and *texture* a lot, and I'd like to describe what I mean. The quick answer is that flavor is what we taste when we eat something, and texture is how it feels while we're eating it. But what am I actually looking for when I want to add flavor and texture to *my* version of a recipe? And what do I spend months— sometimes years—trying to find?

When I decide to work on a recipe—it could be one I remember from the past or something I tried for the first time yesterday—I start with an idea of a dish I would like to make. Next, I might look through the cookbooks in my library and read everything I can about similar dishes. If I have something specific in mind—both flavor and texture—I have a much better chance of getting it right. Then I just start testing—over and over again. I'm really like a scientist and a detective, experimenting until I find the perfect combination of ingredients. Each time I make a dish, I might change one variable to see the effect—*What would happen if I added cognac to this sauce? Or more baking powder to this cake batter?*

My goal in finding the right flavor is to make the dish taste as good as it can taste with as few ingredients as possible. Every ingredient has to earn its place in the recipe. It's not so much about adding flavors as about making the intrinsic ingredients taste like the best versions of themselves. How can I make chicken more "chicken-y," or chocolate more "chocolate-y"? First, of course, I try to start with ingredients that are already the best versions of themselves, such as Lindt bittersweet chocolate or ripe peaches in season from a local farm. Summer peaches need very little to make them taste great, but no matter what you do to a peach in winter, it will probably never taste like a juicy summer peach. *How can I enhance that voluptuous flavor without overpowering it? Or wake it up and give it an edge without pushing it too far in the wrong direction?*

Second, I don't think there should be more than three prominent flavors in any recipe—my brain just can't process more than that without becoming overloaded. And those flavors must play nicely with each other and be perfectly balanced. Roasted carrots, for example, are savory, but they're also sweet, so I cook them in olive oil, salt, and pepper, then add a drizzle of balsamic vinegar, which is both sweet and acidic. Roasting brings out the sugars in the carrots, and the acid in the vinegar gives them an edge and makes the flavors pop.

The most dramatic example of the power of roasting is roasted tomatoes. Plum tomatoes from the grocery store have absolutely no flavor—in summer or winter. If you bite into a raw one blind-folded, I'm not even sure you could identify it as a tomato. But toss it in olive oil, sprinkle it with salt and pepper, and slow-roast it to caramelize the sugars in the tomatoes, and they taste like the best summer tomatoes you've ever eaten. It's like magic!

Almost every recipe, whether savory or sweet, needs an edge. Savory things tend to need something acidic, and sweet things tend to need something bitter to give them more depth of flavor. If you're making something with sweet chocolate, vanilla is an important addition, not only because of its intense flavor but also because it's a little bitter, to balance the sweetness. Good vanilla is one of my favorite ingredients, and I want it to have a presence. I might put in two teaspoons if I'm making something like a chocolate mousse, or even a tablespoon plus vanilla seeds if I'm making something like Crème Brûlée, where vanilla is the dominant flavor. For my Outrageous Brownies, the bitterness of three tablespoons of instant coffee granules and two tablespoons of pure vanilla extract cuts the sweetness of the chocolate and makes the overall flavor so much more complex and interesting. You don't know the coffee and vanilla are in there, but they make the chocolate taste delicious. Similarly, adding brewed coffee to chocolate gives the chocolate more depth of flavor, too. Beatty's Chocolate Cake is actually made with a whole cup of coffee in it. It's stunning what a difference it makes in the cake and frosting, and yet it's hard to identify it as coffee.

A good example of finding the right balance of flavors is a lentil soup I worked on in 2003. I started by sautéing lots of onions, leeks, celery, and carrots with thyme until the vegetables were tender and sweet, then added good homemade chicken stock and French lentils and simmered it for an hour. It was delicious, but there was just something missing. I asked my assistant Barbara to taste it and she thought it was delicious, but it kept nagging at me. What was missing? Finally, I went to the fridge and grabbed a bottle of red wine vinegar and added just two tablespoons to that big pot of soup. I said to Barbara, "Taste it now." The edge of the acidic but flavorful vinegar really brought out all the flavors of the soup. Now it was *really* delicious, and Barbara said, "Wow, that is amazing!" A small splash of the right ingredient transformed a perfectly good soup into something bold and bright that you couldn't stop eating.

I remember another adventure with lentils, when I tried to re-create a classic warm French lentil salad, which is a staple in Paris bistros. I kept making it over and over again, but I kept feeling there was something wrong. I was having lunch with a French friend of mine in Paris, and I asked her about it. She told me the secret that apparently only French people know: take a turnip and cook it with the lentils—and then throw the turnip away! The reason I hadn't been able to figure out the missing flavor was because the vegetable wasn't even in the salad! Only the *flavor* of the turnip was there. I came back to East Hampton, made the warm lentil salad again, and it was exactly what I was looking for! *Done!*

Pairing the right ingredients is also an important part of the process of building flavor. How do I know when it's right? I actually think I have a good flavor memory—if I taste something once, I can usually remember most of the flavors in it. As I said, when I'm starting on a recipe, I need to have a strong sense of where I'm going, or I never actually finish working on the recipe. If I know where I'm going, I keep refining and developing until I hear that little *ping* in my head that says, *Yes! Nailed it!*—and then I know I'm done.

And it's not just that one little taste that's important to me. I also want to know what it's like to sit down and eat it for dinner. Sometimes that one spoonful is deliciously intense for a taste, but maybe it's too intense to eat for the whole dish. I'm thinking about all of this when I'm developing a recipe. I want to know: If you make this dish, will you keep thinking about it because it's so good? Or have you had enough after one taste, and you're done? Does the chocolate cake call my name from the refrigerator, or do I never want to eat it again? I've spent weeks developing a recipe only to discard it entirely because it was a little boring, too flavorful, too hard to make, or the ingredients were too hard to find. Some perfectly good recipes ended up in the "trash" file because they didn't do *everything* I wanted them to do.

Recently, I made a Greek chicken and lemon soup called avgolemono. I love chicken and I love lemon, but each time I make that soup, the flavors leave me confused. This time, I made one that I thought was pretty good, but I still wasn't sure if I wanted to eat an entire bowl. Jeffrey came home, and we had it for lunch. The soup was interesting but a little "quiet" when I started eating it. Then, the more I ate, the more I loved it—an experience I'd actually never had before. The lemon bubbled up and the flavor seemed to get stronger. Did the soup get more intense as it sat in the bowl? Was it like a fine wine that needed to breathe? I don't know the answer, but I'll keep testing until I find out.

Arriving at the right texture is complicated, too. I never want something to be boring, like puréed baby food. One spoonful can be delicious, but if every spoonful tastes exactly the same, I'm bored out of my mind. That's where my need for texture comes in. I have two perfect examples of how to play with texture in *Go-To Dinners*.

Creamy Potato Fennel Soup on its own could be one of those sad, boring purées, which is why I rarely make puréed soups. But I saw that my friend Erin French from the Lost Kitchen in Maine did something with soup that was really interesting. Before she poured the soup into the bowl, she placed delicious garnishes in the center, then poured the puréed soup around the garnishes. I tried the same thing—I put cubed creamy goat cheese, big toasted croutons, and crumbled bacon in the middle of shallow soup bowls and poured the puréed potato fennel soup around it. Now, instead of baby food, each spoonful is a choose-your-own-adventure when the creamy soup combines with each crunchy, flavorful garnish, and it's *never* boring.

Even a salad like Winter Greens with Stilton & Hazelnuts can be a symphony of flavor and texture. The greens—soft butter lettuce, spicy arugula, and slightly bitter, crisp Belgian endive and radicchio—partner with pungent, creamy English Stilton, crunchy hazelnuts, and a bright lemon Dijon dressing to engage all the senses.

Some recipes are more elusive than others. When I make

something over and over and still can't get it right, I generally put it away for six months and then come back to it later. Pity the poor Boston Cream Pie, which is not a pie at all, but a vanilla cake layered with vanilla pastry cream and topped with a shiny chocolate glaze. I'd heard of it and knew what it looked like, but I had never actually tasted one. When I was on a book tour in Boston, we stopped to get a Boston Cream Pie for the trip home (if not there, where?). It was totally disappointing, so I decided to tackle it myself. For the next six years, I promised to include it in my following book, but it was always a sad runner-up, because I was searching for a balanced flavor and texture that I just couldn't find.

I made so many Boston Cream Pies that I could do it in my sleep. The "pie" and I seemed to be heading for a breakup. Each time I made one, I ended up with a cake that was just another boring variation on vanilla and chocolate. Sometimes the chocolate flavor of the glaze was so strong that you couldn't even taste the vanilla in the cake or pastry cream. It's not just the flavors that are important to me; it's how they bubble up and balance each other—you taste one, then the other, then the last—and they all have equal intensity.

I decided what it needed was another layer of flavor that would make the vanilla and chocolate more edgy, so I tested adding an acidic orange note to each element of the cake. I added grated orange zest to the cake batter and Grand Marnier to the pastry cream, and, finally, brushed the cakes with a "soak" of freshly squeezed orange juice, sugar, and Grand Marnier. The cake and pastry cream were now strong enough to balance the chocolate glaze, and oh my God, it was amazing. After all that time and all those failed tests, the recipe finally made its debut in *Modern Comfort Food*. It was worth the wait.

I'm never satisfied with the flavor and texture until I hear that *ping* in my head that signals, *That's it, that's exactly what I'm looking for!* I'm like an orchestra conductor trying to get the carrots and turnips to do what they're supposed to do. *We're working together here. No divas!* It's an arduous process, but I love doing it, and when I'm finished, I know people will love the dish, and I know that when they make it, the recipe will come out perfectly every time.

My television show had to have the right combination of ingredients, too—the recipes, of course, and a theme to pull them together. But it was really important to me that each episode be real—these were my actual friends, not actors playing "friends," and the parties were actual parties that I might have. And, as with any party I might host, they had to be fun.

Fun wasn't even a question when I invited Susan Stroman to come on the show with a Mystery Guest, and she brought her dear friend Mel Brooks. Mel is possibly the funniest man on the planet, but what you might not know about him is that he is a serious wine connoisseur who consults with sommeliers around the world. He is also exceptionally fit. When you dine with him, he's very disciplined and eats only half of what he's served to maintain his fabulous Hollywood physique.

That's *not* the Mel who showed up the day we filmed. I thanked him for coming, and he said, "Free meal!"—which made me laugh uncontrollably. Then he ate that free meal like it was his last supper before the gallows. After the Salmon Blini hors d'oeuvres, I served him a bowl of my Cream of Wild Mushroom Soup. He ate the *entire* bowl and asked for more!! "I want MORE SOUP!"—banging his silverware on the table for emphasis.

"Mel," I warned, "you have to pace yourself because you're going to have to eat several bowls of soup while we film each take for the show." That didn't deter him. He finished the second bowl, then the third, and after that, he dug into the Parmesan Chicken—

again and again! Finally, I put a giant wedge of Stilton and a plate of pears in the middle of the table for dessert, and Mel pulled the cheese close to him and asked, "And what are the others having?"

At the end of the dinner, the man who had arrived chanting "Free meal!" pulled out a hundred-dollar bill, slapped it on the table, and said, "I'm gonna pay for this meal, I insist; I'm not kidding! This is the best meal I've had in years!" (In my mind, I could hear the director saying, "Can I get a close-up of that hundred-dollar bill, please?") It was definitely one of the most fun shows I ever filmed. Just thinking about it makes me laugh.

Another memorable episode was when Elmo, my favorite Muppet, and his creator, Kevin Clash, came to East Hampton to cook with me. The story was that Elmo would stop at Bridgehampton Florist to pick up a bouquet for me while Kevin and I made Maryland crab cakes at the barn. Then Elmo would join us, and we'd go to the beach.

As Kevin and I were cooking, I remember thinking *Oh, I hope Elmo gets here soon so we can leave for the beach.* He was so real to me that, for a moment, I actually forgot Elmo couldn't do anything without Kevin! My Muppet friend is still real to me, and I hope he comes back.

People who didn't understand that the guests on my show were my friends in real life often wrote to see if they could cook with me. Barbara handled my correspondence and always sent polite letters explaining how the show worked. One day, she came to me and said, "I think I did something terrible." She'd offhandedly dismissed a letter from Jennifer Garner because she apparently didn't realize who she was.

Barbara's response to Jennifer was perfectly lovely: these are Ina's actual friends, not famous guests. But I had an instinct about her. She seemed smart, funny, and so grounded, very un-Hollywood. She even had her own national line of organic baby food made from ingredients grown on her family's farm in Oklahoma. I thought she was someone I could have fun with. I reached out to her when we were shooting an episode in Los Angeles, made a date to cook together, and, as we both suspected, felt an instant connection. Jen may be gorgeous and talented, but she also has such depth and an amazing heart. She gets up at five in the morning to make homemade English muffins for her kids. She gardens. And she says her primary job is the work she does for Save the Children. All in addition to being a very busy actress!

I happened to be there on the day of her fortieth birthday, and she invited me to come to her party that night. Not a red-carpet event—a real party for her *real* friends, forty lovely, interesting women who were told to come wearing their sweats, ponytails, and no makeup. It was the warmest, coziest LA party ever.

We've been friends ever since, and I'm a huge fan of her *Pretend Cooking Show*. After one of my events in LA, we planned a dinner that was typically casual—we met at a local In-N-Out Burger, where I released my inner germaphobe by cleaning all the empty tables in the joint (the people who looked up from their burgers to witness the spectacle probably thought I was crazy!) before she arrived. Jen and I can have a good time anywhere.

There have been many high points doing my show, like getting to know Jen, and then sometimes there's magic. I was in the room where it happened when the cast of *Mary Poppins Returns* visited while I was filming my TV series *Cook Like a Pro*. My friends the director Rob Marshall and producer John DeLuca had just finished making *Mary Poppins Returns* and suggested I invite the stars, Emily Blunt and Lin-Manuel Miranda, to be on my show along with them. I loved the idea of cooking with Emily, an actress who starred in so many of my favorite films, not to mention Lin-Manuel, the genius behind *Hamilton* and Emily's costar in the imaginative sequel to the Disney classic.

A few days before we were supposed to film the show, Rob called and said, "I think you should see the movie before we film together." It wasn't out yet, and I was dying to see it! He set up a private screening for me the next day. From the moment the lights went down and I saw the Disney logo, I was sobbing, dancing, singing, and having the time of my life. I thought I was alone and had no idea the projectionist was sitting behind me, watching me act like a crazed ten-year-old.

I couldn't stop thinking about the movie on the way home; then I had a flash of inspiration. *Oh my God, I want the show to look just like the movie.* I called the rental company to get a pink-and-white striped tablecloth. I ordered ribbons and candy-colored *anything* that would evoke a fanciful English tea and planned a centerpiece of meringues, cupcakes, and other confections on cake stands.

Then I realized . . . I'd just been *directed* by Rob Marshall, who did it brilliantly. Instead of telling me what to do, he showed me the film to give me the context and tools to help me find my inspiration. That's why actors love him so much—he gently guides them to where they need to go, and eventually, they get there on their own with their own creativity.

I planned the show so it would be perfect. But when we were getting ready that morning, I felt a little nervous. Olivia, who had been my producer and was now also directing me, came over and said, "You're really worried about this, aren't you?" Worried? "I'm *really* worried," I told her. "I feel like I'm responsible for Rob and John and these great actors, and I want to be sure I do a good job."

She said the words that made me feel a thousand times better: "You don't have to worry about it—they're all professionals. They'll know exactly what to do." Phew! She was so right; I didn't have to control it. I just had to let the magic happen.

Rob and John were entirely at home. Fifteen years of friendship will do that. Lin-Manuel was charming, game for anything, and the first to admit he didn't know much about cooking. Haricots verts? "I have no idea what those are," he said. "I thought it was a type of font, like Comic Sans."

As Mary Poppins would say, Emily was "practically perfect" in the kitchen. Armed with enormous oven mitts and looking gorgeous the whole time, she expertly made her mother's insanely delicious roast potatoes as if she had been doing a cooking show her whole life.

I completely forgot the cameras were there. We all just had a really good time together and made one of my all-time favorite shows.

Emily's English Roasted Potatoes

SERVES 6 TO 8

Kosher salt

3 pounds large Yukon Gold
   potatoes, peeled and 1½ to
   2-inch diced

½ cup vegetable oil

Coarse sea salt or fleur de sel

Minced fresh parsley

Preheat the oven to 425 degrees.

Bring a large pot of water with 2 tablespoons kosher salt to a boil. Add the potatoes, return to a boil, lower the heat, and simmer for 8 minutes. Drain the potatoes, place them back in the pot with the lid on, and shake the pot roughly for 5 seconds to rough up the edges. *Carefully* transfer the potatoes in one layer to a baking rack set over a sheet pan. Set aside to dry for at least 15 minutes. (They can sit uncovered at room temperature for several hours or in the fridge for up to 6 hours.)

Pour the oil onto another sheet pan, tilt the pan to distribute the oil, and place the pan in the oven for 5 to 7 minutes, until the oil is smoking hot. Transfer the potatoes carefully into the oil (I use a large metal spatula) and toss them lightly to coat each potato with the hot oil. Evenly spread out the potatoes and lower the oven temperature to 350 degrees. Roast for 45 minutes to one hour, turning the potatoes occasionally with tongs, until very browned and crisp on the outside and tender and creamy inside.

Transfer to a serving platter, sprinkle generously with 1½ to 2 teaspoons sea salt and parsley and serve hot.

La Vie en Rose

Jeffrey and I found ourselves in a very happy place. It was like we had spent our lives building an airplane, we'd learned how to fly it, and now we could cruise along and just enjoy the ride. I was deep into writing cookbooks and filming the cooking show, and Jeffrey had gone from being the dean to teaching graduate business courses at Yale and writing books, both of which he found very satisfying.

Of course, Jeffrey makes appearances on my show. When he was the dean of the Yale School of Management, a student on the school newspaper came to interview him. The student asked if Jeffrey was actually the "doofus" people see on my show or if that was an act he put on. It makes me laugh every time I think about that question. Jeffrey's not only the kindest, smartest, funniest guy I know, but he has succeeded in three very different worlds—he was a New York City investment banker, undersecretary of commerce in the Clinton administration, and dean of the Yale business school. All the while, he has taught business and foreign policy classes at Columbia University, New York University, and now at Yale; written for *The New York Times* and had a monthly column for *BusinessWeek*; and authored many wonderful books along the way. If anyone thinks that all he does is love my cooking, well, they're partially right, but he is so much more than that.

We had built a great life together, and we were very content, simply enjoying ourselves. It was a time of close friends, wonderful small dinner parties, and traveling to Paris often, with side trips to Amsterdam, Stockholm, Milan, and Provence. I couldn't have known this in advance, but living in Paris is a totally different experience from visiting as a tourist. As a tourist, you check into a hotel and hit the streets to see museums, go to restaurants, and enjoy the nightlife, because you never know when you'll be back. Having an apartment in Paris means that we can enjoy all the comforts of home but still spend our time in different ways than in East Hampton and New York. One of the first things we decided was that we would *not* have a television because we'd rather sit in a café with a glass of wine than binge old episodes of *Law & Order* or rewatch *The Crown*.

Gradually, we developed a routine. We'd get up in the morning, go to a café for breakfast—the *same* café every day—and order the *same* café crème and tartine, which is a fresh baguette slathered with French butter and raspberry jam. (It's so simple and delicious that I joke that if I flew to Paris, had my crème et tartine, and flew home again, the trip would have been worth it.)

While we're having our breakfast, we plan our day, which is basically to follow our noses. Our lives at home are overscheduled, so in Paris we try not to have a plan at all. If it's a beautiful day, we'll walk along the Seine or stroll through the street market, filling my straw basket with fresh vegetables and maybe a rotisserie chicken. Or we'll go back to the apartment and read or, better still, do *nothing*, the greatest gift when you're playing hooky from a busy life.

We love making plans with friends. We've gotten to know so many people there—both French and American—and each one lives in Paris for a different reason. Since Paris is the most popular travel destination in the world, we also have lots of friends come to visit us. My favorite day in Paris is to invite someone to dinner, spending the day cooking something simple and puttering around the apartment. We also love to go out to lunch or dinner with friends—never a big fancy restaurant but rather a small bistro or brasserie. We've enjoyed so many memorable meals and good times, but one that I'll never forget was a lunch with Nora Ephron and her husband Nick Pileggi on the afternoon of Christmas Eve, 2011.

I met Nora for the first time in 1999, when she sat opposite me at our friend James Lapine's fiftieth birthday party. She was sitting next to Jeffrey, and I heard her say, "So, tell me about yourself." Knowing that Jeffrey never talks about himself, I piped up, "If you can get him to tell you anything you're a better reporter than anyone I know!"

She was a great journalist and writer (and the writer and director of many of my favorite films, including *Julie & Julia*), but even she couldn't crack that code. Jeffrey flipped the conversation and started asking *her* questions. A friendship was born, particularly after she sent me the recipe for the insanely delicious truffle sandwich that we both loved from the restaurant La Petite Maison in Nice.

In December 2011, Nick and Nora were in Paris, and we met them with mutual friends for lunch at Le Récamier, a restaurant known for its amazing soufflés. Paris was all dressed up in its Christmas finery, and the winter's day was unusually bright and clear. Inside the restaurant, the conversation was dotted by laughter, and since it was Christmas in Paris, we ordered a bottle of delicious champagne. At one point, Nora raised her glass to make a toast and said, "To better times!" We all laughed hysterically because of course there could be no better time! We all thought, *Life just doesn't get better than this!*

Tragically, Nora died six months later. What no one knew at

the lunch was that she had been battling leukemia and decided to tell no one, so the moment in that restaurant was pure Nora Ephron. The irony of her toast was known only to Nick and herself, and she kept it a secret so the people around her would be happy. I'm glad that a perfect Paris lunch was one of her memories, and will always be one of mine.

Sometimes, when friends come to Paris, we love to plan a special outing. We discovered that there was a Venetian water taxi we could rent for a twilight cruise on the Seine. It's a small, elegant wooden boat that's open in the back, the perfect setting for a picnic of champagne and hors d'oeuvres. When our friends Rob and John came to visit, we took them on a sunset cruise. They were so delighted that they spontaneously stood up and belted out every song from *Gigi* (and any other French songs they knew) while we glided past the Eiffel Tower. It was the best show in Paris that night!

One year, friends were coming to spend New Year's Eve with us, and we decided to take them to a great Paris bar before a midnight dinner of Lemon Capellini with Caviar at home. But which great bar? I made a list of six possibilities, arranged for a car and driver for the evening, and set out with Jeffrey in search of the perfect place. I love whiskey sours, so my test was to see which bar was the most Parisian *and* made the best whiskey sours.

We visited every single one of those six bars. One place was too fancy, another was as quiet as a library, and one, with an underground twenty-something vibe, was *way* too cool for us. I've forgotten the fourth and fifth choices, which evaporated in my whiskey sour haze, but the sixth, the bar at Le Meurice, a hotel built in 1835, had everything I wanted: dark wood, frescoes, soft lighting, comfortable chairs, and a master barman who concocted a flawless cocktail. Just like when I'm testing recipes, I heard that *ping* in my head. This was the perfect Paris bar! After all those whiskey sours, I insisted that Jeffrey take me to Flores for something to eat, but as we were getting ready to leave, someone in the bar decided to send us each a glass of champagne. *I'm going to have to drink this too?!* It was going to be a long night—but a fun one!

One of the things I love most in Paris is being invited to a French dinner party. The evening starts late, usually around nine p.m. One night, our hostess, an incredible cook, served drinks in the living room, and it was casual and fun. But as I looked around, I noticed there was no dining room. *How's this going to happen?* I wondered. But like most Parisian women, she had it all under control.

Offstage, while we were having drinks, a table was set up in the foyer (by elves?), complete with beautiful china, silver, and crystal, and we sat down to the best dinner I'd ever had. My friend had created a menu where each course could be served with my favorite wine—Château d'Yquem Sauternes. In fact, it's one of the best wines in the world, but it's a sweet dessert wine, so it was hard to imagine drinking it through an entire meal. The first course, foie gras, is classically served with Sauternes, so that was wonderful. Then she served lobster with grapefruit, and it was amazing with Sauternes, and finally, my favorite—a French apple tart for dessert. I'll never forget that simple but oh so elegant dinner. Afterward, we moved to her library for espresso, drinks, and chocolates, and when we came out, poof! The table was gone!

There was something magical about dining in an unexpected place. The foyer! The French don't assign a single purpose to a room: their approach is more fluid, and that element of surprise elevates the meal. It was so inspiring to experience this in person.

This is the thing about being in Paris. I always say that you can't be inspired sitting at home alone by yourself. You have to go out into the world and see what people are doing, and that will trigger something else in you, and then you'll do it your way. That's exactly what Paris has done for me. It opened a world I would never have had the opportunity to see or be inspired by. I get ideas about food, flowers, design, architecture . . . everything. As the writer Adam Gopnik wrote, "Everyday things in Paris are wonderful." You don't need to spend a lot of money in Paris to be inspired; you just need to go out in the street and smell the baguettes, watch the people, and breathe it all in. That's what I loved when we went to Paris during our camping trip in 1972, and that's exactly what I love about it today. As Jeffrey said in his letter to me so long ago, *We'll go back to Paris when we can afford an apartment and we'll do exactly the same things we loved when we only had five dollars a day.*

As you know, when life is everything I want it to be, the part of me that thrives on a challenge is always looking ahead to the next one—the puzzle that keeps me thinking, the problem I want to solve, the goal I'd do anything to accomplish, the idea that sticks in my head and gets my adrenaline pumping.

During this time, I thought a way to grow my business could be to partner with food companies to produce high-quality Barefoot Contessa products. Lots of companies, including Target and Williams Sonoma, had approached me. The hard part was knowing when to say yes and when to say no. When I was making those decisions, I never gave a thought to "building my brand."

In fact, I believe that you don't build a brand; you just do what's true for you every day, and then one day, you realize that you have a brand. *I* was Barefoot Contessa, so I had to be my own compass: make the right decisions and hold them to my standards. It's a big responsibility to be accountable to yourself and to figure out what feels right. But it's the only way I work.

Some noes were really easy. One company wanted to make a line of Barefoot Contessa fertilizer! (I thought, *You want to put my name on your shit?*) Another wanted to do a line of Barefoot Contessa clothes, which was bizarre because I notoriously wear the same thing every day. It would be a very small line of clothing.

My choices were always organic. I had originally written cookbooks to help people cook delicious meals easily at home. But some people find cooking very challenging, and although I resisted television because my first experience was so awful, I saw it as an effective way to actually *show* people how to cook—how to cream butter, sift dry ingredients together, and bake a cake. It's not easy, and it's great to see someone doing it. I used to wonder why I had the nerve to write cookbooks and film a cooking show when I have no formal cooking education. But as time went on, I realized that all the things I didn't know how to do when I started became what I could actually teach an audience. No one needs to know how to make spun sugar, but I could answer something as simple as: Should you scrub or peel a carrot, and is it better to cut it straight across or diagonally? (I prefer scrubbing, and diagonally cut looks more elegant.)

Then I thought, maybe I'd take it a step further than TV and cookbooks and partner with a company to develop a cake mix so people can simply open a box, add butter and eggs, and serve the same Coconut Cupcakes as if they'd made them from the recipe in *The Barefoot Contessa Cookbook*.

My friend Frank Newbold and I worked together on this idea, and we approached it by doing local research. We visited specialty food stores all over Manhattan, looking for the products with the best quality and packaging. Stonewall Kitchen was the star on every shelf. I learned that the company was founded in Maine by Jonathan King and Jim Stott, who began by selling their homemade orange marmalade at a local farmers' market. When the line of customers at their table got longer and longer, they turned their hobby into a booming business and distributed their products all over the country. We tested a lot of their products and loved the quality. I sensed we had a lot in common and called them.

Later, they told me they were so thrilled to hear I was on the line that they thought they should keep me waiting for a few seconds, so I'd think they were really busy. We had a great conversation that led to a partnership called Barefoot Contessa Pantry. It was fun working with Jonathan and Jim on the thirty-five recipes we included in the Pantry: Coconut Cupcakes, Outrageous Brownies, all favorites from my cookbooks.

My first goal was to ensure that each product's quality was outstanding. Everything produced by Stonewall Kitchen had to taste exactly like the original recipe, and we tested and retested them until they did. Jim and Jonathan's standards were as high as mine when we developed the products and designed the packaging, so I ended up with exactly what I wanted: good mixes with quality ingredients that people could pull out of their pantry and make at home. The line was a total success.

After five wonderful years with Stonewall Kitchen, ingredient prices were going up, and we were faced with the choice of lowering the quality or raising the price. We didn't think either option was a good one, so we ended the partnership, but I remained friends with Jonathan and Jim.

My second partnership adventure was with a company called Contessa Premium Foods, which had its own set of challenges. Initially, I became acquainted with the company because they were trying to stop me from using the name *Contessa* (a word that's been around since the twelfth century, so what's that about?). I hate litigation—it's an expensive, prolonged, and unhappy process—so when the company changed management and the new CEO called to see if we could find a better solution, I listened. Instead of suing each other, we decided to work together and start a line of frozen Barefoot Contessa dinners.

Now, instead of cooking or even just adding eggs to a cake mix, people could buy my Five-Cheese Penne or Tequila Lime Chicken in the grocery store and keep it in the freezer for nights when there wasn't time to make dinner from scratch. I did all the heavy lifting to make sure that each recipe turned out the way it should. I tasted everything, and if it was off by a single red pepper flake, I corrected it before it went into production.

I was so proud of the products we made—until, a few years into the business, the parent company was sold. The new owners called to assure me that everything was fine and they would take care of everything *for* me, but what I heard was, "Don't worry your pretty little head about this, we'll make all the decisions for you," as though as a woman, I wouldn't be able to make them myself. My "pretty little head" immediately decided to take my name off the products and end the partnership. Fortunately, my contract allowed me to end the deal if the ownership changed.

About four months later, Barbara Libath told me her husband, Tedd, was shopping at a grocery store in Florida and saw that Contessa Premium Foods was still selling my frozen dinners. *What? They can't do that!* I ran to my local grocery store to see if they were there, and they were! The product was our product, the packaging was exactly our original packaging—with our graphics and my actual photograph of the food!—and the only difference was that the tiny photograph of me had been replaced by one of some other brunette, who was supposed to look like me! When I first saw the products, even I was fooled! I was shocked and devastated that these new owners had the audacity to sell my products without my permission!

I had to stop the company from selling the dinners, but they refused. I decided they thought they were dealing with a "girl" and that I would back down, but they clearly didn't know this "girl." Remember, a barrier to me isn't a stop sign; it's a call to action. I called my wonderful lawyer, Chuck Googe at Paul, Weiss, a major big-deal international law firm, who had negotiated the original deal, and asked him to write a letter demanding that they stop. I figured maybe they would realize I meant business, but sadly that didn't work. The next step was to hire a litigator to sue them.

What I didn't know is that IBM and General Electric can afford to hire Paul, Weiss to litigate a case—but a cookbook writer? I had no idea what I was getting myself into. My lawyer kindly called and said, "You know this is going to be *really* expensive, right? Maybe I can recommend someone else to do this?" But I wanted the best team on the case. He introduced me to one of the top litigators in the firm, and I asked her, "How much will this cost?" The answer was that it would cost more than I could possibly sue them for. Yikes! I needed to get my name back from people who were using it illegally, but I hoped it wouldn't bankrupt us in the process.

First, we filed an injunction to stop them from using my name—to remove all the products from all shelves—immediately, *while* we were preparing the lawsuit. After that, we would sue to get them to stop producing the products at all.

Of course, this was all happening while I was filming my show, so I would spend the days filming and the nights trying to figure out how to win this lawsuit.

I decided the only thing that would work was to sue them for a really scary amount of money for damaging my brand. That might get their attention and let them know I meant business! Then, as my father used to advise, I thought, *What do these guys need to get them to stop?* I suspected they needed six months to develop new packaging for their products. I didn't care if they used my intellectual property—the recipes—for a while; I just didn't want my name on any product I had no control over.

The next morning, I called the litigator with my proposal, and she said, "I've never seen that work." But we didn't have a better option, so she made them an offer: pay us and you have six months to change the packaging on the product. She called me the next day and said they agreed. Bingo! I paid the lawyers, I had a very nice bonus left over after my pain and suffering, and they stopped making the dinners. I don't think it was exactly the way Paul, Weiss was used to operating, but hey, it worked. Afterward, Jeffrey said that having Paul, Weiss do this deal was probably major overkill—kind of like asking Tim Cook, the head of Apple, to come fix my computer—but the crisis was averted, and everyone was satisfied. The best advice I got at the time was, when you're involved in litigation, do anything you need to do to end it as quickly as possible. That's precisely what I did.

Despite our best intentions, my partnerships with Stonewall Kitchen and Contessa Premium Foods ended up being troublesome, and I realized I just didn't like partnerships. I want to produce really good cookbooks that I have total control over and to make fun, informative television shows that people like to watch. I like to do things that are out of the box and maybe a little scary. But sometimes they don't work the way I imagined, and I learn a lot from the experiences. I often say, if you never fall down, you haven't skied hard enough, but after "falling down" twice, I decided that I'd rather work with my own team and have a very good time.

Something else was looming on the horizon and I needed to figure it out: social media. Up until this time, my only full-time employee was Barbara Libath, and we were a great team. She was wonderful, and we could finish each other's sentences. I depended on her for everything, and we had the best time together. But both of us had to admit we had no idea how to tackle social media in a world that required it. We needed someone . . . young!

About the same time, a young woman named Lidey Heuck joined our team. With her millennial enthusiasm for social media, Lidey pressed me to start posting on Instagram. I'm not sure I understood what it was, but I was certain I didn't want to do it. I was on Facebook and had zero interest in adding another chore to my life. "I'm too busy," I told her repeatedly. Finally, Lidey just quietly loaded the Instagram app on my iPhone and put it on my desk.

On January 13, 2014, a foggy Monday morning when I was probably looking for a distraction, I picked up my phone and started playing around with the app. *Oh, this is actually really interesting,* I thought. It's a visual medium, and I love photographs. I took a picture of a turkey I was testing for *Make It Ahead,* pushed a few buttons, and there it was—my first Instagram post. How easy was that?

This is the thing—you can't say you don't like something unless you try it. And I had nothing to lose. I could delete Instagram if I thought it was a waste of time. In this case, *no* became *yes,* because I took the time to experience Instagram and was amazed by how quickly I got into the habit of checking it every morning. I loved thinking of new things to share and following friends and designers to see what they were doing, as well.

If I doubted, as I usually do, that anyone would be interested in the pictures I put up, I was wrong. My followers enjoyed seeing windows into my world and what I was doing—a recipe I made, a gorgeous floral arrangement, my garden in different seasons, a moment with a friend—and I liked connecting with them by reading their comments.

Here's what I've learned from my decades of Barefoot business experiences:

First and foremost, stay true to yourself and your vision instead of focusing on becoming a brand. I ask people I trust for advice, but in the end, I have to do what's right for me.

Swing for the fences! You won't hit a home run every time, but that doesn't mean you should never swing at something. Every time you swing, you learn something.

Limit your liability. What's the worst thing that can happen if it doesn't work? Will it change your life or just be a learning experience? Who and what will it impact? What's the upside if it does work?

Never compromise on quality. Ever. Whether an idea or a partnership succeeded or failed, I was absolutely sure that the product was good. And that's more important than the success of any business. Maybe it wasn't the right idea or the right time, but hopefully, no one ever got an inferior product, whether it was a cookbook, a baking mix, or a frozen dinner.

Don't get in your own way. Try something before you decide it's not right for you.

And if you work up the nerve to take a risk and jump into the pond, make sure you can get *out* of the pond if it's not where you want to be. When I agreed to do the cooking show, I committed to thirteen episodes. If I didn't enjoy it, I had a way out, which made it easier for me to give it a real chance. Same with my partnerships: if the business changed, or the relationship with the supplier didn't work, or I lost control of the product, I knew I could get out whole.

Sometimes it's important to control things, but sometimes the opposite is true—you have to be open and let the universe reveal itself. When I put something out in the world, I stay with it, watching how people react and use it. Then I make the product better or more "usable" and watch what happens. My favorite example of this is how Steve Jobs reserved a blank space on the iPhone for apps before he had any idea what they would be or how people would use them. Instead of controlling the space, he left room for creativity and possibility. And, of course, the rest is history. Balancing these priorities is *really* challenging, but that's the fun part!

Nora and I in Town & Country

Nora Ephron

Dear Ina:

The truffle sandwich:

THINLY SLICED COUNTRY BREAD (PREFERABLY POILANE, AVAILABLE AT
VINEGAR FACTORY ON 3RD)
SALTED BUTTER
SEL DE MER
THINLY SLICED BLACK TRUFFLES

BUTTER THE BREAD, LAY A REALLY NICE LAYER OF TRUFFLES ON IT AND
COVER WITH ANOTHER PIECE OF BUTTERED BREAD.

WRAP IN SARAN WRAP AND PUT IN FRIDGE FOR 24 TO 48 HOURS.

REMOVE FROM FRIDGE , UNDO THE SANDWICH AND SPRINKLE A LITTLE SEL
DE MER ON THE TRUFFLES. PUT SANDWICH BACK TOGETHER (YOU MAY
HAVE TO HOLD THE TWO SIDES TOGETHER WITH TOOTHPICKS) AND FRY
(SAUTE?) ON BOTH SIDES IN BUTTER.

It was great seeing you

Nora

2211 Broadway
New York, NY 10024

It's Always Cocktail Hour
in a Crisis

I always thought the best perk of having a Food Network show was that I could get a reservation in almost any restaurant. But in 2014, *Food Network Magazine* approached me with a proposal I couldn't possibly have imagined. Maile Carpenter, the editor in chief, was planning a special music edition where she paired top rock stars with their favorite Food Network people for a photo shoot. To my total amazement, Taylor Swift chose me! I loved the idea of doing a shoot with her because I'm a huge fan and I play her music all the time while I cook. It's impossible not to feel good when you're listening to "Love Story" and "Shake It Off."

As it turned out, while I was listening to her music, Taylor was actually cooking from my books! I had no idea at that time she was a great cook. She told an interviewer that I inspired her to be more confident in the kitchen and to think of cooking as "self-care." How could we possibly not have a fabulous time together?

Instead of just posing for shots, I decided it would be more fun to make something with Taylor and have the photographer take pictures while we cooked. But what should we make? I obsessed for weeks, finally deciding on my Mixed Berry Pavlova because this gorgeous woman reminded me of the dessert named for the famous Russian ballerina Anna Pavlova. It's a beautiful concoction of crisp meringue, airy whipped cream, and (in my version) fresh berries and raspberry sauce.

I prepared all the components, and on the day of the shoot, Taylor and I assembled the dessert together. When we were finished, instead of serving nice little plates of Pavlova, I decided we should just dive in; right there on the counter was my jar of huge silver serving spoons, so I handed one to Taylor and took one myself, and we destroyed that dessert. It was beyond fun, and she was so warm and fascinating. After she left that day, I thought, *Did that really happen?*

The following year, I decided to treat my team to an experience *they'd* never forget, by taking them to Taylor's 1989 World Tour concert at MetLife Stadium in New Jersey. Our squad—Barbara, Lidey, my publicist Kate Tyler, my editor Pam Krauss, and I— put on our Swiftie LED bracelets and entered the stadium, ready for *anything*. Then it was showtime. Sixty thousand exuberant fans cheered Taylor's every move, but it wasn't only her singing that impressed me. She was twenty-five at the time, and between songs, she took a moment to connect with all those young girls— and me! One thing in particular that she said has really stayed with me. She said, "We all get so upset about what's said about us on the internet and social media, but the truth is, what we tell ourselves *about ourselves* is so much worse." I thought it was an incredibly powerful message. Her connection with her audience is much deeper than just entertainment because she relates to how people *feel*. Her songs are about the same struggles that all young women have. She may be Taylor Swift, but she's there for you, listening to and reflecting your inner thoughts. She's not trying to solve your problems, but she's supporting you as you figure them out yourself. And then she tells you to just "shake it off."

One of the highlights in an evening full of highs was when Taylor brought the US Women's National Soccer Team out onstage. They were fresh from their dramatic 2015 World Cup win, and we felt that we were a part of their victory.

The concert ended, but the fun continued at the after-party. After every show, Taylor throws a party for everyone who worked on the show, plus some of her friends. All the eighteen-wheeler trucks that bring the stage sets and equipment make a huge circle in the stadium parking lot, and it becomes a party with music, food, firepits, and Ping-Pong tables. Caught up in the excitement of the night, Kate playfully suggested that we challenge the soccer world champions to a game of beer pong. *Really?*

First, I don't drink beer, and second, I had no idea what beer pong was, so I figured I was off the hook.

"You'll drink wine," Kate said as she dragged me over to the Ping-Pong table to challenge some of the soccer stars. The team accepted our challenge (what were we thinking???), and we were off to the races. At one point, Abby Wambach, one of the most accomplished soccer players in US history, decided to be my coach. The music was so loud that I could barely hear her. "What did you say?" I asked. "Just get the fucking ball in the fucking glass!" she screamed in my ear. That was her advice? I guess that's what works in soccer. Who won? Who cares! We were all winners that night—and confirmed Swifties.

The following years were a time of transition. *Cooking for Jeffrey,* which told our story and included recipes that were special to us, came out in 2016. Then, a sad moment when I had to say goodbye to Barbara, who was retiring and moving to Delaware. It wasn't really goodbye—we were close friends, and she would continue testing recipes. But I wouldn't hear her cheery voice in the morning and know that all was right in our Barefoot Contessa world because Barbara was at its center. She had started working with me when I had begun writing my second cookbook, and she had built the entire business with me. It was heartbreaking to see her go.

We worked on *Cook Like a Pro*, completed the book, filmed the show, and then started a new book and filmed more shows.

Three years passed this way until December 2019, when Lidey left to start her own adventure. I feel that it's my job to teach young people and then send them out into the world to find their own voice. Now I was joined by Rose Brown and Kristina Felix, and with Cindy Massey, my office manager, we established a comfortable routine. But "comfortable" has never been my sweet spot. As I've said before, I need a little edge in my life, a problem to solve, a challenge to meet, and I just wasn't seeing one on the horizon.

My restlessness turned out to be *so* 2019. What happened at the beginning of 2020 gave a new and unimaginable meaning to the concept of challenge. In January, we heard disturbing reports of a deadly new virus in China. By early March, the drumbeats were louder and more insistent. Something was happening, and it wasn't good. I will never forget sitting with Jeffrey and discussing the situation. He was teaching graduate business courses at Yale, and one of the classes was called "Managing Global Catastrophes," covering everything from the space shuttle explosion to Hurricane Katrina and SARS, the virus that was brilliantly defeated by the world health community in 2003. But this deadly virus was spreading much more rapidly—suddenly, the threat was everywhere—and all signs pointed to a shutdown of the economy and a stay-at-home order.

I wanted to be prepared, so I immediately called my team together. I told them that I thought there was a good chance that we would be quarantined in our houses for the next year or two, until a vaccine could be developed. Even that seemed optimistic because at that time, no vaccine had ever been developed in less than four years. I told them to drop everything they were doing and stock up on as many supplies as they might need for a year. I know they thought I'd lost my mind! But how glad I am that we did it.

The problem was figuring out where to store all the supplies so that everyone who worked for me could feed and take care of themselves and their families for at least a year, maybe two. Like many people, I have a basement that serves as a graveyard for the stuff I don't need and never use but can't bring myself to throw away. It was time to be ruthless. Kristina was with me when I was cleaning out a storage area and found two joke gifts banished to a back shelf—a pair of enormous martini glasses (thank you, Jonathan King and Jim Stott) in one corner and an oversized cocktail shaker (thank you, Rob Marshall and John DeLuca) in another. They were funny at the time but had no future, or so I thought. Kristina stopped me just as I was putting them in the trash. "Not so fast," she said. "Maybe we can do something with them." I couldn't imagine their purpose, but I set them aside and continued cleaning and preparing for the worst.

Jeffrey and I watched the evening news with dread. The virus, or COVID-19 as it came to be called, was officially a pandemic. We knew we were fortunate to have each other and our home, but, like everyone else, we felt vulnerable and frightened. My fears were the same as your fears. We had to navigate the protocols for staying safe, which were confusing because they changed whenever new information became available.

The only sane response was anxiety. I was anxious about catching the virus, MORE anxious about Jeffrey getting sick before a vaccine was developed, anxious about filming the television show when I couldn't work with my crew, anxious about my new book coming out and the one I was supposed to be writing. JUST ANX-IOUS. There was too much going on, and I couldn't imagine doing any of it alone in a lockdown.

One day, I was talking to Kate Tyler about the challenges of pandemic life, when she suggested that I offer advice to my followers on Instagram. At this point, everyone had limited access to markets and had to build meals around random products in their pantries, often things that were there because they didn't want to eat them in the first place. Kate thought it would be helpful if I suggested what people could do with all those dried beans they'd stocked up on, or what to do if a recipe called for buttermilk and they didn't have any.

My first reaction was that I couldn't imagine that I would know the answers to all their questions. But the more I thought about it, the more I realized that everyone, whatever their circumstances, felt stressed and overwhelmed by a situation beyond their control. Good home cooking could be the silver lining of this experience. People were even making sourdough bread! Maybe I could help. I posted a picture of my pantry with the caption "I know so many of you are very anxious about what's to come because I am, too. The one thing we CAN do, though, is cook for the people we love who are sheltered in place with us . . . Tell me what's in your pantry, and I'll think of recipes for you to make."

Immediately, nearly nine thousand people commented and asked questions, everything from "What can I do with orzo?" to "How do I use self-rising flour?" Sharp-eyed observers wanted to know if I actually *ate* the ramen noodles they spied in my pantry, so I followed up with a Ramen Chicken Noodle Soup recipe. I answered as many questions as I could and posted recipes that seemed to fit the mood of the time—mostly comfort food, like tomato soup with a grilled cheese sandwich, a waffle topped with peanut butter and jelly, and macaroni and cheese. My Instagram became a community where people posed questions, found solutions to cooking problems, and bonded with each other. I was amazed not only that I could answer a lot of the questions, but also that my connection with people on Instagram made me feel so much less isolated and lonely. Again, you never know the impact of something until you try it. In those early days of the pandemic, my followers on Instagram actually saved me!

Every day seemed exactly like the one before—a giant blur—and everyone was parked under the same black cloud, fearful of catching the virus; depressed by isolation, social distancing, and the sweeping changes in the way we lived; and worried about the future. It was so grim that it was entirely possible no one was thinking about April Fools' Day. I wanted to do an April Fools' post—not a prank, just a little levity to make us forget our troubles, even for a moment. Time to bring out those giant martini glasses!

"It's always cocktail hour in a crisis!" I posted, tongue in cheek. "During these stressful times, it's really important to keep traditions alive," I told the camera (my iPhone) as I mixed a fresh cosmopolitan with an entire bottle of vodka, poured it into a pitcher, and shook it for exactly thirty seconds in my oversize cocktail shaker. Then I poured the mix into one of the enormous martini glasses I'd found in the basement, the one that could easily have been a birdbath, and picked it up with both hands. "Stay safe, have a very good time, and don't forget the cocktails. *Mmm, delicious!*" I said as I took a sip of the gargantuan cosmo, which was especially funny to those who know me because, while I like a good cocktail, I'm *not* a big drinker.

The world took the video in the spirit in which it was created—it was *fun!* Like a match to dry wood, it caught fire and went everywhere, and messages started pouring in. Suddenly, the one thing everybody wanted was an ice-cold pink cosmo, a reminder that it was still possible to have a laugh and a good time during a pandemic. It was a message we all needed to hear.

My friend Erin French from the restaurant the Lost Kitchen in Maine once wrote, "Sometimes you have to trust that the hard times, the pain and the tragedies in life have purpose. They may make no sense at the time, may bring you to your knees and you will wonder why this hell is happening and if you'll ever get through it. But trust is your trajectory, sending you along your path, and if you listen, learn, heal and grow along the way, things will one day make sense."

I hoped she was right, because *nothing* makes sense during a pandemic. I missed my friends and went to great lengths to stay in touch with them remotely. When it became possible to entertain in a safe, socially distanced way, I seated us at a very long table outside, where, dressed in sweaters and coats, we ate individual servings of baked Pasta with Five Cheeses. It wasn't the same as the intimate dinners and communal plates we'd enjoyed before the pandemic, but it was better than isolation.

Meanwhile, I had to film the show, but I was in East Hampton and my director and crew were stuck in London. I figured, if I could single-handedly make a video of myself drinking a huge cosmopolitan, why couldn't I film a whole show on my own? Yes, I would be responsible for everything: doing my hair and makeup, prepping all the food, organizing the props, setting up two iPhone cameras—one for the large shots and one for the close-ups—setting up the microphone, cooking the recipes, talking to the camera, and all the while making sure the continuity was right—all the jobs usually performed by an entire crew. Now it was just me and my two little iPhones!

How hard could this be? I was ready, willing, and able to jump in and do it. Everyone had to be flexible and resourceful while working at home. I made a lot of rookie mistakes in the beginning—I forgot to turn on the microphone; I placed a pot directly in front of the camera; I didn't silence my cell phone. Eventually, I put together a checklist and became comfortable with the process, and we managed to do a streamlined version of the show. After that, any filming I did in the future was going to be really easy.

We all had to be equally resilient when it was time to release *Modern Comfort Food* in October 2020. Whenever a new book comes out, I normally travel all over the country for speaking engagements and book signings, but this time I wasn't going anywhere. We had to come up with alternative ways to connect with readers, so we set up virtual events with bookstores. We'd ask a friend, someone from the store, or a local food personality to interview me on Zoom, then viewers would submit questions, and we all got to do it safely from our homes.

My favorite Zoom interview was with my friend Jen Garner. Nine thousand people joined that call, from every state in the nation and beyond! No one had to get dressed, get in their car, drive to an auditorium, find a parking space, or sit with thousands of other people. Each person had a front-row seat, and they could stay home in their pajamas.

But the best part of the Zoom "tour" was how intimate it all felt. Jen was at her home (in her sweatpants), I was in my home, and we were having a truly intimate conversation, as though there were only the two of us on the call—no distractions of being onstage with the crowds, the lights, the time clock. And people were watching from all over the world. "Hello from Sweden," I'd see in a comment bubble floating up the screen. I enjoyed these interviews so much that I remember thinking this might have been the best book tour I'd ever done! As Jeffrey says, you never know your good breaks from your bad ones.

I was thrilled when readers connected with my book *Modern Comfort Food*. Seven months into the pandemic, *comfort* was the most important word in everyone's vocabulary. People thought it was serendipitous that I came out with a cookbook about comfort food when people needed it most, but I had given a lot of thought to the topic. When I was planning the book in 2018, I looked around and saw a world that was deeply divided and stressed about the upcoming election, and I thought, *Whatever side you're on in 2020, you'll want food that can make you feel better.* Ultimate Beef Stew, Lobster BLTs, Creamy Tomato Bisque, Hot Spiced Apple Cider—these are all foods that are familiar, cozy, and delicious, like wrapping yourself in a big security blanket. I wanted *Modern Comfort Food* to be that security blanket. Little did I know that the book would come out in the middle of a worldwide pandemic, and we would be stuck at home, trying to cook and comfort ourselves!

At this point in my life, I had been writing cookbooks and filming cooking shows for more than twenty years, and it seemed to be time for me to shake things up. But we were in the middle of a pandemic, so the options were limited. Jeffrey explained to me that the companies that stand still during a crisis, stop all investment because they have no visibility, and just wait for the crisis to end don't fare well. He went on to explain that Andy Grove, the legendary CEO of Intel, told him that businesses that reorganize during a crisis and invest in the future come out way ahead of the competition. (How lucky am I to have the dean of the Yale School of Management as my business adviser?)

I decided to do three things differently. I had no idea if any of them would work, but I thought if I tried several things, maybe one would be successful. As I said, sometimes you have to put ideas out in the world and let the universe (or customers) decide what you do next. First, I decided to open up the Barefoot Contessa brand to include more lifestyle subjects. I proposed two more books: this memoir and a design book, not a pretty coffee-table book but something more like my cookbooks, a "how-to" about table settings, flower arrangements, gardens, interior design, kitchen design—all the things I've loved doing for the past fifty years.

Second, I proposed to Food Network that instead of continuing my cooking show, I launch an interview show called *Be My Guest,* where I'd invite someone interesting to spend the day with me at the barn, talking, cooking, and generally having fun together. And finally, because I always love having one personal project, I decided to renovate our house. My kitchen was twenty-seven years old, and it was way past time for a facelift!

This memoir was my first project. I had been approached by a writer who proposed doing my biography, but a friend pointed out that if *anyone* was going to tell my story, it should be *me.* I was skeptical and worried that the story wouldn't be interesting enough. And, if I committed to doing it, I would have to be open, honest, and vulnerable. A terrifying thought. My mantra is "How easy is that?" but life is not easy—*my* life has been amazing, but it hasn't always been easy. I had spent so much time avoiding the painful periods in my past, especially my childhood, that I wondered if I'd be able to open those doors. And what would be behind them? There was only one way to find out—jump in!

Surprisingly, writing the story of your own life requires boots-on-the-ground research. I started with a huge box of letters from Jeffrey that I'd saved for fifty years. I reread them because they were incredibly detailed—almost like a diary—and brought back many forgotten memories and emotions. Did I really climb out a window and barrel down a makeshift slide at a Dartmouth fraternity party to land in a snowbank? Yes! And apparently, I even enjoyed it.

When it was safe to travel, I took a series of trips, hoping my recollections would be more vivid if the places where they happened were right in front of me. First, I went to the house where I grew up in Connecticut. The neighborhood was prettier than I remembered (the bush where I hid my ugly snow pants so I wouldn't have to wear them to school was still there), but my memories of feeling lonely and unloved were the same: intense and disturbing. It was like visiting a house of horrors. I knew the past couldn't hurt me now, but it's always there deep inside. It's what we do with those feelings that can determine the rest of our lives.

I also went to Washington, DC, to remind myself of our early years there. I visited our first house (which was so much smaller than I remembered) and the second, the enormous one we bought in a rush of optimism and sold with an even greater rush of relief. Then the third house, where we lived for several years before I spotted that advertisement for Barefoot Contessa and made the wild and crazy decision to buy a specialty food store in the Hamptons.

Standing in front of that house, I had an out-of-body experience. I was transported back to 1978, when Jeffrey and I had sat on those front steps, uncertain if our marriage had a future—when he was still hopeful, but I had serious doubts. I didn't have a crystal ball then, so I had no way of knowing the real stakes, that walking away would have meant missing out on a lifetime of happiness. I felt sick thinking I came *this* close to losing Jeffrey and the life we shared. Rationally, I knew we created a better outcome by discussing our issues and working together to solve them. Still . . . what if?

I've never told the story of our near breakup before this memoir, but I hear so much about "Jeffrey and Ina #relationshipgoals" that I decided it was important to talk about it. The crisis was real, and we could have made a terrible mistake. Instead, we listened to each other, changed the things that caused our unhappiness, and ended up with a much stronger relationship. It was a process—even the best marriages are not easy or perfect, and there will always be "for better or for worse" times. What carries you through is how you feel about each other and mutual respect. My friend Maile Carpenter, the remarkable editor of *Food Network Magazine*, who's wise beyond her years, told me that the definition of a good marriage is that each person thinks they got the better deal. That's exactly how I feel about Jeffrey as we approach our fifty-sixth anniversary, and I know he feels the same way about me.

The second idea I had for changing my business came up during the pandemic, too. I've been interviewed so many times in the past twenty years, but now, for the first time, I was getting requests to interview other people. I would be the interviewer, not the subject, which surprised me because I'm not a journalist. Typically, I answer the questions, but now I would be asking them. It was a new frontier, and I was intrigued to see where it would take me.

My first interview was with John Grisham, one of the bestselling authors in the world. I discovered that I loved preparing for the interview, rereading his books, exploring his life, and thinking of questions that would spark an interesting dialogue. John's a great conversationalist with wide-ranging interests, including, surprisingly, Paris and cooking! We had a great time talking on his Zoom book tour, and he explained that he started writing books because his life as a courtroom lawyer wasn't as exciting as he'd thought it would be. He decided to write the stories he wished he'd experienced in court. I asked him, "When did you know your books were going to be successful?" and I was shocked when he told me his first book was a total disaster—no one bought it! No one? John Grisham?

Anyone else would have been defeated by the first failure and thrown in the towel, but John was motivated and did something else—he wrote another book and set it up for success. This time, his agent sold the movie rights first, then the book rights, generating great buzz around the project. That second book was *The Firm.* Thirty-seven consecutive number one bestsellers later, the same John Grisham who couldn't sell a book has become one of the most popular storytellers in the world.

I found his story fascinating, because everybody thinks that successful people are smarter, more talented, or just plain lucky. I don't think it always works that way. The people I've known who are successful have faced enormous challenges, but they didn't let the challenges stop them—they figured out some way over the wall or around the wall, or they just smashed the wall down. In fact, it was exactly those challenges that shaped their success. My conversation with John Grisham, plus my desire to connect with people, inspired me to create my interview show, *Be My Guest.*

Sometimes, if you're lucky, the person sitting next to you at a dinner party turns out to be really interesting, and you have a lively conversation that makes you think, *I want to know more.* I envisioned re-creating that feeling for my viewers by sitting with my guest at the table in the barn and sharing stories about the experiences—including the failures and detours—that made a difference in our lives. We'd talk and bond over a little cooking, because food always brings people together.

When we started filming, my first guest was the best—or maybe the worst?—choice. The best because I had the pleasure of sitting opposite the charming Willie Geist. The *worst* because

Willie is one of the best interviewers in the business—I watch him regularly on NBC's *Sunday Today*—and I must have been crazy to think it was a good idea to start with the master of entre nous. This skilled raconteur talks to actors, singers, writers, entrepreneurs, and politicians without breaking a sweat. He'd interviewed me twice, so I knew firsthand how good he is.

I prepared—well, I overprepared—to the point where I knew more about Willie than his mother and had enough questions to fill multiple interviews. I had no reason to worry. Willie was candid about his setbacks. He said that when he turned twenty-nine, he questioned his career choice and wondered if he even had a future in television. Two of his shows had been canceled, and he was unemployed with no prospects. He considered pivoting to another profession—maybe law?—and a lot of soul-searching followed. But his wife, Christina, always believed in him. Then he received an offer from MSNBC to produce *The Situation with Tucker Carlson,* and one success led to another. Today, Willie Geist is all over NBC, but he didn't get there with a road map or a grand plan. He worked hard and made the most of every opportunity, even when it meant doing a show at four o'clock in the morning.

Every guest was a puzzle waiting to be solved. If I did my homework and found the right pieces, the story would come together. Julianna Margulies told heartbreaking stories about her nomadic childhood and some of the difficult choices she had to make after she became successful. But those choices led her to the life she had always wanted with her wonderful husband, Keith, and son, Kieran. Julianna and I had just met, but our connection was so real—when she cried, I cried with her.

Misty Copeland's story is stunning. As a young girl, living in a motel with her mother and five siblings, she joined the local Boys & Girls Club, where a dance teacher took her under her wing. Misty fought her way through poverty and prejudice, breaking barriers, making hard choices, and becoming American Ballet Theatre's first Black female principal dancer. And that's just the beginning of her amazing story.

My guest Marcus Samuelsson survived the devastating loss of his mother in childhood in Ethiopia. He and his sister were adopted by a family in Sweden, where his adopted grandmother taught Marcus how to cook and set him on the path of becoming an internationally acclaimed chef and philanthropist.

My dear friend Rob Marshall's story is equally inspiring. He was a very successful dancer on Broadway, starring in shows like *Cats,* until an injury dashed that dream and forced him to pivot to a different career—first as a choreographer, then as a Broadway director, and finally as a movie director. Ultimately, Rob, with his partner John DeLuca, won the Academy Award for Best Picture for their first film, *Chicago.* Would that have happened if Rob hadn't injured himself? Who knows?

Another guest was my friend Emily Blunt, who had a terrible stutter as a child and never thought about acting as a career until a teacher noticed that she didn't stutter when she entertained her friends with funny accents. The teacher suggested she try out for the school play. Acting onstage gave Emily the confidence and skill to manage her stutter and, as we all know, changed the course of her life. Emily had thought she would be a translator, but thankfully, that one teacher saw something no one else did.

In each case, my guests' successes were hard-won. I learned, and continue to learn, from their stories that seemingly insurmountable problems not only make us who we are but can propel us to exactly the place we want to be.

Here's what I've learned from my own difficult childhood. It's true that what goes in early goes in deep. I will never truly lose that critical voice in my head that says, "Don't do it, it will turn out badly," for as long as I live. But I also think that those years of debilitating fear taught me enormous compassion, maybe even for my parents. One day, well into my adulthood, my father told me how bad he felt about his cruelty to me when I was growing up. He knew he was wrong and was sorry. It brings a tear to my eye even thinking about it twenty years later. The fact that he acknowledged his behavior made it possible for us to have a better relationship and spend more meaningful time together before he died. Unfortunately, I didn't have that experience with my mother, because she couldn't express emotion. It still hurts to remember how my parents treated me, but I understand that they spent their entire lives trapped in their own cages with the doors wide open.

The second thing a troubled childhood taught me is to work hard and swing for the fences. What's the worst that could happen if I failed? Everything I experienced made me stronger, and I'm ready to deal with whatever comes along.

Today, when I walk up the street, and someone smiles, leans in, and whispers, "Ina, I love you!" I always remember my father telling me, "No one will ever love you." It's like this private cosmic joke for me. Did my life unfold this way *because* I wanted to overcome my parents' harsh criticism? Or *despite* it? I'll never know, but one thing I know for sure is that everything changed when I met Jeffrey. This is when my life began. We all need only one person to believe in us, and for me, that person is Jeffrey. With his love and support, I learned to believe in myself and found happiness and peace.

Epilogue

I was planning the next season of *Be My Guest* when I received word that *60 Minutes* wanted to film a segment about me. *60 Minutes*? Wouldn't my parents have been shocked to see me interviewed on the show? I've watched *60 Minutes* since it debuted in black and white in 1968. On Sunday nights, I have a Pavlovian response to the familiar sound of the ticking stopwatch. I curl up on the couch and don't move until it's over. Sometimes when I meet with my team on Monday mornings, I have to tell them all about the show the night before.

I wasn't sure how I fit into the most successful show in television history's award-winning investigations and profiles of legendary artists like Paul McCartney. But they seemed to have a plan.

The producer Michael Karzis and his team lived up to their reputation for stunning excellence. They were forensic in researching the details of my biography and fact-checked to the point where I found myself having to dig deep in my memory to answer their questions—and this was my life!

I'm not going to lie. I was pretty nervous the day we filmed. While the *60 Minutes* crew set up the shoot, I set up the drink I would make and prepared for the sit-down interview. I was going to be in the hot seat, and my one goal was to not say anything I'd regret later, because I knew I'd regret it for the rest of my life.

Wait, I know how this works, I reminded myself when I sat with Sharyn Alfonsi, the Emmy Award–winning correspondent conducting the interview. On *Be My Guest,* when I'm the interviewer, I try to make each person feel relaxed, comfortable, and safe, which is exactly what Sharyn did with me. We had such a good time! I stopped thinking about the camera as soon as we started talking.

Sharyn began the interview by saying, "Everyone sees you as just walking around with a big cosmopolitan in your hand, having a very good time. But you worked really hard to get there—before buying Barefoot Contessa, while you worked in the White House, you went to business school, taught yourself how to cook, and renovated old houses in Washington." Sharyn went on to say that my success hinged on "hard work, shrewd business sense, and leaving nothing to chance."

I was stunned. Sharyn and *60 Minutes* had a view of my life that was completely different from the story I had told myself—and others. I had always thought that I did what I loved and just got lucky along the way. In fact, when I was given a Matrix Award for women in media, that's exactly what I said. Addressing my fellow honorees—amazing women like Tina Fey and Sheryl Crow—and the audience, I spoke about how lucky I was at each phase of my career because it seemed that whatever I was most interested in doing was exactly what the world wanted at that time. I was lucky that I was interested in food and cookbooks at a time when the world was interested in food and cookbooks. I was lucky that Food Network was looking for home cooks when they found me, and lucky that they refused to take no for an answer. Lucky.

I finished and took my seat on the stage, right next to Oprah.

Immediately, she turned and smacked me on the arm, saying, "You weren't lucky. You make your own luck."

Did Oprah just smack me in front of a thousand people?

"Actually, I have been lucky," I started to say.

And then she smacked me again.

When Lesley Stahl got up to introduce the next person, she said, "Why do successful women always say they're lucky, and successful men say they got there by the force of their talent?"

Wait? Did Lesley Stahl just smack me, too?

I kept thinking, *Am I crazy? Haven't I been lucky? How much does luck really count in success?*

Soon after the *60 Minutes* filming, I had dinner with my friends Rob Marshall and John DeLuca, and Rob shared a story that answered that very question. When he was all of twenty-three and the dance captain of *The Rink,* the Tony Award–winning Broadway show starring Liza Minnelli, she told him something that stayed with him his entire life—and I'm paraphrasing here—"Be ready when the luck happens."

It turned out *60 Minutes* was right about me, and I had never realized it! My story was about hard work *and* luck. I never had a five-year plan when I taught myself how to cook, bought the store, got up in the middle of the night to make a thousand baguettes, tested recipes for thirteen cookbooks, or agreed (reluctantly!) to do a television show. I concentrate on what's in front of me and work hard because I *love* what I do, and I have fun doing it.

And then I leave the door open, so I'll be ready when the luck happens.

Thank You!

So many people helped me with this memoir. First and foremost is my dear friend Deborah Davis, who has been part writing partner, part therapist, part researcher, but, above all, an amazing collaborator. This was her idea, and I admit that I was skeptical when we began, but it has been the most interesting project I've ever worked on.

At Crown, I want to thank David Drake for always being so supportive, Gillian Blake for being a stunningly good editor, Kate Tyler, Marysarah Quinn, and Chris Brand. Thank you, especially, to my wonderful agent, Esther Newberg, for always believing in me and to my speaking agent Steven Barclay, for always taking good care of me.

There are many people who contributed their memories to the book: James Lapine, my dear friend since we were teenagers, and other high school friends, including Janet Sloatman Files, Wendy Herlands Barensfeld, and Christine "Buzzy" Bruckner, whom I hadn't seen for almost sixty years. I've loved reconnecting with them.

I'm grateful to Sarah Esterling, Lee Esterling, Shawn Warren, Martine Sharp, Bettina Thompson Stern, T. R. Pescod, Hunt MacWilliams, and Tedd Libath—for sharing stories about Barefoot Contessa and reminding me that those early days were intense and crazy but so much fun.

Thanks also to longtime friends Frank Newbold, Susan Newbold, Carolyn Kastner, and Claire Roth. They helped me to relive the good times we shared, as did the late Dick Erb, who was such a huge influence on my style of cooking. I also appreciate the recollections of Chip Gibson, my first publisher and champion; Pam Krauss, who has guided my cookbooks with a kind and steady hand; Eileen Opatut, Rachel Purnell, Olivia Grove, Helen Shabason, the late Roy Finamore, and Sarah Chase.

Barbara Libath and Suzanna Giuliano worked with me for decades, and we built the business together. I've also had the pleasure of working with Cindy Massey, Lidey Heuck, Kristina Felix-Ibarra, Rose Brown, and Mica Bahn, who have contributed untold ideas and inspiration and have made it fun to come to work every day. I love them all.

Cecily Stranahan is all over this memoir, because her wisdom and guidance have saved me in so many ways. Truly, none of my story after I met her in 1985 would have happened without her wise counsel. Just when I thought my career was over, Cecily guided me to do what I never even knew I wanted to do—write cookbooks. My heart is full of love and gratitude for her.

One of the extraordinary results of writing this memoir has been reconnecting with my brother, Ken. Two children growing up four years apart often have totally different memories of their childhoods. I was stunned not only that Ken and I had the exact same memories, but that he even used some of the same words. I'm so grateful to him for helping me understand what happened to both of us.

And of course, for the past sixty years, there has been Jeffrey. We all need just one person to really believe in us in order to realize our dreams. None of this would have been possible without his constant love and support.

ABOUT THE AUTHOR

Ina Garten is a *New York Times* bestselling author and the host of *Be My Guest* and *Barefoot Contessa* on Food Network and streaming on Max, for which she has won five Emmy Awards and three James Beard Awards. She lives in East Hampton, New York, with her husband, Jeffrey.